Measuring Information

Library and Information Science

Consulting Editor: *Harold Borko*
Graduate School of Education and Information Studies
University of California, Los Angeles

Harold Borko and Charles L. Bernier
Abstracting Concepts and Methods

F. W. Lancaster
Toward Paperless Information Systems

H. S. Heaps
Information Retrieval: Computational and Theoretical Aspects

Harold Borko and Charles L. Bernier
Indexing Concepts and Methods

Gerald Jahoda and Judith Schiek Braunagel
The Librarian and Reference Queries: A Systematic Approach

Charles H. Busha and Stephen P. Harter
Research Methods in Librarianship: Techniques and Interpretation

Diana M. Thomas, Ann T. Hinckley, and Elizabeth R. Eisenbach
The Effective Reference Librarian

G. Edward Evans
Management Techniques for Librarians, Second Edition

Jessica L. Milstead
Subject Access Systems: Alternatives in Design

Dagobert Soergel
Information Storage and Retrieval: A Systems Approach

Stephen P. Harter
Online Information Retrieval: Concepts, Principles, and Techniques

Timothy C. Craven
String Indexing

The list of books continues at the end of the volume.

Measuring Information

An Information Services Perspective

Jean Tague-Sutcliffe
School of Library and Information Science
University of Western Ontario
London, Ontario
Canada

Academic Press
San Diego New York Boston London Sydney Tokyo Toronto

This book is printed on acid-free paper. ∞

Academic Press, Inc.
A Division of Harcourt Brace & Company
525 B Street, Suite 1900, San Diego, California 92101-4495

United Kingdom Edition published by
Academic Press Limited
24-28 Oval Road, London NW1 7DX

Library of Congress Cataloging-in-Publication Data

Tague-Sutcliffe, Jean, date.
Measuring information : an information services perspective / by Jean Tague-Sutcliffe.
p. cm. (Library and Information science series)
Includes bibliographical references and index.
ISBN 0-12-682660-9
1. Information science--Statistical methods. I.. Title.
II. Series: Library and information science (New York, N.Y.)
Z669.8.T345 1995
020.'21--dc20 94-30926
CIP

PRINTED IN THE UNITED STATES OF AMERICA
95 96 97 98 99 00 BB 9 8 7 6 5 4 3 2 1

To Robert Fairthorne, the frog-prince, who, many years ago, set me on a trail that led to this destination.

Contents

Preface xi

1

Introduction

1.1 What Are Information Services? 2
1.2 What Is Information? 3
1.2.1 Lakoff's View of Meaning 5
1.2.2 A User-Centered Definition of Information 8
1.3 Measuring Information 15
1.3.1 Why Measure Information? 16
1.3.2 How Can We Measure Information? 17
1.4 Measurement in Information Services 19
1.4.1 Collection 20
1.4.2 Description 22
1.4.3 Retrieval 23
1.4.4 Packaging 25
1.5 Problems of Aggregation 26
1.6 Overview of the Book 29
1.7 Questions for Discussion 30

2

Measurement in General and Information Measurement in Particular

2.1 A Theory of Measurement 32
2.1.1 Ordinal Measurement 37
2.1.2 Additive Measurement 41
2.1.3 Aggregation of Ordinal Measures 43
2.1.4 Hypergraphs and Chains 45

2.2 Reasonable Properties for a Measure of Information 46
2.2.1 Domain and Range of Informativeness 47
2.2.2 Informativeness of Record Sets and Sequences 49
2.2.3 Informativeness of Information Services 53
2.2.4 Use of an Informativeness Measure 54
2.3 Summary 55
2.4 Review Problems 55

3

A Review of Earlier Measures of Information

3.1 Probabilistic Measures 58
3.1.1 Shannon's Measure 58
3.1.2 Extensions of the Shannon Measure 63
3.2 Semantic Measures 68
3.3 Statistical and Decision-Theoretic Measures 74
3.4 Algorithmic Measures 81
3.5 Summary 83
3.6 Review Problems 83

4

An Ordinal Measure of User-Record Informativeness

4.1 Measuring User–Record Preferences 86
4.2 Standardizing the Informativeness Measure 95
4.3 Summary 100
4.4 Review Problems 101
Appendix A4.1 Algorithm to Determine the Informative Chains 102
Appendix A4.2 Proof of the Existence of an Ideal Chain When Query Aspects Are Ranked 107

5

Aggregation of the User-Record Informativeness Measure

5.1 Retrieval Trails 112
5.1.1 Relationship of Informativeness to Other Retrieval Evaluation Measures 125
5.2 Use Trails 126
5.3 Service Delivery 132
5.4 Summary 138
5.5 Review Problems 139

6

Evaluation of Information Services

6.1 Determination of Overall Informativeness 143
6.2 Testing for Differences in Informativeness 153
6.2.1 Evaluation of Collections or Databases 155
6.2.2 Evaluation of Descriptions 161
6.2.3 Evaluation of Search Strategies 166
6.2.4 Evaluation of Packaging 171
6.3 Summary 175
6.4 Review Problems 176
Appendix A6.1 Comparing Informativeness Using the Analysis of Variance 178
A6.1.1 ANOVA Test for a Difference in Informativeness, Single-Factor Design 178
A6.1.2 ANOVA Test for a Difference in Informativeness, Single-Factor, Repeated Measures (within Subjects) Design 179
A6.1.3 ANOVA Test for a Difference in Informativeness, Two-Factor Design with Equal Observations per Cell 181
Appendix A6.2 Comparing Informativeness Using the Meddis Rank-Based Approach 183
A6.2.1 Rank Test for a Difference in Informativeness, Single-Factor Design 183
A6.2.2 Rank Test for a Difference in Informativeness, Single-Factor, Repeated Measures (within Subjects) Design 185
A6.2.3 Rank Test for a Difference in Informativeness, Two-Factor Design with Equal Observations per Cell 187

7

Conclusion 191

References 195
Index 199

Preface

I have been fascinated by the problem of defining and measuring information ever since I worked as a doctoral student at the Center for Documentation and Communication Research at Western Reserve University in the early sixties. There, a number of other student assistants and I worked as "evaluators." It was our function to go through the abstracts of articles retrieved from what was then the only commercial computer-based retrieval system (that of the American Society for Metals) to choose those we should send to the user. Because this was long before the days of online systems, queries and results were communicated by mail (snail mail, that is).

I had already spent several years in the library profession, but it was not until I became an evaluator that I realized the essential difference between records—abstracts, articles, books, **things**—and what the reader got from them, what they told the reader—**information.** Winnowing the possibly informative from the clearly noninformative articles made me aware of the great divide between what the machine matched and what the user wanted.

During that time in Cleveland, I was lucky to meet Robert Fairthorne, an eccentric visitor from the Royal Aeronautical Establishment in England. Though I found much of what he said baffling, he helped me realize that information, although not something that could be held in the hand, was something that could be talked about in the abstract, described by properties related to the use of the word in ordinary language. Information could be modeled and even measured. Rereading him today, I find his perceptions as fresh as they were in the sixties and much more understandable, as a result of my own experience and growth in knowledge. Fairthorne's insight that every use of the word "information" refers to something useful to someone is a cornerstone upon which this book is built.

Measuring Information: An Information Services Perspective reflects more than thirty years of thinking about the problems of measuring information. Many people have helped and stimulated me in this odyssey. My faculty colleague Michael Nelson has been a continuing sounding board for my ideas, and his help in shaping them has been immeasurable. For this particular book, discussions with doctoral students at the University of Western Ontario, especially James Blustein, Stephen Downie, Trevor Richards, Patrick Rocca, and Elaine Toms, have refined a great deal of my initial thinking. My editor, Harold Borko, has been very encouraging and has helped me present this material in ways that are understandable to more than a few readers. The reviewer made a number of comments that forced me into a greater understanding of my own theoretical perspective. My family (Bill, Chris, Eliza, Fred) tolerated my neglect and supported me in countless unchronicled ways during this consuming preoccupation.

Some of the material in this book was presented in a earlier form at the 1991 Sarada Ranganathan Lectures in Bangalore, India; at the 1992 International Conference on Research and Development in Information Retrieval in Copenhagen, Denmark; and at the 1993 International Conference on Bibliometrics, Informetrics, and Scientometrics in Berlin, Germany. In all cases, but especially in Bangalore, discussion with and suggestions by the participants have been valuable in clarifying my own thinking about the nature of information.

Finally, I thank the Natural Sciences and Engineering Research Council of Canada, whose continuing financial support over a number of years for studies on the modeling and design of information retrieval systems has provided me with the resources to develop and test many of the ideas contained in this book. I also thank the University of Western Ontario, which granted me a study leave in 1991–1992 and thus provided me with time away from administrative duties to work through what has become a life-long obsession: determining how we can measure the amount of information provided in formal information service environments.

Jean Tague-Sutcliffe

1

Introduction

It is commonplace to say that we live in an age of information. Life is no longer physically hard, but for many it is mentally hard, that is, confusing. Filling our needs, from the most basic to the most sophisticated, is information dependent. Survival is not so much a matter of *doing* (growing, hunting or catching food, building shelter, making clothes) as of *knowing* (how to get a job, what kind of education to pursue, how to apply for benefits, where to get help). In a complex, highly structured society, information has become like the air we breathe, so pervasive that we scarcely notice its existence and yet so essential that we cannot live without it.

Organized information services are a product of our need for information. These are services that supply the information we require in order to function in our society, but that we cannot obtain from our immediate environment. Information services appeared, first, as adjuncts of other agencies and institutions in society: educational institutions such as schools, colleges, and universities; social welfare organizations such as charities and hospitals; private enterprises such as industrial and business firms or membership-based lending libraries. They arose, in large part, because society developed ways of recording and storing information.

In the present age, information services come in many forms. They form a substantial part of the services provided by our large libraries, public, academic, and national. They exist as a functional unit in most private- and public-sector agencies, as information management departments or corporate information centers. Provision of information to the public is a major service of a number of commercial, governmental, and nonprofit organizations: commercial online database vendors, tourist bureaus, travel agencies, community information centers, various kinds of "hotlines," and many others. Professionals in the health care and legal fields increasingly see the provision of information as a significant part of their function.

In a society with a high level of technical expertise as well as a high level of expectation among its citizens, there are many, frequently conflicting demands for resources. Information services must compete with other services for resources within the society and within individual organizations.

It is important that information services be able to provide to their governing bodies and funders a clear picture of the role they play and the value they contribute to their communities. The extent of the resource they provide, information, needs to be determined in some way so that it can be judged against societal needs. Measuring information is an essential part of evaluating information services.

1.1 What Are Information Services?

Before considering measurement, let us explore what we mean by an information service. An information service is a resource, in the form of a separate agency or a unit or a defined function within an agency, which has as its purpose the provision of information to a user community. This information may be provided in either verbal or recorded form, that is, in a conversation with the user or as a printed, electronic, audio, or video record.

An information service is characterized by the kinds of information it can provide and the kinds of user it serves. Information management units within private- and public-sector organizations serve the needs of managers and employees for information about the past and present activities of the organization and for the information about both the internal and external environment that is significant for future decisions. Their users are primarily internal. Other information services provide information to the general public: community information centers about human support services available in the user's community, various hotlines about services available to respond to personal needs or problems (employment, counseling, crisis intervention); travel agents and tourist bureaus about transport, accommodation, and attractions. Online services provide up-to-date information resources to such professionals as technical, medical, and legal workers. Public libraries provide broadly based information resources to the general public, and university libraries provide information to students and scholars, primarily through recorded rather than verbal information. School libraries provide information tailored to specific curriculum needs of their students.

The information provided by these services is associated, for the most part, with records, that is, with relatively permanent and cohesive physical representations. Language-based collections of records, such as books, journals, reports, and databases are called text, whether in printed or electronic form. In this book, we will be primarily, though not exclusively, concerned with the information provided by text. Much of what we develop, however, can be equally well applied to other language-based products such as audio recordings and to structured graphic information records such as graphs, diagrams, and maps. This book is *not* intended to deal with records developed primarily for aesthetic or entertainment purposes, though often it is difficult to separate these purposes from the informational. Sometimes we will use the word document to represent a set of records created as an information package, an article, a chapter in a book, a report, and so on.

1.2 What Is Information?

Before we can measure information, we must first define it. Most people have an understanding of the word "information" as it is used in ordinary language. We get information all through the day, by viewing, reading, listening. On our way to work, the car radio gives us information about the weather. At work, we check the files for information about previous correspondence with a client. We call the travel agent for information about flights and hotels for a trip we are planning. We go to the library seeking journal articles for information that will help in an upgrading course assignment. We use an online database to get information about a company in which we might invest. We scan our cookbooks for information about a new dish we want to cook for dinner. We watch the eleven o'clock news for information about the latest developments on the national and international scene.

Information is what humans and human-produced records communicate to other humans over space and over time. Like life itself, it has many different forms, depending on the environment. We all use information, but, for all its familiarity, its essential nature has proved difficult to define.

There has been no lack of attempts. Fairthorne (1975), in fact, suggested that the word information is simply a labor-saving device. He says:

> It is after all a nuisance to make up one's mind as to whether one is talking about signals, the marks on paper, the marked paper, changes in the state of one's knowledge caused by the meanings of the marks on the paper, and so on. It is easier to let the reader do this for you.

Fairthorne suggests that previous investigators have provided both objective and subjective definitions of information. Information has been viewed as associated, solely, with a record (document, text, message, answer, etc.). It has been defined as the record itself. For example, Buckland (1991) has recently suggested that when we speak of information systems, as is common today, we are using the word information in the sense of a thing, since information systems act on things: records, text, data. He concludes that there are many things that can be information, including not only textual items, but also pictures, recordings, museum objects, natural objects, experiments, events. In fact, anything might be information, depending on the situation.

One problem with defining information as a thing is that two different things may convey the same information, as the word is commonly used. A weather report in English conveys the same information as one in French. Another problem with defining information as a thing is that one thing, one record, may mean different things, and hence provide different information, to different people, because of the knowledge they bring to the record. We speak of records not as equivalent to information, but as containing information. However, this shift really does not help much, if it still characterizes information as something physical, as "stuff." As Fairthorne says:

> This substance is squeezed from books like water from a sponge, and can be stored and pumped around. This notion of an "informational essence" has less excuse than the notion of Phlogiston or of the lumineferous aether.

These problems with a definition of information as a thing, a physical entity, have led to definitions in which information is considered to be an intangible attribute of a record, an abstraction associated with the record, a construct.

One such intangible attribute is uncertainty. Since the 1940s, the name of Claude Shannon has been intimately connected with the scientific study of one kind of information. Shannon and Weaver (1949), in their pioneering work on the transmission of signals, introduced the notion of information as the removal of uncertainty. This definition would seem to represent an abstraction, but uncertainty is as difficult to define as information itself, though the mathematical theory of probability provides a convenient framework for its measurement. It is important, however, that we distinguish information itself from the *measurement* of information.

Derr (1985) also defined information as an abstraction; for him it is a meaningful representation of determinations that have been made of objects. He suggests that information should not be regarded as involving the cognitive structure of an individual, for example, the reader of the record, but that it should be regarded as an objective abstract entity. However, it is not then clear what the *representation* in his definition actually is. If it is not physical (the record) or mental (the concept), what exactly is it? The question is really a broader one: to what extent can abstractions (information, truth, justice, beauty, etc.) be said to have objective existence, independent of a conceptualization by an individual?

Information has sometimes been identified with the *meaning* of a record. However, Fox (1983) has pointed out that in ordinary discourse the two words are used somewhat differently. We do not normally say that one record has more meaning than another, whereas it is common to say that one record contains more information than another. Also, we think of information as being true or false in the real world (though we may not know which), whereas meaning is true or false only of the symbol. We say, for example, that "added weight to," not "annoyed," is the true meaning of the word "aggravated" (the relationship between the word sequences in quotes is true). On the other hand, we say the statement, "The president's visit aggravated the difficulties," is giving us true information only if we believe the statement represents something that happened in the real world.

1.2.1 Lakoff's View of Meaning

Despite these differences in definition, there is clearly some relationship between the meaning of a record and the information it provides. Meaning itself is a difficult concept to isolate. In the classical approach to semantics, words are seen as having lexical and referential meanings, the former connecting them with other words, the latter with "referents," things or events or states in the real world that they represent. However, this approach to meaning has been criticized by Lakoff (1987) on the basis of ignoring the way humans conceptualize. Lakoff proposes, instead, an experiential approach to meaning, which characterizes meaning in terms of the nature and experience of the beings doing the thinking, not just as individuals but also as members of a physical species and a social community.

Lakoff's view of meaning uses a view of thinking based on conceptual (cognitive, mental) structures that are *embodied* and *imaginative*. They arise from our bodily experiences, classified as: (1) basic-level experience, including gestalt perception, bodily movement, and mental images; and (2) experience of image-schematic structures, simple structures that occur regularly in our daily experience, entities such as containers, paths, links, forces, and relations such as front–back, up–down, and center–periphery. These two kinds of experience are the basis for what might be called physical concepts. More abstract conceptual structures arise, first by metaphorical and metonymic projection from the physical to the abstract and, second, by projection from basic-level categories to supercrordinate and subordinate categories.

Lakoff's concept of meaning makes it internal to human beings; however, to the extent that their bodily experiences are similar, total subjectivism or relativism (meaning is subjective or relative to the individual) is ruled out and shared conceptual structures are possible.

The foundation of Lakoff's approach to meaning, then, is provided by basic-level and image-schematic cognitive structures that arise from the preconceptual experiences of everyday life. These structures are not atomic building blocks, but rather lie at an intermediate level, at neither the highest nor lowest level of a conceptual structure hierarchy. Thus, *dog* or *car* or *running* is basic level, rather than *animal, vehicle,* or *movement,* on one hand, or *poodle, Ford,* or *sprinting* on the other. With these foundations, humans are able to reason abstractly by projecting metaphorically from the physical domain to the abstract and by forming complex concepts. For example, the abstract notion of quantity can be structured from our perception of up/down relationships: more is up, less is down. The abstract notion of a family can be structured metaphorically, from our basic-level experience of bearing and caring for young.

Lakoff distinguishes various types of more complex conceptual structures or cognitive models: propositions, scenarios, feature bundles, radial categories, and graded categories. These will be briefly described, to provide a better understanding of his multidimensional approach to meaning.

Propositions are statements in a logical calculus. Simple propositions assign a property to an entity. More complex propositions are constructed from these using quantifiers (*for all, for at least one*) and logical operators (*and, or, not, if . . . then*). For example, reading a weather report in the newspaper might create a propositional model of the form:

> *It is going to rain today.*
> *When it rains, I take an umbrella.*
> *Therefore I will take an umbrella today.*

However, conceptual models are not constructed solely by this kind of reasoning. Some aspects of the models are, in a sense, assumed. A scenario is a conceptual model with a number of slots or characteristics that have default or assumed values. For example, if I read that an orchestra performed at a local concert hall last night, my cognitive model assumes, unless I read otherwise, that there was an audience, an orchestra, a conductor, most of the audience were seated, the members of the orchestra played violins, flutes, trumpets, and the like, the audience applauded at the end of selections, and so on.

Many conceptual structures are based on categorization. In Lakoff, traditional categories, that is, categories defined by a number of properties, are called feature bundles. For example, if I see a book called *Communication among Mammals,* my cognitive model of a mammal is of an animal who bears its young alive and has milk-producing organs to feed its young.

Lakoff defines two additional types of categories besides feature bundles. Radial categories have central and peripheral members. When I read the word bed, for example, my concept will probably be of a piece of furniture with a mattress and four legs, used for sleeping. However, I would be willing to admit as peripheral members futons or even sleeping bags. I would also admit, as peripheral members, a garden plot containing strawberries or the ground where a road is built. Graded categories are like radial categories in that things have varying degrees of membership in the category, depending on the context. The boundaries of the category are fuzzy. For example, someone may not be a member of the category *children* in the sign *Children admitted half price,* but be a member of the category *Children inherit equal shares of the estate* in a will.

Language thus has meaning in terms of these cognitive models. The meaning of a text is what the user understands from the text. Nothing is meaningful in itself; meaning derives from the experience of functioning as a certain sort of being in a certain sort of environment. Text is understood if the words are meaningful, that is, correspond to the reader's existing conceptual structures. Text is not just a representation of a single external reality.

Truth is a correspondence between a person's understanding of the text and understanding of a situation in external reality. When different people understand the text and the situations differently, then truth will be relative. However, as members of a community share many basic-level experiences, their truth values are likely also to be shared. There is also a kind of feedback. Since we act in accordance with our conceptual systems and since our actions are real, our conceptual systems have a major role in creating reality.

Lakoff's conceptual models resemble Schutz's (1970) earlier idea of provinces of meaning, that is, sets of experiences of a specific cognitive type. These provinces include the world of physical things and bodily movement (Lakoff's basic-level experience), dreams, fantasies, scientific theories, experiencing works of art. Within one of these provinces, Schutz suggests, a person has a theme (the present object or aspect of concentration) and a horizon (the physical space, autobiographical experiences, and social background that are *potentially relevant* to the theme). Schutz distinguishes three kinds of relevance: topical, interpretive, and motivational relevance. Topical relevance determines what is separated from the horizon, in voluntary or imposed fashion, to form the theme. Thus, from the viewpoint of a reader and a book, the part of the book the reader is actually reading has topical relevance. Aspects of past experience to which the topical theme may be compared have interpretive relevance, and aspects that determine which of several alternative interpretations will be selected have motivational relevance.

A cognitive scientist, Johnson-Laird (1983), has carried out a more detailed examination of what Lakoff calls propositional models. He sees understanding as having several steps:

1. The meanings of the words are mentally represented.
2. Sentences are parsed to form a propositional representation.
3. The propositional representation is used as the basis for the construction of a cognitive model, guided by contextual clues and implied references based on general knowledge.

Johnson-Laird comments that the original record or utterance is more like a clue to the design of the cognitive model than a blueprint. In constructing cognitive models, people use inference, a process of thought that leads from one set of propositions to another. However, inference is not equivalent to formal logic; rather, it is a kind of reasoning in which they search for counterexamples to tentative conclusions. He suggests that these models play a central role in representing objects, states of affairs, sequences of events, the way the world is, and social and psychological actions.

Language, says Johnson-Laird, gives us the ability to produce records that are not under the immediate control of the local environment but that can intentionally refer to other states of affairs, including hypothetical ones and imaginary ones. A word is not just a stimulus that elicits the corresponding object in the real world. Words, even on their own, have a multiplicity of associations and relationships, varying from one person to another. The meaning of a sentence or a record will be even more complex and individual, combining as it does the meaning of the individual words and parts according to grammatical rules and conventions of discourse.

Johnson-Laird's view of cognitive models, which he calls mental models, is similar to Lakoff's. He distinguishes physical models derived from perception (Lakoff's basic-level models) from conceptual models (Lakoff's abstract models). He differs from Lakoff in believing that cognitive models are computable, that they can be constructed from tokens arranged in a particular structure to represent a particular state of affairs. Lakoff believes that the correspondence between the token structures and states of affairs in the world cannot be constructed within this scheme. If it can, he asks, to what does *correspondence* correspond? There is no one-to-one, objective relationship between cognitive models and states of affairs. Lakoff, further, believes that the computational model is inadequate because it lacks what he has called *conceptual embodiment*. He says, (Lakoff, 1987, p. 349) "An adequate theory must take into account how the content of a concept is related to bodily experience. And that is outside the realm of the algorithmic mind." The tokens used in computer computation are meaningless, whereas the tokens used in thought are meaningful.

1.2.2 A User-Centered Definition of Information

If we accept Lakoff's model of meaning, then the information provided by a record can be seen as what the reader understands by the record. This information will depend on the reader's present cognitive structure as well as the record. If the author's conceptualizing mechanism is different from the reader's conceptualizing mechanisms, what the reader understands from the language in the record may be different from what the author intended.

Similarly, two readers may differ in their understanding. With texts relating to commonsense or basic-level experiences, the information obtained from a text may be the same for all readers because their basic-level structures will be similar. However, more abstract domains are understood much less directly and may involve different uses of imaginative capacity, different conceptualizing mechanisms by different readers.

Information is thus the cognitive structure in the user's mind that results from the interaction of the user and a record. It is important to remember also that the records, the information sources, are for the most part products of human minds. As Froehlich (1991) has pointed out in his discussion of the relationship of Lakoff's work to information science, citations and texts are not simply things, but language products that bring into play the reader's understanding of the language and his or her cultural background and subject matter knowledge as they bear on the text. Information, in a sense, results from the interaction of two minds, via the medium of the record.

How does information differ, then, from meaning, since the meaning, also, has been defined as what the user understands by the record? As we pointed out earlier, information has the property of being true or false, while meaning does not. But there is another distinction, also initially pointed out by Fox (1983). Even though the information may be false, at some point in the user-record transaction the user is prepared to entertain the possibility of its truth, because of the perceived authority of the creator of the record. A record that informs is believed to be true, at least in some of its aspects. Information is, in a sense, what we got out of the record, not just what we understood by it.

Fox has presented what is probably the most thorough investigation of the word information as it is used in natural language. He defines information as a mental state associated with text. The information carried by a text is defined as the conglomerate proposition or assertion expressed by the text, or that which is told (by a text, a person, an object, etc.). This is the definition that was initially presented by Machlup (1983). However, Fox adds to Machlup's definition the qualification that the originator of the text is in a position to know, thus distinguishing, by the authority of the originator, informing from telling.

Fox makes a further stipulation when information is being transferred to another human: the information is the conglomerate proposition expressed by that part of the text, if any, which the recipient can understand. More formally:

A source of messages X informs a receiver Y that P is the case if

1. there exists a set S of sentences, that is, a message, such that
   a. X sends S to Y in context I

b. Y receives and understands the sentences of S
c. P is the conglomerate proposition expressed by S in context I.

2. X is in a position to know that P is the case.

Thus, P, a proposition, is the information X imparts to Y. It is information because X has authority, is in a position to know that P is true. Fox sees misinforming as less general than informing. Misinforming means that X tells Y that P is the case, X is in a position to know that P is true, but in fact P is false. Informing does not imply that P is actually true, nor even that X knows it to be true. Information is that which is conveyed when X informs Y that P is the case. It is what X tells and Y learns.

A problem with Fox's definition is that it restricts information to propositions. In classical logic, a simple proposition assigns a predicate (attribute) to an argument (entity). Complex propositions are formed by substitution, quantification, complementation, conjunction, disjunction, negation, and multiplace predicates, where semantic relations (agent, object, instrument, etc.) may hold among the arguments. However, the propositional is only one kind of cognitive model; Lakoff's work has pointed to the importance in human affairs of others such as scenarios, feature bundles, radial categories, and graded categories. Also, the propositions are understood, in Lakoff's approach, not just through formal classificatory properties, but also through metaphors, metonymy, and image schemas. What needs to be changed in the Fox definition is the restriction to propositions. Information is what the reader understands from the text, whether that understanding is by means of a propositional model, a metaphoric one, a metonymic one, an image-schematic one, or some other.

Information has been defined as an aspect of the transaction between a record and a user by other earlier writers, notably Belkin and Robertson (1976), Brookes (1983), Machlup (1983), Nauta (1972), and Schreider (1965). Machlup ties the meaning of information clearly to human communication: he states that the noun "information" has essentially two traditional meanings: (1) the action of telling or the fact of being told something; and (2) that of which one is apprised or told. Any other meanings, he suggests, are analogies or metaphors.

Information is often related to knowledge or seen as something that creates knowledge. According to Machlup, information is different from knowledge in several ways: (1) information is piecemeal, fragmented, particular, whereas knowledge is structured coherent, and often universal; (2) information is timely, transitory, perhaps even ephemeral, whereas knowledge is of enduring significance; (3) information is a flow of messages, whereas knowledge is a stock; (4) information is acquired by being told, whereas knowledge can be acquired by thinking.

Machlup insists that information is addressed to human minds and received by human minds; the informant or author intends to inform, though the recipient need not always be chosen in advance. However, Machlup does not really suggest what Lakoff's model would imply, that different minds will receive different information from a text depending on the existing cognitive structure of the reader's mind (though he does not deny this viewpoint either). He does, however, complain that the restriction of the word "information" by specialists makes it harder for nonspecialists to understand what it means. In particular, he says:

> The requirement of truth or correctness should exclude false or incorrect messages; the requirement of value or usefulness should exclude messages not helpful in decisions and actions; the requirement of novelty should exclude repeated or redundant messages; the requirement of surprise should exclude messages that the recipient expected; the requirement of uncertainty-reduction should exclude messages that leave the recipient's state of mind unchanged or increased . . .

He suggests that, because we can, in fact, speak of false, useless, redundant, old, or confusing information, these restrictions are invalid.

Both Machlup and Fox restrict information to what is understood from a human-created source. Records are created by human agents. It is not clear that this restriction is necessary; an individual may, indeed, find "tongues in trees, books in the running brooks, sermons in stones . . ." (*As You Like It,* act 2, sc. 1). For this book, we will consider that a record in an information service has been created with some degree of human intervention, if only at the level of selection or isolation from other parts of the environment. For example, data generated by medical monitoring devices will be considered to be records.

We will therefore modify Fox's definition as follows:

I is the information provided to a user Y by S in context C if

1. there exists a record S such that
   a. Y reads or otherwise perceives S in a context C
   b. Y uses his or her conceptualizing capacity to understand S
   c. I is the conceptual structure that Y understands by S.
2. Y views context C, in general, as a source of true sentences.

The latter requirement retains Fox's notion that informing differs from telling in that the source of the information has some authority for the recipient. It differs from Fox in that it allows conceptual structures other than propositions and makes the context, rather than a person, the authority.

Let us summarize our definition of information at this point. Information is an intangible that depends on the conceptualization and the understanding of a human being. Records contain words or pictures (tangibles) absolutely, but they contain information only relative to a user. The information is what the user understands by reading or otherwise cognitively processing the record. The information does not really have a separate existence external to the things that contain it or to the reader or listener who perceives it. Information is associated with a transaction between text and reader, between a record and user. It is what the user understands from the record during the time user and records are in contact.

In looking at an aspect of the transaction between user and record, we cannot ignore the user's motive in consulting the record. The user may have a need for a particular kind of information, a problem for which she or he hopes to find a solution in the record or a curiosity about some phenomenon. On the other hand, the user may access the record simply for entertainment or to pass the time. If the user has an information need or interest, this will act as a filter on what she or he understands from the record. For example, if I want to determine the weather forecast for today for my locality, I will scan the daily forecast in the newspaper and "understand" only that relating to this particular interest.

Information thus involves an understanding in short-term memory that is affected by the context of the need and the state of the user. Of course, understanding is not necessarily the totality of the interaction between user and record. Before understanding, the user may need to decode or translate the record, a process that may require special techniques or equipment (a record does not tell you much if you do not have a record player). After understanding, the user may reorganize his or her other conceptual structures, his or her knowledge structures, in various ways. He or she may ignore the text, take it as a confirmation or refutation of something, develop a new conceptual structure, fill gaps in an existing one, know how to do something. If it contains nothing new, nothing that the user does not already know, there may be no change in the long-term cognitive structure. On the other hand, his or her degree of belief in some event or proposition may be changed simply as a result of the repetition. If the record describes a situation previously unknown to the user (a rare event for the user), the change in the user's cognitive structure may be considerable. If the user is tired or feels overburdened with information (information overload), reading the record, despite its novelty, may produce no change at all.

Another aspect of the process by which a record *informs* a user is that it does not occur in isolation. Records, like words, do not exist independently; they have many possible relationships to one another. One text may explain another that the user has read, confirm it, contradict it, reinforce it, extend it, provide an illustration of it, make a generalization of it, partially duplicate it, criticize it, summarize it, analyze it, satirize it, to name but a few of the possible relationships. The reading of two or more records in one sequence may lead to different kinds of understanding, and hence provide different information to the user, than reading the records in some other sequence. The effect of the records on the cognitive structure of the reader may not be independent of the order in which the records are read.

This user-based view of information is a useful one for the evaluation of information services. Services collect, store, and organize and make available records, but these are only tools for accomplishing their real objective, facilitating the acquisition of information, not records, by the community they seek to serve. In measuring its value to this community, the service needs to look at the extent to which the information requirements of the community are satisfied, rather than at the number of records acquired, organized, retrieved, or circulated.

Is the definition of information that we have just presented consistent with the categorizations and approaches to information of the other information scientists, listed above, who also saw it as a product of the interaction between record and user?

Of these earlier writers, Schreider (1965) has a view of information that comes closest to the one we have presented here. He defined information as corresponding to a change in the receiver's (i.e., the user's) thesaurus (i.e., knowledge structure) as a result of a received text. In Schreider's view, two texts carry the same information, even though they may differ physically, if they produce the same transformation of the recipient's mental state. The change affected depends on the recipient's existing state of knowledge as well. As Schreider says, someone who has learned a discipline well will derive more from a text in this discipline than will someone who is ignorant of it. Moreover, an expert, someone who already knows everything about the discipline, may receive little information from the same text. Schreider's description of the thesaurus, however, limits it to propositional models, rather than the more extensive set of cognitive models described by Lakoff. Also, Schreider defines information as involving the long-term memory effect of the record, rather than the immediate, short-term understanding.

Nauta (1972) described an information process as one involving several elements: the information vehicle or record, an interpreter (the user), the interior state of the interpreter, described in terms of an information network or map (the user's existing cognitive structures), a purposeful state of the interpreter, determining what information and which responses are relevant, and a filter on the interpreter's perceptions and decisions (e.g., a specific need or question). The record is interpreted via the interior state and, if it is admitted by the purposeful state of the interpreter, the record is said to have a connotation for the interpreter. The record is said to have a denotation if there are entities in the interpreter's environment that correspond to the connotation (i.e., if the user sees the record as true).

Nauta's process is similar to the one we have proposed, though it is not entirely clear what he means, specifically, by information. He says,

"Information is news," but, also, "Evolution is an informational process." His idea of connotation seems closest to what we have called the user's cognitive structure. Nauta says that "something (a discernable form) can be information only for an interpreter with a certain structure." Thus, he recognizes the importance of the user's existing mental state in defining information. He seems to equate what we call understanding with the process of interpretation and admission by the purposeful state of the interpreter. He also distinguishes the syntactic aspect of information (the vehicle) from the semantic (understanding) and the pragmatic (use). In our approach, we define information, generally, on the basis of understanding, but will look at use, later, in relation to particular user situations.

A few years after Nauta, Belkin and Robertson (1976) and Belkin (1978) defined information in a way that fits more clearly with Lakoff's cognitive models. The information associated with a text, according to them, is the generator's conceptual structure, which underlies the surface structure (language) of the text. They suggest that the surface structure may be modified by the generator's purpose, intent, and knowledge of the recipient's state of knowledge. It is not clear, though, whether Belkin and Robertson saw the information as also dependent on the reader's cognitive structure, as our approach implies. They did say that the phenomena of interest to information science include: (1) the text and its structure; (2) the image structure of the recipient and the change in that structure; (3) the image structure of the sender and the structuring of the text. Their viewpoint seemed to be that information is associated with (3) the sender, rather than (2) the receiver.

In later papers, however, Belkin (1980) suggested that a user comes to the information service because she or he has recognized an anomalous state of knowledge (ASK) and that she or he evaluates the information obtained from the system in terms of the ASK and her or his conceptual state. This view is close to the one we have presented, though it is perhaps concerned more with defining the *effect* of information than information itself.

In 1974, Brookes defined information as "that which adds to or modifies in any way the knowledge structure with which it reacts." Pratt (1982) presents a similar definition of information as being "that which occurs in the mind upon absorption of a message," though he goes on to suggest that the word "emmorphosis" be used for this concept, since it has the same etymological structure as "information" but with Greek rather than Latin roots.

Brookes later (1983) suggested that a context for this definition had been provided by Popper (1972) in his *three worlds:*

> . . . we may distinguish the following three worlds or universes: first, the world of physical objects or of physical states; secondly, the world of states of consciousness, or of mental states, or perhaps of behavioral dispositions to act;

> and thirdly, the world of objective contents of thought, especially of scientific and poetic thoughts and of works of art . . .

Popper goes on to say that, among the inmates of the third world, are theoretical systems, problems, problem situations, critical arguments, state of a discussion or argument, and the "contents" of journals, books, and libraries. What he calls the third world thus seems to contain the cognitive models that are widely shared by a community, be they scientific, artistic, linguistic, geographic, or some other. However, these are "objective" only to the extent that they *are* shared by the community; individuals outside the community, for example, might understand the "contents" of a book differently. Indeed, from the viewpoint of an information service, a problem in satisfying user needs is that the user's understanding of how an author would describe the needed information may differ from the way authors actually write about it.

Green (1991) presents three cognitive models of information that she developed through a linguistic analysis of phrases incorporating the word "information" from a sample of abstracts in the LISA database. The theoretical approach described earlier in this chapter is that which she identifies as the "information-seeking model" in that the process is seen as under the direction of the user rather than the system. Green found that information, in this model, is described as a "bridge across a need gap" or as that which is "used to fill the need container."

1.3 Measuring Information

Although information is an intangible aspect of the interaction of a text and a reader, it does, according to the way the word is used in ordinary language, sometimes appear to have magnitude. We say one text contains more information, is more informative, for a reader than another text. Or we say that a text is more informative for one reader than another reader. Usually we make this distinction when the reader begins with a question or problem or educational need that acts as a filter on the information taken from the text. For more random kinds of reading, for example, browsing the magazines in the dentist's office, we are unlikely to be able to make such a distinction.

Let us consider what we actually mean when we say one text is more informative than another in satisfying some need. We mean that, in some sense, one text helped us understand an issue or problem better or taught us more about a subject than did the other. We do not necessarily mean that, because we have read the former, we need not read the latter. The first text may offer some basic ideas without which the second would not be understandable. Or our understanding of the first text may be extended by what is in the second. In most cases we will prefer to read a more informative text before a less informative one, but that need not always be the case. For example, one text may contain a few definitions that are essential to understanding another more substantial text, but otherwise contribute little to resolve an information need. We may not be able to compare all records as to the amount of information they contain. Some pairs of records may relate to our understanding of different concepts or aspects of the problem that brought us to the information service. In this case, we may not be able to say which has more information.

If information has magnitude, at least as it relates to one user's problem or query or to several users with the same or a similar problem, can this magnitude then be measured? *How* can we measure amount of information or what we shall call informativeness? Since Shannon, many writers have discussed measurement of information. However, almost all have defined information as a property solely of the record or message, not of the interaction between a record and a user. An exception is Jumarie (1990), who states that all information should be regarded as information relative to a given observer. The observer, says Jumarie, in an approach consistent with the one we have just presented, mainly relies on a pre-existing internal model that she or he has about the observable under consideration, that is, a set of expectations. The observer may be passive (a physical device) or active (a person who reads the message and then compares its semantic content with what is already available in memory).

The view of informativeness presented here is similar to the view of the relevance of a record to a user presented by Schamber *et al.* (1990), namely that, "Relevance is a dynamic concept that depends on users' judgments of the quality of the relationship between information and information need at a certain point in time." Relevance is seen as a measurable concept "if it is approached conceptually and operationally from the user's point of view." Thus, relevance appears to be related to the amount of information, or informativeness, though relevance may carry more of a connotation of value to the user than does informativeness.

A number of questions must be asked about informativeness. Why should we want to measure informativeness? Can it be measured directly, like length, or only indirectly, through other measures? What is the scale of measurement: ordinal, interval, ratio? To answer these questions, we need to look at the problem of measurement in the social sciences.

1.3.1 Why Measure Information?

Wittgenstein (1958) has said, "An inner process stands in need of outward criteria." We have defined information as an intangible product of an inner process, a reader's understanding of a physical record. In an information services environment, why do we need outward criteria? What kind of outward criteria do we need for this inner process?

An information service consumes resources provided by its community. In the normal course of events, it must justify its use of these resources. Senior management, the board of directors, the trustees, the municipal council, the electorate, the funders want to know what benefit the community is reaping from the information service, be this community the employees of a company, the residents of a city, the students and faculty at a university, the customers of an online service, the citizens of a country, the members of a profession, or some other.

Benefits can, of course, be described qualitatively and, indeed, should be so described for a broad understanding of what the service is doing for the community. What are all the benefits, tangible and intangible, provided by a public library, from making the current best sellers available for leisure-time entertainment to providing a place for latchkey children to go after school to providing a place where small businessmen can access online financial services? What is the benefit of having an integrated information management service in an agency, from one-stop information shopping to rationalized use of resources?

Quantitative descriptions of benefits complement, rather than replace, qualitative ones. Quantitative descriptions can be more precise. Quantitative measures lend themselves better to summarization and to comparison. For example, how can we compare two branch libraries or two online search services as to the benefits they are providing to their communities? How can we compare last year to this year? The broad description of services may be the same. If we ask users and nonusers for their opinions, we will get thousands of different descriptions, difficult to summarize accurately. The answer lies in describing benefits quantitatively as well as qualitatively.

Measurement is assigning numbers to events. It is undertaken for purposes of evaluation, prediction, and justification. Measuring the information provided by a service to its user community enables us to evaluate how well it is fulfilling its mandate with respect to its user community. It enables us to predict the effects of changes in the way the service is offered. It enables us to justify the expenditure of resources to maintain or expand the service. Measurement is one aspect of survival and of achieving excellence.

1.3.2 How Can We Measure Information?

Measurement has long been an essential part of the physical sciences. It is only in the present century, however, that it has been adopted by the social sciences, of which information science is one, since it deals with an aspect of human society, the interaction of users with records. The past few decades has seen the development of a measurement theory specifically related to the social sciences. How this theory can be applied to the problem of measuring information will be considered in Chapter 2.

We have said that information is what the user understands from the record. What outward criteria are possible for such a nebulous inner process? Phillips (1987) warns that, though it is reasonable to suppose that it is the cognitive structure resulting from reading the record that allows an individual to act in a certain way after reading, it does not follow necessarily that the structure can be inferred from data that are only about the individual's actions. One may look, for example, at success or failure in a task or time to react or to do a task in order to measure informativeness of instructional material. However, many alternative structures may lead to the same success/failure or response-time pattern. Informativeness is a construct, rather than an observable variable, and so we need to consider ways of constructing the measure and ways of determining its validity.

Phillips believes the answer to this problem lies in Karl Popper's view of the scientific method. Popper suggests that any scientific theory must be prohibitive, it must forbid certain things to happen. A theory that is not refutable by any conceivable event is nonscientific. Every genuine test of a theory is an attempt to falsify it or refute it.

How can this philosophy be applied to measuring the quantity of information provided by an information service to a user, measuring its informativeness? We have said that whatever measures are proposed must be tested, must be subjected to external validity tests. However, since the information in a record differs for different people, this validation is *not* a matter of having replication of the information measurement for a particular record by another individual. Another user might well find the record provides a different amount of information, since a different cognitive structure results for him or her.

What we are asking is not whether the user has assigned an appropriate informativeness value to a particular record. What we are asking is whether a way of assigning numbers to a set of user-record interactions makes sense with respect to the ordinary meaning of the phrase "amount of information." It may be possible, by having independent judges (i.e., people other than the users) look at the informativeness values of a set of interactions and the actions that the users subsequently took, to assess the appropriateness of the measures. For example, if the informativeness values that students assign to their interaction with a retrieval system and the use students make of retrieved items in their assignments are both recorded for a number of student users of an information service, external assessors could decide whether or not the informativeness values seem appropriate in the light of the student actions. This technique will be pursued at greater length in Section 5.1.

1.4 Measurement in Information Services

The ultimate question that one would like to be able to answer about an information service is: how much information does the service provide to its community, relative to the information needed by the community over some period in time? This question presupposes, through the term "needed," the existence of an ideal information service, with ideal collection, description, retrieval, and packaging functions, filling all the information needs of the community in an optimal fashion during this time period.

A related, though different, question is: how valuable has the service been to the community? Filling all the information needs of the community in an optimal fashion may not necessarily be of greatest benefit, when benefit is measured by some other economic or social criterion. However, one would expect most generally used measures of social and economic value to relate positively to increased knowledge within the community. We discuss further this second question in Section 1.5.

In general, it will not be possible to describe completely the ideal service. However, the lack of a totally delineated ideal service does not mean evaluation is impossible. The informativeness of an information service can at least be estimated by looking at how it is used by its present community (users and nonusers) and how satisfied they are with this use. How this estimation and evaluation can be done is the subject of this book. The approach will be to postulate an ideal service, estimate this ideal, and then compare the actual service with the ideal.

Functions performed by an information service can be described as: creation or collection of records, enabling access to records by classifying, cataloging, indexing, extracting, abstracting, and otherwise describing them; retrieval of records in response to user needs; extraction of answers to questions; analysis; and synthesis of information in records to respond to user requirements. These functions might be summarized as collection, description, retrieval, and packaging.

Information services vary in how they carry out these functions. Libraries typically collect records produced by others: books, journals, reports, disks, videos, and so on. Corporate and governmental information or records management departments typically collect records produced internally. More public-oriented services, such as community information centers and tourist information centers, usually create their own databases of records and, as well, collect material from external sources. To facilitate access to the stored records, information professionals classify, code, and organize them, create indexes or abstracting tools for the collecton, and develop procedures or software to retrieve records relevant to a user's needs. In some information services, to respond to special user requirements, information professionals also package information and create new records specifically tailored to the user, by analyzing, synthesizing, and reformulating existing records. For each of these functions, information measurement can serve an evaluative, predictive, and justificatory role. For each function, particular problems arise, particular questions are asked, and particular approaches to information measurement may be taken.

Because information occurs as a result of the interaction of a user and a record, we define the atomic event to which an informativeness value can be assigned as one user using one record at one point in time. Whether or not this event occurs, that is, whether the user gets this information, depends on the collection, organization, description, retrieval, and packaging functions of the service. To evaluate these functions we need to be able to discriminate the extent to which the total amount of information that the user receives from the service is a result of the way a particular function is carried out.

Disentangling the effect of each function on the informativeness of the resultant interaction (or noninteraction, if the record was not one presented to the user) would be difficult to do. However, one can assess the relative informativeness of the way a particular function is carried out by comparing it with other ways, other approaches to the same function. This is done by aggregating or averaging informativeness of individual transactions separately for the two or more alternative approaches and then carrying out appropriate statistical tests to compare the resulting aggregated informativeness. Looking at the effect of different approaches to the functions of collection, description, retrieval, and packaging on the overall informativeness of an information service is important, because often the community served or the managers or funders of the service want to compare the cost effectiveness of these alternative ways of serving the users.

To elaborate on the ideas in this section, let us examine how this approach can be applied in developing measures to answer specific questions concerning the four processes of an information service.

1.4.1 Collection

Collections of records represent some aspect of the world of objectified knowledge. Although we have said that this world (Popper's Third World) does not exist independently of the minds of indivduals, it has an independent existence to the extent that it corresponds to the cognitive models, the understanding, of groups of individuals. Thus, widely accepted observations, scientific theories, religious beliefs, aesthetic judgments can be said to be part of this world of objectified knowledge. To a large extent, these shared structures are communicated from one individual to another by records.

In developing collections of records, the information needs of some user group, present and perhaps future, are considered. These needs may be for specific information or general educational and cultural development. Sometimes the information service administrators' general sense of what these information needs are or should be is codified in a formal collection policy. Sometimes, user information needs are estimated based on past use or nonuse of the collection. In either case, these approaches provide clues to the ideal collection, the collection that covers just those areas of knowledge which the users will want to access and no others.

Collections may be evaluated at the macroscopic or microscopic level. In the first case, we are asking how much information the collection as a whole provides to its user community. In the second case we are asking how much information a single record provides to the user community. With microscopic evaluation, we are aggregating informativeness of a record in the collection over users and their needs; with macroscopic evaluation, we are aggregating informativeness over users, needs, and records.

Macroscopic evaluation is an evaluation of the collection policies of the information service. How well does the collection cover the area of knowledge or type of material it is meant to cover? Since we do not know what this ideal collection is, the best we can do is compare the informativeness of the given collection with that of other collections, standard bibliographies, items indexed by online databases, or collections defined by user known-item or topic requests, for example. Microscopic evaluation is an evaluation of collection decisions (acquire or discard, convenience of access) relating to single items: how much information will this item add to or remove from the collection?

For example, consider an evaluation of the collection of a special library such as a law library, medical library, or engineering library, which serves the needs of a well-defined professional group. It provides the materials (papers, books, technical reports, government publications) needed by the professionals and paraprofessionals in their current work. Thus, evaluation of the collection can be carried out relative to these needs. We might ask: what is the informativeness of the present collection relative to one in which located gaps have been filled? Or if users of the library may access materials externally, as on online information services, as well as in the internal collection, we might also ask: what is the relative informativeness of internal and external sources?

As another example, consider a community information center, which develops and accesses a database providing information about human services available in a region. To evaluate such a service, we need to assess the informativeness of the database that the center creates relative to potential and actual users in the community. The determination of the ideal database will be based both on collection policy and user requirements, with the collection policy essentially indicating user service priorities, that is, which users the center considers most important to serve.

1.4.2 Description

Few information stores or collections consist simply of a random set of records. To facilitate access, records are classified, arranged, cataloged, indexed, abstracted, and otherwise described. These devices provide information to users directly and make possible access to informative records that would otherwise not be found. Their value lies in the assistance they provide in satisfying users' needs for information. Of course, whether or not a record is found depends also on the amount of effort the user or intermediary puts into the search for relevant records. This factor can be neutralized by comparing the informativeness of one kind of description with that of another over many uses of the service.

One cannot directly compare the informativeness of different kinds of descriptions for a single user need, since what the user understands from one description may affect what she or he understands from another. Thus, comparisons must be made using different needs for different methods of description and then aggregating the informativeness values for the two or more methods. It may be important, in so doing, to distinguish different types of users. In any case, once informativeness values are aggregated, we can compare the information gain or loss of one description method relative to another.

Description of records facilitates access via two distinct methods: classification and record surrogation. Classification involves organizing records in the store, according to some scheme. This organization may involve the actual physical arrangement of the records or a logical arrangement, accessed via an index. To evaluate a classification scheme we ask the question: how much information is gained or lost through using one classification scheme rather than another, or through using a classification scheme rather than random ordering?

Record or document surrogates are created by the process of indexing, cataloging, abstracting, and extracting. To compare different kinds of surrogates we ask a question similar to that proposed for classification: how much information does a surrogate provide about the original record or relative to another type of surrogate for the same original record? How much more informative, for example, is an abstract than an extract or a simple citation?

How much more informative, in an index, are descriptors selected from a controlled vocabulary than keywords selected from the text? In some situations, we may want to compare the informativeness of the surrogate with that of the original record. For example, an information service may consider keeping only abstracts rather than original reports because of space considerations and may wish to evaluate the amount of information that would be lost by this decision.

1.4.3 Retrieval

Users (clients, customers, patrons) come to an information service when they have some interest or problem in their lives that they believe can be satisfied or resolved, at least in part, by additional information, when they encounter what Belkin and Robertson (1976) call an information anomaly. The information need may be as simple as the address of an agency that could help the client or the source of a statement a manager remembers a supplier made in earlier correspondence. It may be practical: how to fix a car engine of a specified make and model; how to make some exotic dessert. It may be a long-term project: understanding and experiencing transcendental meditation; learning how to program in C. It may be complex and difficult to define: a research problem in molecular biology or epistemology.

In some information service uses, called searching, users may provide a verbalized statement of the problem or interest (a query) as a starting point for retrieval. In other uses, called browsing, users may peruse the collection or database without a focus or clear definition of the problem or interest.

The response of an information service to a user with an information need can take a number of forms, depending on the form and description of the collection or database and the policies of the service. Users may search sets of electronic surrogates, such as cataloging, indexing, or abstracting databases, and then locate the printed full-text items in the collection. This is the normal practice in university and public libraries in North America. Users may search a surrogate database or a full-text database or both online or ondisk and then copy in print or electronic form those parts of the database that are of interest. Many online information services now provide this facility to their users. Professional intermediaries may assist users with the search, acting as consultants when the user has problems. In totally delegated searches, users explain their information requirements to professionals, a query is formulated, and the intermediary then carries out the search of the database. In some environments, for example, community information centers or organizational information management centers, the professional then provides information in verbal, printed, or electronic form to the user based on the retrieved records and their own expertise. In other environments, for example, special libraries, users are provided, following the search of a surrogate database, with lists of references, are allowed to select those of interest, and are provided with full-text copies.

The capability of browsing is also important for many user communities. It may involve scanning the shelves of a library or the records of a database. It is facilitated by the availability of different access orderings of the records in the collection, through a number of different classifications or through hypertext links.

A number of measurement questions arise in evaluating the many varieties of the retrieval process. How much information does the result of an information retrieval process provide to the user with respect to his or her underlying information need? How much information does the set retrieved in a search of the surrogate database provide about the informativeness of the full-text record to which the surrogate points? How informative is each record as it is visited during the user's search of the database, or as it is scanned in the intermediary-provided search output? How much information is missed in the search?

In traditional information retrieval testing, based on queries, the value of a search is measured by the recall and precision of a search output, measures defined using the concept of a relevant set of records. Recall is the proportion of relevant records that are retrieved and precision is the proportion of retrieved records that are relevant. A relevant record is sometimes defined to mean a record that is about the query and sometimes defined to mean a record that is useful to the user. Neither concept exactly mirrors the concept of informativeness, which measures the amount of information the record provides to the user, but they are related to it, as we noted earlier.

The information problem or interest that brings the user to the information service, or the query, in the case of a delegated search, acts as a filter for the searcher, determining both the strategy (the sequence in which records are examined in the search) and what information is extracted from the record. However, the informativeness of a record is unique to the user, at least at a particular point in time. Two users with similar information problems may examine the same sequence of records but extract different information and different amounts of information from them. A single user, at different times, might extract different information and different amounts of information from the same sequence of records. Thus it makes sense to ask not how much information the record provides in general, but how much information the record provides at a particular point in time to the user relative to the information problem that brought the user to the service.

Often, of course, users of an information service will have more than one interest or problem that might be resolved by information. If the user carries out the search, he or she may examine records for information relating to more than one need. Thus, it may become more difficult to decide on the information provided by a record relative to each problem or interest. Search process analysis, that is, detailed questioning of the user or taping user's comments while searching (search protocols) can be of value here.

1.4.4 Packaging

Retrieval results in the user perusing a sequence of records, containing varying amounts of information relative to his or her need. Sometimes this examination of records satisfies the user's need. However, in many situations, the users place additional requirements on the information service.

Users may want answers to specific questions of the what, where, who, when, which, and whether variety, extracted from the records. What is the Canadian dollar exchange rate? Where is the head office for IBM? Which airlines have daytime flights from Toronto to London? Who said, "Nothing endures but change"? Particularly in situations where the information service supports managerial or professional staff, information professionals are expected to provide exact answers, not documents that may contain the answers.

Sometimes, professionals in the information service are also expected to analyze and synthesize records for the users. An information specialist member of a research team is expected to compile reviews and summaries of new acquisitions in the topic area of interest to the team. Managers require information professionals to provide statistical and financial summaries of the raw data files that an organization's information center collects.

These activities provide added value to the users of the information service but require additional professional resources. Can we assess how much information is gained or lost by this processing? Does the resulting text have more or less information for a user, compared with the original records? The extracting, summarizing, and statistical and financial processing activities reduce the amount of text the user must examine and so may omit aspects that may be informative for the user. The user benefits, however, by having less text to examine. Can we measure informativeness of one text relative to others on which its content is based?

1.5 Problems of Aggregation

If informativeness is to be used to evaluate how well information services serve the needs of their communities, it must be possible to measure it at a number of levels:

- the informativeness of a record with respect to an individual user's information need;
- the informativeness of a sequence of records provided by a service in response to an individual user's information need;
- the informativeness of a sequence of uses, possibly by different users, of a single record over a specified time period;
- the informativeness of an information service with respect to the needs of a user community over a specified time period.

Thus, we would like, for evaluation purposes, to be able to aggregate the information measure over records, over users, and over the needs of the user community in some time period. However, it will not necessarily be the case that a measure of the informativeness of a set of records for a user at one point in time will be additive, so that one can simply add the informativeness values for individual records to determine the informativeness, say, of a search output. The reason is that records interact, so that the informativeness for the user of a set of records in one sequence is not the same as the informativeness of the set of records in another sequence.

Evaluating the informativeness of a single record used several times over some period of time, again, is not necessarily a matter of adding the informativeness values for each use. Even if we assume independent uses, the informativeness values for each use may be calculated relative to the needs of that user, that is, may use a unique scale of measurement. We need to find a measure, related to individual informativeness, which can be used to cumulate informativeness of a record over different users.

If we think in terms of the problems and interests of a community or a society rather than individual users or records, maximizing the response to the information needs of each single user at a particular point in time will not necessarily maximize the response to the information needs of the community served. The response to an individual user may be too late to do any good. There may be members of the community with information needs that were never addressed by the service. Indeed, the question of information needs is a complex one because user needs are not isolated but arise from and depend on those of other users. Frohmann (1992) suggests that, in information science research, by focusing on mental events of individual users, we ignore the social, political, and economic forces that may have shaped these events. We need to examine not just the total amount of information provided to individual users, but the relationship of this total to the information needs of the community.

Informativeness has already been distinguished from the value of information. Information has some peculiar properties when we consider it at the macro level as a social or economic good. Bates (1988) sees these properties as falling into three areas: indeterminacy of the value of information, value of information versus value of the record, and the ancillary value of information.

The indeterminacy arises because the value of information to an individual in a community comes from its use at some future point in time and is influenced by the circumstances of that use. For example, if a user seeks and finds records relating to some problem, she or he may not know until later whether or not the information from the records really solved the problem. The value of information versus the value of the record distinction arises because records may be used by more than one individual in the community, so that the information from the record is received by many. Determination of the value of the record then becomes difficult, because it involves multiple uses and future as well as past uses. Finally, information has ancillary value because it may create value not only for the user, but for others through the acts of the user. The use of information may result in changes in the social, physical, and economic environment, and these changes will have value.

Bates (1988, p. 81) says:

> The use of information changes the system, not only for the individual using the information, but for others as well. Clearly, such changes in the system can result in changes in the status, relationships, and opportunities of others within the system, effectively creating (positive or negative) value, ancillary to that received by the user of the information—shifts in value that can, however, be attributed to that use of information.

In a community of users, some record-sequence user interactions will have more value than others to the community as a whole, when one examines the overall "good" of the community. It may be important that certain users receive certain records early, and such a distribution may in fact eliminate the need for other users to receive the records at all. On the other hand, optimal social value may result from all users receiving the same set of records at the same time.

For example, there has been a lot of discussion in the media about warnings of the harmful effects on the human body of the reduction in the ozone layer. To what extent does the release of this information to the general public before it is thoroughly validated provoke an unnecessary panic situation? Should it be released only to scientists who can assess its implications? Another example is information about proposed new remedies or therapies for AIDS. What degree of testing should take place before the information is released to commercial firms and to patients?

The question here concerns the ultimate value of information, relative to other social constructs such as justice, security, culture, and individual rights, and relative to physical requirements such as food, clothing, and transportation. This is an important question, but it is not something this book will attempt to answer. To answer this question we would have to convert informativeness values and measures of all of these other constructs and requirements to the same scale (e.g., dollars). This is an important economic question, but not one with which this author is ready to grapple at this time. We must first learn how to count oranges before we can assign a dollar value to a dozen of them.

The focus in this book will be on counting oranges, on evaluating how well an information service does what it has been set up to do: getting information to those who need it in the service's community. Usually, the service itself will define the community it intends to serve in terms of geographical, topical, temporal, organizational, and other boundaries. However, an important part of the evaluation process is determining whether or not these boundaries are appropriate: are there people with information needs that could be filled by the service that are not presently reached by the service?

As well, an evaluation of an information service's performance should look at the extent to which it gets information to those who need it *at the right time*. Delays, in many cases, discount the value of the information. A battered wife and mother needs information about community "safe" houses at a particular, critical point in time. Does the community information service provide it at that moment? This is an important evaluation question.

Thus, the question of the optimal interaction sequence for the community will be replaced by the simpler one of asking what records should get to which members of the community at what time. The actual service sequence, that is, the user-record sequence interactions that did occur, will be examined for four kinds of divergence in assessing the value of the service to its community:

- divergence in the retrieval set from the set of records that should have been presented to the user, divergence caused either by omitting informative records or by including noninformative records;
- divergence from the optimal order of record presentation for the user;
- divergence from the optimal time of service, that is, service delays;
- divergence in the set of users served from the set of members of the community whose information needs could have been or should have been served, that is, unmet needs.

1.6 Overview of the Book

The purpose of this book is to develop a general framework for measuring informativeness and to apply this framework and develop specific measures that will be useful in the evaluation of information services of all kinds.

The next four chapters present a theoretical basis for the measurement of information in information service environments. Chapter 2 provides some background about the mathematics of measurement in the social sciences, based primarily on the work of Roberts (1979). It then proposes some reasonable properties for a measure of informativeness.

Chapter 3 provides a review of earlier measures of information relative to these properties. Most of these earlier measures assume that information is associated with the record alone, rather than with the interaction of a record and a user. As well, they assume that the record is in some kind of canonical form: probabilistic, logical, statistical, or algorithmic. The earlier measures will be reviewed according to these categories.

Chapter 4 develops the framework that will provide an integrated approach to information measurement for information services. The reasonable properties for a measure of informativeness introduced in Chapter 2 are expanded and formalized as a set of axioms, a set of conditions that can be assumed to hold for all information measurement in an information services environment. A general measure of information is derived from the axioms.

The problem of aggregating informativeness values in order to evaluate the service an information agency provides to its community is then addressed in Chapter 5. As we have seen, because of the peculiar nature of information, this informativeness is not necessarily a simple sum of the informativeness for users of the service. From the point of view of the community of actual and potential users, the information service is operating optimally if it provides records to members of the community in ways that will satisfy the needs and interests and solve the problems of the community in the shortest time. An aggregated informativeness measure is developed that reflects the degree to which the service achieves this ideal.

Chapter 6 is concerned with the use for evaluation purposes of the proposed measure in an operational environment. It considers the questions of sampling and experimental design that must be addressed if the measure is to be used to answer some of the questions posed in Section 1.4 of this chapter. Recall that these questions related to the relative informativeness of different approaches to the processes of collecting, describing, retrieving, and packaging records in an information service. For each process, we will consider how the measure may be used to compare different approaches and relate it to measures proposed by earlier writers.

1.7 Questions for Discussion

This chapter has set the definitional framework within which the theory and practice of information measurement will be developed. Some of the questions that readers should consider in assessing this framework are given below. These might, for example, be used as a starting point for a class discussion of the material presented in this chapter.

1.7.1 Based on your own usage of the word, how would *you* define "information"?

1.7.2 Can abstractions be objective? Is there a "world of objective knowledge" in the Popperian sense?

1.7.3 "Information is what the user understands from the text." "Information is a reorganization of conceptual structure." Are these two statements incompatible?

1.7.4 Can we compare the informativeness of records only as they relate to an information problem or interest?

1.7.5 How can we validate a measure of informativeness?

1.7.6 Do the functions of collection, description, retrieval, and packaging adequately classify the activities of an information service? Are there other functions not covered by these four?

1.7.7 An ideal information service has been defined as one that gets the right information at the right time to those who need it. What are the ambiguities in this definition?

2

Measurement in General and Information Measurement in Particular

In the preceding chapter, we saw that information forms a part of many different situations or frames. Reading a record provides general information to the reader, the information he or she needs to solve a particular problem or to answer a particular question. One record, a review or an abstract or a translation, provides information to the reader about another record. As a series of records provides information to a user there may be redundancy and interactions among the records in the information each provides, in what is understood by the user. At an aggregate level, an information service provides information to a community of users and potential users. A record in the information services database or collection has potential information for some or all members of this community.

We would like to develop a measure of information general enough to describe all of these and similar information-providing frames. However, it may be that information measurement is easier in some situations than in others, or even that information measurement is possible in some situations and not in others. In order to investigate this problem further, we will in this chapter first examine some fundamentals of measurement in the social sciences. These fundamentals will be used as a framework for developing a set of reasonable properties for a measure of information.

Measurement is a process in which a variable, a quality of something, is differentiated, discriminated from other qualities, and then assessed in some fashion. Some variables can be observed directly. Others are inferred from a set of indirect indications. For example, height can be observed directly, mathematical ability must be inferred from other indicators such as test scores. Usually, physical variables may be observed directly and cognitive or attitudinal variables indirectly. With the definition of information that we presented in Chapter 1, informativeness is clearly an indirectly observed variable.

Some writers limit the term measurement to assessments that are numeric in nature. However, a more general approach, and the one we shall follow here, sees numeric measurement as simply one type, one scale, of measurement. Other scales are ordinal measures or rankings and nominal scales or categories. A measure of informativeness might be ordinal or nominal, rather than truly quantitative. However, one of the premises of this book, based on the use of the word information in ordinary language, is that a measure of information in the context of a user need is *at least* ordinal (i.e., not nominal).

Measurement may be objective or subjective. Of course, all measurement depends on the accuracy of the measuring instrument, and so, if a person is doing the measuring, the value obtained will vary from person to person. Even measuring the height of an object is subjective in this sense. However, in this case, we do assume that there is a "true" value of the height and that measurements by individuals display "errors" from this value. In objective measurement, we assume the existence of a true value, independent of an individual, which we attempt to determine through an unbiased and precise measurement procedure. In subjective measurement, however, the "true" value is unique to the individual in the sense that it is a property, not just of an object, but of an object interacting with an individual. The time it takes to read a book is a property, not just of the book, but of the book and the reader. It is another premise of this book that information measurement is subjective.

2.1 A Theory of Measurement

Roberts (1979), whose book on measurement theory has become a classic, notes that a major difference between a "well-developed" science such as physics and some of the less "well-developed" sciences such as psychology or sociology is the degree to which things are measured. Roberts extends ideas in the measurement theory of the physical sciences to measurement of social and psychological properties, of which we consider information to be one. He distinguishes different scales of measurement and develops conditions on individual or social judgments, preferences, reactions, and the like for each of these scales. His approach to measurement is one we will follow and will now summarize. Many readers of this book will already be familiar with the notions of a set, relation, and function. However, the following paragraphs provide a brief review of these notions.

Basic to a theory of measurement is the idea of a set, a collection of elements. We will follow the usual practice of listing elements of sets in brackets, for example, the set C of colors as

C = {*black, blue, brown, gray, green, orange, pink, red, violet, yellow, white*}.

The expression a ∈ A indicates that a is an element of the set A. Thus, red ∈ C.

A relation in a set or among sets is an association among some of the members of the set. For example, "adjacent in the color spectrum" is a relationship between elements in the set C. Relations are categorized by the number of elements related, so that a binary relation associates two elements. Such a relation can be represented as an ordered pair. For example, we can represent the fact that red and orange have the relation "adjacent in the color spectrum" by the pair (red, orange). If R is the adjacency relation in the color spectrum, we can represent it by a set containing all the ordered pairs of colors that display this relationship, that is,

R = {*(blue, green), (blue, violet), (green, blue), (green, yellow), (orange, red), (orange, yellow), (red, orange), (yellow, green), (yellow, orange), (violet, blue)*}.

We can also represent the fact that, for instance, red and orange have the relationship R by the notation: red R orange.

Relations often indicate ordering; the color adjacency relation R given above indicates a partial ordering, or ordering of some of the elements, of the set C, namely

<red, orange, yellow, green, blue, violet>.

Notice that some elements, those in the set

{*black, brown, gray, pink, white*}

are not ordered by R.

There can be more than one relation defined on a set. The alphabetical ordering of the color names is defined by a relation. The statement "color a is a combination of colors b and c" defines a ternary relation R′ on C:

R′ = {*(orange, red, yellow), (violet, blue, red), (green, yellow, blue), (gray, black, white), (brown, black, yellow), (pink, red, white)*}.

A function associates or relates one element in a set to *each* element in the same or another set. Thus it is a mapping or correspondence between elements of two sets, the first, say, X, called the domain of the function and the second, say, Y, called the range of the function. This mapping is frequently represented by the expression y = f(x), where x is an element of the domain X, and y is an element of the range Y. The symbol f represents a rule or mathematical expression that allows us to associate a value from Y to each value in X. Another way of representing a function is by means of the "arrow" notation: f:X → Y means that f is a function that maps elements from a set X to elements of a set Y.

For example, squaring a number is a function y = x^2, which associates with each real number another real number, called its square. Notice that each real number (a number that can be represented by a decimal expansion, possibly nonterminating) has a square, but each real number is *not* the square of another number. Thus, not all real numbers are in the range of the function, though all are in the domain. Functions need not be mathematical. For example, the function "has the biological mother" assigns a mother to each person in some set. Again, every person is in the domain (has a mother), but not every person is in the range (is a mother).

An operation in a set is a function that assigns an element of the set to an ordered pair of two elements of the set. The arithmetic operations of addition, multiplication, subtraction, division, exponentiation, and so on assign a number to pairs of numbers. Another example is concatenation, putting together two character strings to form another string.

Measurement can be defined as assigning numbers to each element in a set in a way that corresponds to or represents or preserves observed relationships and operations in the set. Given a relational system $<A, R_1, R_2 \ldots O_1, O_2 \ldots>$, where A is a set of objects, R_i, $i = 1, 2 \ldots$ are one or more relations on the set, and O_i, $i = 1, 2 \ldots$ are one or more operations, a measure is a function or mapping from A to the real numbers, which preserves the relations and operations. By preserves, we mean there are corresponding relations and operations in the real numbers for the relations and operations in the original set. A function with this property is called a homorphism. Sometimes, there is more than one measure, more than one function with this property.

For example, in the relational system $<A,R,O>$, A might be a set of issues of a journal, R the binary relation "is longer than," and O the operation of concatenation (binding together) of issues. In the set of real numbers, the relation R might be "is greater than" and the operation O addition of numbers. A measure defined as the number of pages in the issue or issues would represent the length relation "is longer than" numerically and would be preserved under concatenation in that the number of pages in two concatenated issues would be equal to the sum of the number of pages in each. However, number of pages is not the only measure of length in this situation. Number of words or number of paragraphs might also serve this purpose.

The triple consisting of the observed relational system, the mapping system, and the numerical system is called a measurement scale. Scales are categorized by the relations and operations that they preserve. An ordinal scale preserves order; an interval or additive scale preserves an addition operation. For example, let A be the set of books in a library classified by the Dewey Decimal Classification. Let R be the relationship a R b, a, b $\in$ A if and only if a is before b on the shelf. The Dewey number is an ordinal measure that preserves this ordering. However, it is not additive, since there is no operation on books that corresponds to the addition of two Dewey numbers. Two books with, say, Dewey numbers 210 and 514, when bound together (i.e., concatenated) do not have Dewey number 724.

Sometimes it is not possible to find a measure that preserves order and operations. Sometimes there is a measure, but it is not unique. It may be possible to apply a mathematical transformation to the original mapping and obtain another measure that still preserves the desired relations and operations. Another way of determining the scale type is by looking at the mathematical transformations that can be performed on the original measure without invalidating it, that is, that still allow it to preserve desired relations and operators.

Roberts defines the following scale types in terms of admissible transformations:

Scale Type	*Admissible transformations*	*Example*
Absolute	Identity f(x) = x	Counts
Ratio	Similarity f(x) = ax	Times, sizes
Interval	Positive linear f(x) = ax + b	Temperature, calendar year
Ordinal	Strictly monotone increasing	Ratings, rankings
Nominal	Any 1 to 1	ID numbers

Counts are an example of absolute scales; they cannot be transformed in any way: 20 of something, for example, 20 loan transactions, cannot be transformed into any other number. Time units, like seconds, minutes, hours, and measures of size, like meters or grams, are ratio scales. For example, 20 hours can be transformed into 1200 minutes and 20 meters to 2000 centimeters by multiplying by a suitable constant (60 and 100, respectively). Examples of interval scales are temperatures and calendar years: 20 degrees Celsius can be transformed into 68 degrees Fahrenheit and the year 2000 in the Christian calendar to the year 1378 in the Muhammadan calendar by suitable multiplications and/or additions. Ratings such as *excellent, good, satisfactory, fair, poor* can be represented by any set of numbers that preserve this ordering, for example, 5,4,3,2,1 or 95, 80, 60, 50, 30, and hence are an ordinal scale. The order of winners in a race, first, second, third, and so on, is another example of an ordinal scale. Any kind of transformation can be applied to ID numbers; for example, the numbers assigned to members of a hockey team can be permuted in any way so long as distinct numbers are assigned to distinct individuals. Hence this is an example of a nominal scale.

Ordinal scales can be used to make comparisons of size. Interval scales can be used to make comparisons of size and of differences in size. Ratio and absolute scales can be used to make comparisons of size, differences in size, and ratios of sizes. For example, if we use the librarian's subjective ordinal rating scale ("light," "moderate," "heavy") for the demand for a publication, we can say only that publication a is in greater demand than publication b; if we use date since last use (an interval scale), we can say that the demand for publication a exceeds that for publication b by x days; if we use number of times circulated per year over the past ten years (a ratio scale), we can say that the demand for publication a is x times that for publication b.

There are a number of different kinds of ordering, determined by the presence or absence of certain properties. These properties include reflexivity, symmetry, transitivity, and completeness, defined in Table 2.1, where A represents a set of elements a, b, c . . . , R = a relation on A, and a R b states that element a has relation R to element b.

In the examples, the relation "longer than" with texts is asymmetric, transitive, and negatively transitive, but is not reflexive or complete. However, the relation "of at least equal length with" would be complete. The relation of equality with numbers is reflexive, symmetric, transitive, and negatively transitive but is not asymmetric or complete. The relation of adjacency of colors in the spectrum is symmetric, but not reflexive, asymmetric, transitive, negatively transitive, or complete. The relation "greater than or equal to" with numbers is reflexive, transitive, negatively transitive,

Table 2.1
Properties of Ordering

Property	Definition	Example
Reflexivity	a R a (Any relation an element always has with itself)	Numbers with equality relation (a = a, a number is equal to itself)
Symmetry	a R b Implies b R a (any relation that holds regardless of order)	Colors with adjacency relation (if a is adjacent to b in the spectrum, b is also adjacent to a)
Asymmetry	a R b Implies not b R a for all a, b ∈ A	Text with "longer than" relation (if a is longer than b, then b is not longer than a)
Transitivity	a R b and b R c implies a R c	Text with "longer than" relation (if a is longer than b and b is longer than c, then a is longer than c)
Negative transitivity	Not a R b and not b R c implies not a R c	Text with "longer than" relation (if a is not longer than b and b is not longer than c, then a is not longer than c)
Completeness	a R b or b R a or both for all a, b ε A, a ≠ b.	Numbers with "greater than or equal to" relation (either a is greater than or equal to b or b is greater than or equal to a or both)

and complete, but is not symmetric or asymmetric. An example of a relation that is transitive but not negatively transitive is "has the same length" for texts. If a has the same length as b, and b has the same length as c, then we can conclude that a has the same length as c. However, if a does not have the same length as b, and b does not have the same length as c, we cannot conclude that a does not have the same length as c.

2.1.1 Ordinal Measurement

Ordinal measurement is sometimes called preference measurement. Given a relational system <A,R>, an ordinal measure m(a) for $a \in A$ is a function from A to the real numbers satisfying the condition that a R b (sometimes read as "a is preferred to b") for $a,b \in A$, if and only if $m(a) > m(b)$. Thus, an ordinal measure preserves the ordering of the set A. Roberts shows that the function m exists if and only if <A,R> is what is called a strict weak order. This relational system may be defined in two ways.

Definition 1

A strict weak order is a relational system that is asymmetric and negatively transitive, that is, for which

(1) a R b implies −b R a (asymmetry)
(2) −a R b and −b R c implies −a R c (negative transitivity).

In other words, (1) if a is preferred to b, b is not preferred to a, and (2) if a is not preferred to b and b is not preferred to c, then a is not preferred to c (the symbol − represents a logical not). Notice that the ordering of items in A is not necessarily complete; some pairs may be incomparable in that you can neither say that you prefer a to b nor that you prefer b to a; you are indifferent between a and b.

An equivalent definition of a strict weak order is the following.

Definition 2

A strict weak order is a relational system that is asymmetric and transitive and defines an equivalence relation a E b by:

a E b if and only if −a R b and −b R a.

In other words, a is equivalent to b if and only if it is neither the case that a is preferred to b nor that b is preferred to a.

An equivalence relation is a relation that is reflexive, symmetric, and transitive. The equivalence relation in preference orderings represents indifference between two elements of the set A. The total requirements for a strict weak order using Definition 2 are:

a R b implies −b R a	Asymmetry of ordering
a R b and b R c implies a R c	Transitivity of ordering
a E a	Reflexivity of equivalence
a E b implies b E a	Symmetry of equivalence
a E b and b E c implies a E c	Transitivity of equivalence

This definition, though longer, is usually easier to check with a particular relational system.

Ordinal measures are sometimes called ordinal utility functions. To determine whether such a function can be found, it is necessary to check whether the properties in Definition 1 or Definition 2 hold for all pairs of elements a and b, that is, whether the expressed preferences satisfy these properties. However, there is an easier way to determine if an ordinal measure exists, which will now be described.

Let m(x) be the number of times a in A = {a_1, a_2 . . .} such that x R a (x is preferred to a). Construct a matrix W whose rows represent the elements of A in decreasing order by values of m(x) and where W_{ij} = 1 if a_i R a_j, and 0 otherwise. If the zeros in the matrix are not all in the lower left-hand triangle of the matrix, this is not a strict weak order and no ordinal utility function exists.

Example A user compares each pair of a set of publications as to their informativeness with respect to a query. The results are as follows:

Publication (x)	a_1	a_2	a_3	a_4	a_5	*Utility m(x)*
a_1	0	1	1	1	1	4
a_2	0	0	1	0	1	2
a_3	0	0	0	0	1	1
a_4	0	0	0	0	1	1
a_5	0	0	0	0	0	0

An ordinal function does not exist because a_2 is not more informative than a_4 and a_4 is not more informative than a_3; however, a_2 is more informative than a_3. Thus, the preference ordering does not satisfy the property of negative transitivity in Definition 1. This situation might arise if the query had several aspects and a_2 and a_4 were about different aspects of the query and so were difficult to compare and, similarly, a_4 and a_3 were about different aspects and so could not be compared, but a_2 and a_3 were about the same aspects and b was the more informative for the user.

Schreider (1975) has proposed a relation called tolerance to represent situations in which items can resemble one another, that is, where items are comparable in some aspect or feature, but not in others. This kind of relation is exhibited in the work of the Dutch artist M. C. Escher (see Figure 2.1), where birds adjacent in a row or column resemble each other, but

Figure 2.1
Night and Day, by M. C. Escher. This drawing illustrates the concept of a tolerance relation, based on pairwise resemblances.

from beginning to end of a row or top to bottom of a column the birds change to plots in the landscape, and there is no resemblance. Thus, resemblance is not transitive.

A tolerance relation is reflexive and symmetric, but not transitive. Objects resemble themselves and if object a resembles object b, object b resembles object a. A resemblance relation cannot be used directly to partition the objects in a set into disjoint subsets, since if we form a subset of objects that resemble one another, there may be other objects that resemble some but not all objects in the subset. However, it is possible to describe a minimal set of possibly overlapping tolerance subsets such that any two tolerant items will appear together in at least one of these tolerance subsets, and if any tolerance subset is omitted, at least one pair of tolerant items will not appear together in a subset. As Schreider says, each element carries some definite information about the elements resembling it, but not all such information. Within tolerance subsets, items may be ordered.

A tolerance relation in a set of documents can be defined by the different descriptors of a query. Suppose we had the query: genetic studies of the evolution of the human race. Documents might deal with any combination of the three descriptors "genetic studies," "evolution," and "human race." Each descriptor defines a tolerance class, namely all documents described by that descriptor. However, these tolerance classes might *not* correspond to the user's comparable sets if the user is using some aspect other than the query terms to make decisions about comparability.

More concretely, consider a set of six documents retrieved in response to the sample query. Suppose the query descriptors assigned to each of the six documents are as shown in the following table, where a 1 indicates the document is assigned the descriptor and a 0 indicates that it is not.

	Query Descriptor		
Document	*Genetic Studies*	*Evolution*	*Human Race*
a_1	1	1	1
a_2	1	1	1
a_3	1	1	0
a_4	1	0	1
a_5	0	1	0
a_6	0	0	1

If the four documents relating to each aspect defined by a query term are comparable as to informativeness relating to that aspect, the initial descriptor-based tolerance classes would be:

$$\{a_1, a_2, a_3, a_4\}, \{a_1, a_2, a_3, a_5\}, \{a_1, a_2, a_4, a_6\}.$$

However, suppose a user's preferences produced the following comparable subsets:

$$\{a_1, a_2, a_4\}, \{a_1, a_2, a_3, a_5\}, \{a_6\}.$$

We see that the first set of comparable records corresponds to the intersection of the "genetic studies" and "human race" initial query-based classes and that the second set of comparable records corresponds to the "evolution" initial class. However, the third set does not correspond to any of the initial classes nor their union or intersection. Thus one suspects that some aspect other than the query descriptors (e.g., "overviews") is being used by the user in his or her preference assignments.

Schrieder shows that, not only do sets of features or aspects of records define a tolerance relation on the records, but, as well, grouping records or other items into comparable or tolerance classes provides us with a set of arbitrary or canonical features. When a tolerance relation is defined through a set of initial features (i.e., when two items are tolerant if they have at least one feature in common), the canonical features that are not initial features can be obtained by applying the operations of union and intersection to a collection of sets, where each set contains those items that possess one of the initial features.

Thus, in retrieval, the sets of comparable records correspond to the canonical features. If these are not consistent with the initial features, that is, with sets of documents assigned each of the query terms or their unions and intersections, then some other set of initial features must have generated the comparable sets. Determining these initial features is the key problem in retrieval.

2.1.2 Additive Measurement

If some kind of operation combining two or more elements is defined on a set, we may want to find a measure that can be added to represent the effect of the operation. For example, when we measure the size of a book by counting the number of pages, we know that we can measure the size of two books bound together by adding the number of pages in each. However, though we can measure both an amount of sugar and an amount of water in cups (or liters), the amount we get when we combine them is not the sum of the two separate amounts because the sugar dissolves in the water. Additive measures are not appropriate when the operation causes an interaction between the elements.

There are conditions on a relational system with an operation <A,R,O> for the existence of an additive measure, that is, a function m such that m(a O b) = m(a) + m(b). According to Roberts, these conditions are, for any a,b,c $\in$ A:

1. <A,R> is a strict weak order. In other words, if an additive measure exists, the relational system will satisfy the requirements for an ordinal measure, as described in the last section.

2. a O (b O c) = (a O b) O c. In other words, the operation is associative; the result is independent of the sequence in which it is applied. Multiplication is associative because, for example, $12 \cdot (6 \cdot 2) = 12 \cdot 12 = 144$ and also $(12 \cdot 6) \cdot 2 = 72 \cdot 2 = 144$. However, division is not associative because, for example, $12/(6/2) = 12/3 = 4$, but $(12/6)/2 = 2/2 = 1$.

3. a R b if and only if (a O c)R(b O c). In other words, the operation is monotonic; the relationship continues to hold between a and b when we apply the same operation to both. Thus, with numbers, if $a > b$, then if we add 2 to both a and b we will have $a + 2 > b + 2$.

4. a O b = b O a. In other words, the operation is commutative; the order of the elements is immaterial in applying the operation. For example, multiplication is commutative ($3 \cdot 5 = 5 \cdot 3$), but division is not ($3/5 \neq 5/3$).

5. If a R b, there is a positive integer n such that, for any c and d, (na O c)R(nb O d). By na we mean that we apply the operation n times to a. This condition is called the Archimedean property. It means, roughly, that if a is greater than b, in some sense, then, by taking a sufficient number of "copies" of a and b, that is, n copies, and "adding" them, respectively,

to c and d, we can always make the combination with c greater than that with d, even if, initially, d was greater than c. This condition clearly applies to numbers and the operation of adding. For example, $5 < 10$; however, $6 * 2 + 5 > 6 * 1 + 10$. However, in order to apply it to other sets, we must be able to define what we mean by n copies of an element of these other sets.

Example of an Additive Measure

Let a and b be texts and let a O b represent the operation of reading text a followed by text b (concatenation). Let the informativeness of a text x be defined by

$$I(x) = n(x)$$

where n(x) is the number of pages in x. Since the number of pages in a followed by b is n(a) + n(b), I(a O b) is an additive measure, that is,

$$I(a \text{ O } b) = I(a) + I(b).$$

However, this definition of amount of information, though additive under concatenation, does not seem valid in terms of the way we use the word information. For example, the Archimedean property, though formally true, does not seem to relate to the information provided by records. Reading a record *n* times does not seem like an operation that will increase its informativeness *n*-fold for the reader. Yet this is what the Archimedean property requires.

Suppose that, instead of defining the informativeness of a text as number of pages, a user determines, for all pairs of texts, whether one is more informative than the other. Will the five conditions for an additive measure be satisfied? His preferences would have to follow the axioms of a strict weak order, as described earlier for an ordinal measure to exist. Associativity would not be a problem since the nature of the text sequence does not really change under grouping. However, monotonicity is a problem, since it says that if a is more informative than b, a followed by another text c will be more informative than b followed by c. But this may not be the case because of interactions of a and b with c. For example, if c contains a definition of terms in b, then prefixing c to be may make it more informative than prefixing it to a, where terms were already defined. The Archimedean property is unlikely to hold, also, since, as we have suggested, reading a text additional times may not increase its informativeness. Commutativity, also, may not hold because, for example, a provides information needed to understand b.

As we have seen in the previous section, it is not always possible to find an ordinal utility function for information. There is a *representation* problem. One reason for this problem is that the indifference relationship is not necessarily transitive. In the example, because there were various aspects to the user's query, the user was indifferent between documents that covered different aspects, but could compare as to informativeness documents about the same aspects. An additive informativeness function is even more difficult to attain, since it requires that the information provided by one document be independent of that provided by another, that is, when two documents are read, there is no interaction between them in terms of the amount of information they provide to the reader. This is a virtually impossible requirement, for example, in considering the effect of rereading the same document.

2.1.3 Aggregation of Ordinal Measures

The preference situation becomes even more difficult when we need to aggregate values over a number of judges, as might occur in group decision-making situations. For example, several judges might rank the importance to the user community of a number of different proposed new services for an information service: a CD-ROM collection, a video collection, a software collection, and commercial online systems access. How do we combine their rankings into a consensus function?

Situations in which a group of individuals each indicate preferences between pairs of items are called pair comparison systems. Such systems are described by a set of items A and the function p_{ab}, $a, b \in A$, which represents the proportion of individuals in the decision-making group who prefer a to b. In a sense, p_{ab} measures the strength of the preference for a over b or the degree of consensus among the group.

We want to find a measure of this strength of preference, a measure f(x) for all items x in A, which is an ordinal utility function, that is, for which

$$f(a) > f(b) \text{ if and only if } p_{ab} > p_{ba}.$$

To derive the function f, which is called a probabilistic consistency measure, we define a relation W as follows:

$$a \, W \, b \text{ if and only if } p_{ab} > p_{ba}.$$

Then the ordinal function f exists if and only if the relation W is a strict weak order, as we saw in the previous section. If such a function f is possible, we can define f(a) as the number of items $x \in A$ such that a W x, that is, the number of items compared to which a was preferred by a majority of the judges. Thus, f(x) is our consensus function.

The strict weak order condition means that the preference relation W must be transitive, a condition that does not always hold. For example, if a is a CD-ROM collection, b is a video collection, and c is a software collection, we might have

$$p_{ab} = p_{ba} = \tfrac{1}{2},\ p_{bc} = \tfrac{1}{3},\ p_{cb} = \tfrac{2}{3},\ p_{ac} = \tfrac{3}{4},\ p_{ca} = \tfrac{1}{4}.$$

Then a W c and c W b, but not a W b.

An alternative consensus function to the probabilistic consistency measure is the Borda count g. Assume each judge's preferences define a strict weak order. Let $g_i(x)$ represent the number of elements to which x is strictly preferred (ranked above) by the *i*th judge. Then let

$$g(x) = \Sigma g_i(x)$$

and let a be preferred, by the group, to b if and only if $g(a) > g(b)$.

Even if each judge's preferences satisfy a strict weak order, the probabilistic consistency measure and the Borda count may be incompatible. We may have $g(a) > g(b)$, but $f(a) < f(b)$. This is shown in the following example.

Example A sample of four judges from a user community rank three searches, s_1, s_2, s_3, as to informativeness as follows:

	Judge's Preference			
Comparison	*J1*	*J2*	*J3*	*J4*
s_1 vs. s_2	s_1	s_2	s_1	s_1
s_1 vs. s_3	s_1	s_3	s_3	s_1
s_2 vs. s_3	s_2	s_2	s_3	s_3

Judge J1's preference ordering is s_1, s_2, s_3. Judge J2's preference ordering is s_2, s_3, s_1. Judge J3's preference ordering is s_3, s_1, s_2. Judge J4's preference ordering is s_1, s_3, s_2. Thus p_{xy}, the proportion of judges who prefer x to y, is given by

$$p_{12} = \tfrac{3}{4};\ p_{21} = \tfrac{1}{4}$$
$$p_{13} = \tfrac{1}{2};\ p_{31} = \tfrac{1}{2}$$
$$p_{23} = \tfrac{1}{2};\ p_{32} = \tfrac{1}{2}.$$

Thus, f(x), the probabilistic consistency measure (the number of items to which x was preferred by three or four judges), is given by $f(s_1) = 1$, $f(s_2) = 0$, and $f(s_3) = 0$, and so, $s_1 > s_2$, $s_1 = s_3$, and $s_2 = s_3$.

The Borda count g(x) is given in the following table:

	Number of searches ranked below		
Judge	s_1	s_2	s_3
1	2	1	0
2	0	2	1
3	1	0	2
4	2	0	1
g(x)	5	3	4

and so $s_1 > s_3 > s_2$.

Thus, the probabilistic consistency measure, based on proportion of judges, results in a nontransitive measure, in which s_1 is superior to s_2, but indifferent to s_3, while s_2 and s_3 are indifferent. The Borda count, on the other hand, results in a transitive measure, in which s_1 is superior to s_2, which, in turn, is superior to s_3. The reason for the discrepancy is that the probabilistic consistency measure simply looks at proportion of judges preferring x to y, whereas the Borda count also looks at the distance in ranking between x and y for each judge. Thus, the Borda count is, in a sense, a more discriminating measure.

As with measures for single users or judges, an important consideration is the transitivity of preference and indifference. If judgments are not transitive, neither the probabilistic consistency measure nor the Borda count provides an ordinal measure. Thus, an important consideration in developing a measure of information is the question of whether or not informativeness is transitive. Can we assume, if record x is more informative than record y, and record y is more informative than record z, that record x is more informative than record z? Can we make similar assumptions regarding indifference? These are questions that must be answered, not by mathematical theory, but by empirical observation of how people make informativeness judgments.

2.1.4 Hypergraphs and Chains

In developing a mathematical model for information measurement, we have described the records read by the user simply as an unstructured set. However, some writers (see Tompa, 1989; Watters and Shepherd, 1990; Tague *et al.*, 1991) have suggested that the database or collection of an information service can best be modeled by a mathematical structure called a hypergraph. A hypergraph is a mathematical generalization of the mathematical structure called a graph, which consists of a set of nodes and a set of links joining the nodes.

A hypergraph H is described by a pair of sets (T,E), where T is a set of nodes representing records and E is a family of nonempty subsets of T such that any record $t \in T$ is included in at least one subset of E. (See Figure 2.2.) A chain $C = (E_1, E_2 \ldots E_k)$ is a sequence of edges and represents a weak ordering of some of the records of T, in which all records in E_i precede any record in E_{i+1}, though within the subsets the order of elements may be random. The subsets might represent all records that have the same degree of informativeness, and the chain, subsets of increasing informativeness.

The mathematical formalism of edges and chains will be useful in developing a theory of information measurement for the retrieval function of information services. They are more complete and more discriminating

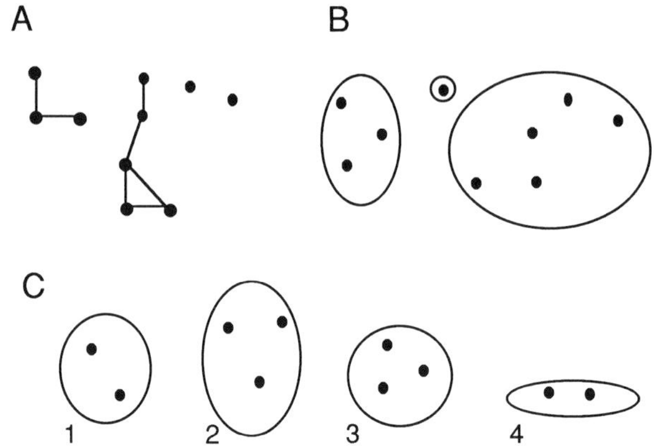

Figure 2.2
A diagrammatic representation of a graph (A), a hypergraph (B), and a chain (C).

than other models that have been proposed for information retrieval, such as the vector space model, the Boolean model, and the relational model. (For a comparison of these models, see Tague *et al.*, 1991.) We will use this formalism in developing a general measure of informativeness in Chapter 3.

2.2 Reasonable Properties for a Measure of Information

Given the definition of information developed in Chapter 1 and the mathematical properties of measures just described, what formal properties would we expect of an informativeness measure in the context of information services? The following seven properties are suggested as consistent with this definition of information and the need for evaluative measures for information services. As in earlier sections, we will speak of the informativeness of records, where the term record means a sequence of text, graphics, sound, and the like, which is meaningful to some of the users of the service. The seven properties are grouped into four areas. In the first section, domain and range of informativeness, we look at the properties of a measure as they relate to a single record–user interaction. In the second section, we look at the joint informativeness for a user of record sets and ordered sets, or sequences. In the third section, we look at the overall informativeness of an information service as it serves some community over a period of time.

2.2.1 Domain and Range of Informativeness

Property 1 Informativeness is a nonnegative number associated with the *interaction* of a record and a user.

Informativeness is a measure of the extent to which a record provides information to an individual, the user. Information is what the user understands from the record, which depends on the cognitive state of the user. The record contains potential information before it is read, but the actual information will be determined by what the user is seeking and by her or his knowledge store at the point in time the record is read.

Information is the conceptualization the record produces in short-term memory and informativeness measures the extent of this conceptualization. Some of this information may also produce a change in the user's stock of knowledge, in long-term memory. By specifying that informativeness is nonnegative, we are saying that understanding either occurs to some degree or not at all. It cannot reduce short-term conceptualizations because of their transience. Not all writers agree that informativeness cannot be negative. Jumarie (1990) suggests that some records may be so confusing or misleading as to reduce the individual's store of knowledge. However, Jumarie seems to be defining information as long-term memory rather than short-term memory conceptual structures.

Corollary 1 The informativeness of a record may vary from user to user.

Because information is what the *user* understands from the record and may depend on what she or he already knows or is seeking, different users may receive different amounts of information from the record. However, the extent to which users have a common information need or reason for reading a record and a common knowledge base will determine the extent to which the informativeness value of a record will vary or be constant over the user group. As Schreider has pointed out, someone who is familiar with an area of knowledge will probably derive more from a new text in this area than someone who is totally ignorant of the area. However, there may be a saturation point, beyond which the expert will not receive any further information from new texts in the area of knowledge.

Corollary 2 Informativeness is not totally determined by some special aspect of the record, for example, its probability or its syntactic or logical structure or the computational process used to produce it.

Because information services collect such a wide variety of text, graphic, sound, video, and other kinds of records, and collect records in such large numbers, any measure of information that depends on special properties of the record, probabilistic, logical, syntactic, or other would be, at the least, impractical and in many cases impossible to determine. As we shall see, logical and syntactic measures would require a translation of the original records into a special form. Computational measures would require knowledge of the program used to produce the record. Probabilistic measures would require the determination of probabilities for all user–record interactions.

It is certainly not self-evident that information, in the sense we have defined it, as what the user understands from the record, is completely determined by such properties, although it may certainly be affected by them. What the user understands may be affected by the probability, that is, the surprise value, of the record, by the logical propositions it implies, by the complexity of its syntactic structure, by the effort required to produce it. However, none of these properties vary from user to user. Thus, they do not reflect all of the potential variation in information that different users will get from the same record.

Property 2 Information has magnitude, but the amount of information in a user–record interaction, or informativeness, cannot, in general, be measured directly. However, user preferences or rankings of records relative to amount of information preserve any ordering of the informativeness values.

We thus are hypothesizing that there is an underlying, unobservable amount of information in a record for a user. This unobservable variable may be ordinal, interval, ratio, or absolute in scale; we have insufficient evidence to decide. However, what *can* be observed, at least in some situations, are user preferences as to the informativeness of records. It is sometimes possible for individual users to compare two records with respect to their relative informativeness. However, we do not assume that all records can be compared as to informativeness, that is, we assume that the user may sometimes be unable to say which of two records is the more informative. Most likely, it will be possible to rank records when the user has a well-defined problem that the information in the record can help solve. Given any two records, therefore, a user can say one of the following:

1. record a is more informative than record b (a > b),
2. record b is more informative than record a (b > a),
3. records a and b are equally informative (a = b),
4. records a and b cannot be compared as to informativeness (a ~ b).

If both of two records deal with only one aspect of the user's information need, the user will probably have no difficulty with the decision about which is the more informative, or whether they are equally informative. However, sometimes the information need will have several aspects, and if the two records deal with more than one aspect of the problem, the user may not be able to compare them as to informativeness (i.e., he or she may be indifferent to both of them). One record may be more informative with respect to one aspect and the other record more informative with respect to another aspect. If the user *can* always order any two records that deal with several aspects of the information need, it will usually be the case that some aspects are more important than others; the user can order aspects as well as records, and judges the record to be more informative if it is more informative with respect to a more important aspect.

Thus, in this approach to informativeness we do not assume that the user can do more than order records with respect to their amount of information. We do not assume that she or he can assign a *magnitude,* a real number, to represent the amount of informativeness, in the sense that one can assign a real number to represent the height or the length of a record. Our approach, if informativeness is seen as similar to relevance, diverges somewhat from that of Eisenberg (1988), who uses magnitude estimation techniques to measure relevance. Our view is that individuals cannot reliably judge informativeness beyond the ordinal level, though there may be an underlying value that forms part of a continuum. The situation is similar to judging the loudness of sounds. Most individuals can say which of two sounds is the louder; however, they cannot provide the number that measures the sound in decibels. For informativeness, there is no audiometer for making individual judgments more precise.

2.2.2 Informativeness of Record Sets and Sequences

Since the informativeness measure will be an ordinal one, records can be assigned informativeness values only relative to other records in a set of records with which the user has interacted. With a set of records, records may be combined or concatenated into a sequence, and we need to consider how the informativeness measure will be assigned to sequences as well as individual records.

Property 3 Records may be concatenated and informativeness measured for individual records and for their concatenation. Informativeness is not necessarily commutative or additive under concatenation.

Concatenation of two records means that they are both read, one after another. The order in which records are concatenated may affect their informativeness ranking. For example, if one record (1) explains or defines concepts used without definition in another record, (2) the concatenation ba would be confusing, whereas the concatenation ab would be clear. If records are independent, the informativeness of ab and ba will be equal. In general, though, the informativeness of a set of records may depend on the order in which they are read. For example, Eisenberg and Barry (1988) found that users assigned documents to different relevance categories vis-à-vis a query depending on the order in which the documents were presented. Also, the informativeness of concatenated records is not necessarily additive, since records may interact, providing more information, or be repetitious, providing less information, than the two records considered separately.

Property 4 Some subsequences of records are also records (i.e., meaningful) and can be assessed as to informativeness. The total informativeness of the record is invariant under partitioning into record subsequences of differing granularity.

An essential characteristic of text is that substrings (subsequences) of text are also texts (subtexts) above some atomic level such as a sentence or other kind of meaningful unit. We have seen in Property 3 that the informativeness of a text is not necessarily the sum of the informativeness values of a set of subtexts that partition the text because of interaction effects. However, so long as the order of the sequence of subtexts remains the same, partitioning into finer and finer units (increasing the granularity), for example, into sections, paragraphs, sentences, will not affect the total informativeness of the text, provided the user reads in the same sequence.

Property 5 When records are ordered according to nonincreasing user preference (i.e., with the most informative records first but with ties in ordering permitted), the informativeness of a subsequence is approximately proportional to the logarithm of the number of records in the subsequence.

This requirement reflects a kind of law of diminishing returns when we read records about a particular topic or for a particular need (a query). Early items provide the most information, in terms of adding to what we already know; later ones will repeat at least some of this additional knowledge. In probabilistic terms, the probability we have already acquired the information in a record increases as we read more records. Thus, in terms of an underlying informativeness continuum, the density of information drops.

There is scattered evidence that such a logarithmic law of diminishing returns exists for the informativeness over all records of records relevant to a topic or information need. Bradford's law (Bradford, 1948) of journal or source productivity, which has been validated for many topic areas, stipulates a logarithmic relationship between number of journals or sources, when these are ranked by number of records relating to the topic and the cumulated number of relevant records provided. In retrieval experiments, plots of the number of items retrieved against number of relevant items retrieved usually show a logarithmic relationship. An example is given in Figure 2.3, which shows the number of retrieved items needed to obtain a specified number of relevant items for a search described in Salton (1975). May (1968) evaluated the literature of a field of mathematics (determinants) and found that the number of new papers grew exponentially over time

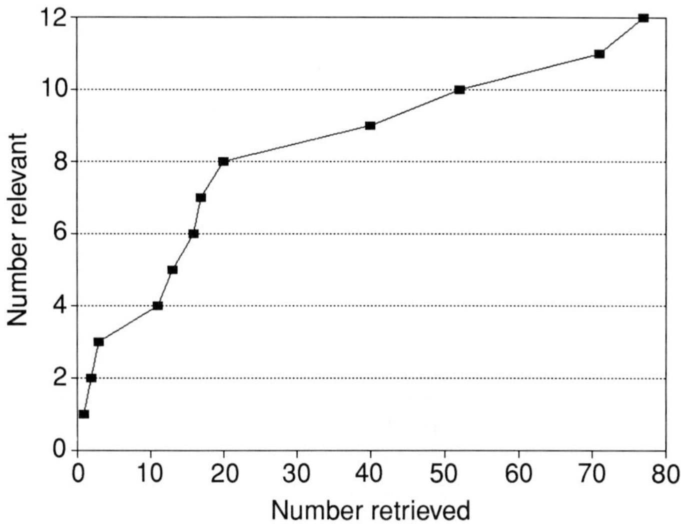

Figure 2.3
A graph showing the approximately logarithmic relationship between number of relevant items and number of retrieved items in a ranked search output, based on a search reported in Salton (1975).

but the number of new ideas grew only linearly. Transformed to a logarithmic scale, this result shows that number of papers published and number of new ideas have the same relationship as numbers retrieved and numbers relevant in a database search.

A logarithmic law is consistent with the Weber-Fechner law that the magnitude of a psychological response to a stimulus varies directly as the logarithm of the magnitude of the stimulus. A number of writers have suggested that the Weber-Fechner law can also be applied to the processing of information, among them Brookes (1980a,b) and Resnikoff (1989). Brookes suggests that if, as claimed by the Weber-Fechner law, our sensory mechanisms behave according to a logarithmic law, it is possible that all of our neural mechanisms behave in this way.

A logarithmic law is, of course, also consistent with the most widely accepted measure of information, that of Shannon, which, as we shall discuss in Chapter 3, is based on the idea that the information provided by a "message" is inversely related to the *logarithm* of its probability. Although we do not take a probabilistic approach in general, the informativeness measure we shall develop in Chapter 3 can be considered as a generalization of Shannon's, taking into account the interaction of the sender and receiver.

Property 6 The informativeness of the response of an information service to a user query is related to the completeness and ordering of the records perused in the retrieval process with respect to those in an ideal chain of records, where this chain represents the records that will completely satisfy the user's information need.

For each query, or verbalized information need from an information service user, there are one or more ideal answers, a chain of records that completely satisfies this need. Recall that a chain is a weak ordering of a subset of records of the database. An ideal chain represents the ideal sequence of records for the user. Because, for some information needs, there may be alternative ways of satisfying the user's need, there may be more than one ideal chain for a user with a query.

Queries can be categorized in terms of the number of records in the ideal chain, the number of alternative ideal chains that could be provided, and the extent to which the records and ordering of the ideal chain will vary from person to person with the same query. For example, queries requiring short, factual answers, queries of the "who," "what," "where," "when" variety, will have short ideal chains (usually one record) and will vary little from one user to another. There may be more than one ideal chain, for example, single record, which satisfies the user. On the other hand, a background study for a major research thrust will have a single ideal chain of many records for one researcher, and two researchers embarking on a study of the same problem may vary in the records they would want to examine, that is, in their ideal chains.

The retrieval trail, that is, the record sequence that a user peruses in the database or collection of the information service, varies in size and ordering depending on the search strategy. The amount of information provided by the retrieval trail, or its informativeness, will depend on the degree to which it provides the user with the records in an ideal chain, rather than noninformative records, and whether it provides them in the optimal reading or perusal order for the user. The information provided by a record is order dependent or context sensitive, thus the order of the retrieval trail is important in determining its informativeness for the user. This order effect, for example, is evident in the study of Eisenberg and Barry (1988), who found that order of presentation of documents to users affected relevance judgments.

The ideal chain is similar to the relevant set of earlier studies but differs in two ways. First, an ideal chain contains only as many records as are needed to satisfy the user's information need, not all records that are "about" the query in some sense. Second, the records in the ideal chain are weakly ordered as to degree of informativeness.

How can an ideal chain, an ideal output of the system for the user be determined? This problem is an old one in information retrieval testing, under the guise of the determination of absolute recall. How can one distinguish the sequence of records, the trail the user *should* have followed, from the one actually followed? It is probably unrealistic to expect that we can obtain perfect knowledge of an ideal chain. It is not unrealistic, however, to expect that we can estimate divergences from this chain in the retrieval trail and that our estimates will be more or less valid depending on the procedures we use. We will return to the question of determining the ideal chain in Chapter 6.

2.2.3 Informativeness of Information Services

Property 7 The informativeness of an information service organization to a user community (actual and potential) is a measure of the extent to which the service satisfies the information needs of the community. It is a function of the degree to which community needs are served by the organization and the timeliness and informativeness of each service.

The informativeness measure must be capable of aggregation over records and users if it is to serve as a basis for information service organization evaluation. To fulfill this purpose, the informativeness of the service is assessed at a number of levels:

- the informativeness of a sequence of records provided by a service in response to an individual user's information need at a particular point in time;
- the informativeness of a sequence of uses of a particular record over a period of time;
- the informativeness of an information service with respect to the needs of a user community over a period of time.

Thus, we would like to be able to aggregate the information measure over records, over users, and over time. However, it will not necessarily be the case that a measure of the informativeness of a sequence of records for a user at a point in time will be additive, so that one can simply add the informativeness values for individual records to determine the informativeness, say, of a retrieval trail. The reason is that information is dynamic, so that the informativeness of a set of records in one sequence is not the same as the informativeness of records in another sequence.

It is similar with a set of users. The overall needs of the community may best be served by making available certain information to certain members of the community at a certain time. Its performance should, in some sense, be compared with this ideal. For example, it may be the case that some members of the community are currently nonusers, but the community would benefit, in terms of having its information needs better met, by having specific records provided to them. It may be the case that some users should have seen some records earlier than they did. For a user community, we assume there is an optimal sequence of user–record interactions or information service. To determine the overall value of the actual service to the community, we compare it with an estimate of this ideal.

2.2.4 Use of an Informativeness Measure

Aggregation of the informativeness measure provides us with a way to answer the evaluation questions about the functions described in Chapter 1, Section 1.4. These functions of an information service were summarized as collection, description, retrieval, and packaging. The questions were as follows:

Collection

1. How much information does the collection or database contain for its user community, compared to other collections or databases?
2. How much information for the user community does a single record provide to the user community over some period of time? How much will it provide in the future?

Description

3. How much more informative for users in general and for particular groups of users is one type of description than another, where description includes all varieties of indexing, abstracting, classifying, cataloging, extracting, and so on?

Retrieval

4. How much information does the record sequence retrieved by a search strategy provide to the user with a particular information need at a particular point in time? How much information that, potentially, could satisfy this need is missed?
5. How much more informative is one type of strategy than another in satisfying the needs of the user community?

Packaging

6. How much information for the user community does a record surrogate provide about the original record?
7. How much information is added for the user community in general and for particular user groups by the analysis and synthesis of records by an information professional?

2.3 Summary

We have looked at measurement as a function from a set of items to the set of real numbers that preserves certain relations and operations of the set of items. We have distinguished ordinal measurement, which preserves a preference relation among the items of the set, from additive measurement, which, as well, preserves a combining or concatenating operation among the items of the set.

Following this introduction to the concepts of measurement theory, *we defined informativeness as a subjective, ordinal-level, cumulatively logarithmic, noncommutative context-sensitive measure of the information produced by the interaction of users and records.* In Chapter 3, we will examine measures of information suggested by earlier writers to determine the extent to which they satisfy these criteria.

2.4 Review Problems

2.4.1 What are the scale types (nominal, ordinal, interval, ratio, absolute) for the indicated measures of the following conceptual variables? If necessary, you may contextualize the variable in order to arrive at a measure.

Variable	*Measure*
Computer use	Connect time in seconds
Geographic location	Postal code
Amount of unemployment	Monthly unemployment rate
Intelligence	IQ scores
Voter intentions	Opinion polls
Popularity of a TV show	Neilson ratings
Academic achievement	Grade point average
Demand for a database record	Number of times accessed

2.4.2 The teacher of a course on research methods rates five books as possible texts for the course by means of a set of binary preferences. Let B = {a,b,c,d,e} represent the set of possible texts, and the symbol $>$, the relationship "is preferred to." The preferences are as follows:

$$a > b,\ a > d,\ b > c,\ e > b,\ e > d.$$

Can an ordinal measure be found for this preference relation? If yes, provide one such function. If no, explain in what way the negative transitivity requirement is not satisfied.

2.4.3 A class of students S all read a section of the course textbook. We let the information provide to any student s by this section be measured by the number n(s) of questions the student answers correctly on a test about the material in the section. Is this measure additive over the class of students, that is, is the information provided by the section to two students the sum of their scores on the text?

2.4.4 Five instructors of different sections of a course wish to select a text from among four possibilities: a, b, c, d. The preferences for each instructor are as follows:

	Instructor number				
Comparison	*1*	*2*	*3*	*4*	*5*
a vs. b	b	a	a	a	b
a vs. c	c	c	a	a	c
a vs. d	d	d	d	a	a
b vs. c	c	c	b	c	b
b vs. d	d	d	d	d	b
c vs. d	d	d	d	d	c

Determine a consensus function for these preferences relating to texts using (1) the probabilistic consistency measure and (2) the Borda count. Which do you think should be used to reach a decision about the text?

2.4.5 Carry out an online or manual search of a library catalog or commercial database for records pertaining to a topic of interest to you. Keep a log of the items retrieved and the items found informative. Based on this log, answer the following questions:

- Plot the number of informative items against the number of retrieved items. Is this plot approximately logarithmic in shape?
- Can you compare all items as to informativeness? Does an ordinal measure of informativeness exist based on your preferences?
- Can you determine the order in which it would have been most useful to access the informative records?

3

A Review of Earlier Measures of Information

This chapter reviews measures proposed by earlier writers of the information provided by records, texts, messages, propositions, and similar entities. They will be examined for consistency with the seven desirable properties presented in Chapter 2 of a measure of information for information services, namely: subjectivity, ordinality, nonadditivity, invariance over granularities, logarithmic relation to size, order dependence, and delay discounting.

In this review we will classify earlier measures on the basis of the particular model or structure that must be imposed on the record in order for an informativeness value to be calculated. These models may be categorized as probabilistic and related set theoretic, semantic or logical, statistical, and algorithmic. A good overview of these measures and their application in a variety of fields will be found in Losee (1990).

Probabilistic measures, sometimes called entropy or selective measures, assume that the informativeness of a message in a communication system is inversely and logarithmically related to its probability or likelihood of occurring in some context. Set-theoretic measures are extensions of probabilistic measures, but assume that information, rather than probability, is an atomic property of an event. Semantic information measures are of two types: logical measures and linguistic measures. Both assume that the language of the record can be formally described. Logical measures are concerned with the informativeness of statements in first-order predicate or the propositional logic. Linguistic measures are based on the properties of a semantic network or a tree representation of text. Statistical measures are concerned with the information provided by a sample in statistical inference or decision making. Algorithmic information or computational measures determine the information in a computer output on the basis of the length of the algorithm needed to produce it.

3.1 Probabilistic Measures

3.1.1 Shannon's Measure

The best-known measure of information is that developed by Shannon in 1948 as part of a mathematical theory of communication. This theory was concerned primarily with signal transmission, that is, with efficient ways of coding and transmitting messages. It was also concerned with sequences of characters, not with their content or interpretation. The components of the Shannon model are conventionally pictured as follows:

$$\textit{Source} \rightarrow \textit{Encoder} \rightarrow \underset{\substack{\uparrow \\ \textit{Noise}}}{\textit{Channel}} \rightarrow \textit{Decoder} \rightarrow \textit{Destination}$$

The source generates a finite set of messages. The encoder assigns a code word (set of symbols) to each distinct message. A message may be thought of as a sequence of characters or what we have called a record. The message is transmitted through the channel but may be distorted because of noise, with the result that the received coded message is not the same as the message sent.

Shannon associated a quantity called uncertainty with each message, equal to $\log_2 1/p$, where p is the probability of the message. Thus, the larger the probability, the smaller the uncertainty and vice versa. For a source X, a quantity called H(X) entropy, or average uncertainty, is defined by

$$H(X) = -\Sigma_i p_i \log_2 p_i$$

where p_i represents the probability of the ith message generated by the source, and the summation is over all messages. Entropy represents the uncertainty removed or information provided by revealing the message, and hence is in a sense a measure of information.

Shannon showed that a function must have this form if it is to satisfy three intuitively appealing properties:

1. If $p_i = 1/n$ for all of a total of n messages, H(X) is a monotonically increasing function of n. In other words, if all messages are equally probable, average uncertainty increases as the number of messages increases.

2. If X and Y represent two independent sources, the joint average uncertainty associated with the two messages, H(XY) is the sum H(X) + H(Y) of the two separate entropies. When X and Y are dependent, H(XY) < H(X) + H(Y). In other words, two sources together can never have greater uncertainty than the sum of the two uncertainties.

3. H has its greatest value, for a fixed number of messages, when all messages are equally probable.

The Shannon measure is a measure of the surprise value of a message. It is purely a function of the probabilities of the messages. It is not a direct measure of the information in a message in the sense we have defined above, that is, it does not depend on what the user understands by the message, only on its probability. The probability of a message could certainly be one aspect of its informativeness, but need not be the only aspect. Informativeness primarily depends on the meaning of the message to the user. A needed telephone number may be less surprising but more informative to a user than the largest prime number.

The Shannon measure of information is a ratio scale, since there is a natural zero ($\log_2 1 = 0$), and an equivalent scale can be derived by multiplying by a constant. In particular, the logs may be taken to any base, since

$$\log_k p = \log_2 p / \log_2 k.$$

However, it is convenient to take two as the logarithm base, since then one unit of information, called a bit, is associated with the transmission of one of two equally probable messages.

Entropy also measures information in the sense that it is the minimum average number of yes–no questions needed to determine which message occurs. Suppose the message was the number of dots on the upturned face of a single die, when it has been tossed. There are six possible messages (1,2,3,4,5,6); each message has a probability of $\frac{1}{6}$, assuming the die is a fair one, and

$$H = -\Sigma p \log_2 p = -6(\tfrac{1}{6})\log_2(\tfrac{1}{6}) = \log_2 6 = 2.58.$$

The decision tree for determining the number (X) on the die with a sequence of yes and no questions is shown in Figure 3.1.

Summing the lengths of all possible paths on the decision tree and dividing by six, the number of paths, we find that the average number of questions is 2.67. There is no way the decision tree can be drawn with one fewer question, since in that case the average number of questions would 2.5, that is, less than the entropy value of 2.58.

Picard (1980) has generalized this notion of information as an average number of questions to what he calls a questionnaire, by which he means a connected graph consisting of nonterminal nodes called questions and terminal nodes called answers. Each directed link (arc) <i,j> from node i to node j is assigned a probability value p(i,j). Then, the information processed by answering a question i is the sum

$$J(i) = \sum_j \frac{p(i,j)}{p(i)} \log_2 \frac{p(i)}{p(i)},$$

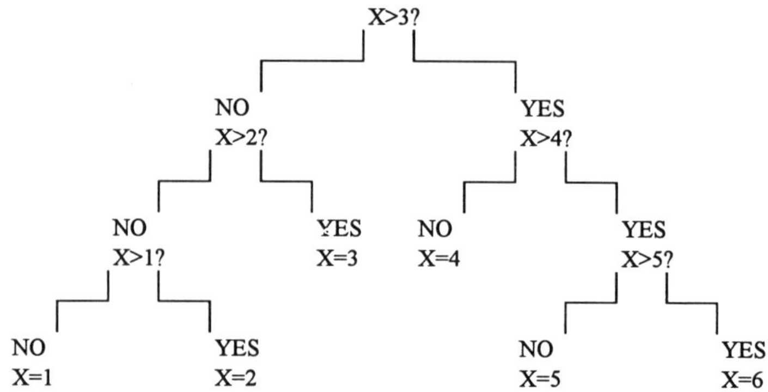

Figure 3.1
A decision tree for determining the number X on a single die using a sequence of YES and NO questions.

where the sum is over all arcs for which i is the initial node and $p(\mathrm{i}) = \Sigma_{\mathrm{j}} p(\mathrm{i,j})$. The total information transmitted by the questionnaire is

$$\mathrm{J} = -\Sigma_{\mathrm{i}}\, p(\mathrm{i}) \log_2 p(\mathrm{i}),$$

where the summation is over all terminal nodes i.

In a similar way, entropy provides a lower bound on the average length of a codeword when there are a fixed number of symbols to code, but codeword lengths need not be equal. For example, if there are six symbols to code, the average codeword length will be at least 2.58. If codewords are to be equal length, the length will have to be 3. However, if length may vary and if symbols are not of equal probability, the minimum average codeword length is obtained by letting the length n_i for the *i*th symbol be

$$\mathrm{n}_i = -\log_2 p_i,$$

where p_i is the probability of the *i*th symbol. Pierce (1965) has determined that if we encode English text letter by letter, disregarding the relative probabilities of letters, we require 4.76 bits of information, whereas if we encode word by word, taking into account the relative probability of words, we require only 2.14 bits per letter.

A measure associated with entropy in informatin theory is redundancy, defined as:

$$\text{redundancy} = 1 - \mathrm{H(X)}/\mathrm{H}_{n,\max}(\mathrm{X}) = [\log_2 n - \mathrm{H(X)}]/\log_2 n,$$

where H(X) is the entropy of the set X of messages and $\mathrm{H}_{n,\max}$ is the maximum entropy value when there are *n* messages in the set X. Thus, using the figures given above for coding English word by word, the redundancy of the English language is $1 - 2.14/4.76 = .56$. This means that, in effect, considered strictly as a coding device, English spelling is not particularly efficient, and we could transmit the same thing with fewer characters. For example, we could transmit the word "the" as a single character (as stenographers already know). However, redundancy may assist in reception when the channel is noisy or in human communication, when the message is difficult to understand.

A similar interpretation of the Shannon measure is given by Bookstein and Klein (1990), who show that, given a probabilistic message generator, the information contained in its message set can be defined as the smallest amount of storage, on the average, needed to store the encoded output of the generator. Let p_i be the probability and l_i the bit string length of a compressed representation of the ith message generated by the source. The average compressed message length is then

$$L = \Sigma p_i l_i.$$

The entropy of the source is the minimum value of this length, where the minimum is taken over all possible compression procedures. Using Lagrangian techniques, they show that the average length is minimized when $l_i = -\log p_i$, that is, when the average length is given by the Shannon formula.

Shannon also defined the properties of joint entropy and conditional entropy for two message sources. Let X and Y be random variables representing two message sources. For example, X might be the transmitted message and Y the received message. The joint entropy H(XY) represents the uncertainty associated with X and Y together. The conditional entropy H(X/Y) represents the uncertainty associated with X given that Y is known. This uncertainty in transmission is caused by noise in the channel. If $H(X/Y) = 0$, the channel is said to be noiseless.

If p_{ij} is the joint probability of values x_i and y_j, p_i, the probability of x_i, and q_j, the probability of y_j, then the joint entropy is defined by

$$H(XY) = -\Sigma_i\Sigma_j p_{ij} \log_2 p_{ij} = H(YX)$$

and the conditional entropy is defined by

$$H(X/Y) = -\Sigma_i\Sigma_j p_{ij} \log_2 p_{ij}/q_j.$$

Shannon defined the information about X provided by Y as

$$I(X/Y) = H(X) - H(X/Y).$$

It can be shown that, with this definition, $I(X/Y) = I(Y/X)$, that is, the information X provides about Y and the information Y provides about X are equal.

Cole (1993) has pointed out that, in fact, the word "information" is used ambiguously in Shannon. From the perspective of the source-generating messages, it is equivalent to uncertainty, the information we obtain by knowing which message has been sent from the source. From the perspective of the receiver, it is equivalent to a reduction of uncertainty, the information the received message reveals about the transmitted message.

The fact that I(X/Y) and I(Y/X) are equal, and other consequences of the definitions of joint and conditional entropy in the Shannon model, are problematic for our concept of informativeness. From the second Shannon axiom, $H(X,Y) \leq H(X) + H(Y)$, with equality holding if the two sources are independent. If we identify H(X,Y) with the uncertainty of a concatenation of X and Y, this requirement eliminates the possibility of interaction between two messages, the possibility that this interaction will provide a quantity of information that is greater than the sum of that provided by each message considered independently. Also, H(X,Y) does not take into account the order in which the messages are received, so that $H(XY) = H(YX)$. Thus, the Shannon measure is commutative or symmetric under the concatenation, while we have stated that we cannot assume commutativity of information under different message orderings in all cases.

Another problem with the probabilistic approach to information is that when we consider record–user interactions, or even records alone in a database or collection, it is difficult to see how a probability value can be assigned to them. Probabilities are normally defined in connection with a chance situation, situations in which there are a number of outcomes, only one of which will occur. The probability may simply be a measure of how often the outcome has occurred in the past (the classical approach) or a measure of degree of belief in the outcome (the Bayesian approach). The probability of a user–record interaction given a certain retrieval strategy is different from the informativeness of the user–record interaction. Similarly, the probability a particular record will be in the collection given a certain collection policy is different from the aggregated informativeness of the record for the community of users.

Thus, although it satisfies the logarithmic requirement, the Shannon measure, as originally proposed, is not sufficiently general for our purposes. It really measures efficiency of signal transmission, rather than informativeness. It is an average, over a number of possible messages, rather than an information value for a particular message. It does not relate to the content of the message and its meaning to the user, only its probability. It is not based on a definition of information in the broader sense in which we have defined it, as what the user understands from the record. It does not permit sequence or interaction effects among several records. It is constructed from another measure, probability, which may itself be more complex and more difficult to measure than informativeness.

3.1.2 Extensions of the Shannon Measure

Various writers have proposed extensions and interpretations of the Shannon measure in order to make it applicable to situations other than efficiency of signal transmission. It has, for example, been applied in genetics, perception, evolution, mechanics, and computer storage to name but a few other areas of application. We shall not examine all of these applications here, but focus on a few that appear to have some relevance to the evaluation of information services. A survey of both the theory and applications of the Shannon measure will be found in Guiasu (1977).

Guiasu and others have incorporated notions from utility theory in defining the entropy with utility of an experiment (i.e., a channel) as:

$$H(X) = -\Sigma_i u_i p_i \log_2 p_i,$$

where u_i is the utility or value of the *i*th outcome or message. This measure might be applied to situations in which certain messages are more critical than others. For example, in a laboratory test to detect cancer, the four outcomes are: (1) cancer is present but not detected; (2) cancer is present and detected; (3) cancer is not present but detected; and (4) cancer is not present and not detected. The consequences of (1) would seem to be the most serious, since there might then be no further treatment or testing. Hence, one might want to assign a large negative utility to (1) in evaluating the measure. As in many utility theory applications, though, difficulties could arise in assigning reliable utilities to outcomes. Hayes (1993) suggests that the utility or weight can be identified with the relevancy of a document to a request by a user. Thus different users would assign different utilities.

Dretske (1981) considers that information is what a message carries that is capable of telling us *truly* about another state of affairs. He is concerned primarily with the information generated by a particular signal or event, rather than averages, as in the Shannon approach. He follows this approach, though, in suggesting that $-\log_2 p(x)$, where $p(x)$ is the probability of the message or event, can be used as a measure of this specific information. However, he admits that, in many cases, the probability would be difficult to assess because the set of all possible messages is not known. He is in agreement with the view presented in this book in suggesting that we can compare the informativeness of two messages. For example, he suggests that a more specific message contains more information than a less specific one.

Dolby (1977) believes a form of the Shannon/Weaver measure can be used as a measure of the ambiguity in descriptions such as subject headings and classification codes of longer text objects (papers, books). He suggests that the amount of ambiguity may be measured by:

$$A(X) = \log \pi\, n_i! = \Sigma \log n_i!,$$

where n_i is the number of objects with the ith description. The product π of all such numbers represents the number of different arrangements of the classified objects. The number of different arrangements of the original, unclassified objects is $n!$, where n is the total number of objects. The information loss associated with a description is

$$I(x) = \log n! - A(X)$$

and indicates how much "uncertainty" we have lost by classifying the objects.

Several writers have suggested entropylike functions for evaluation of information retrieval. Guazzo (1977) suggests that a form of the Shannon measure can be used as a retrieval performance measure. Let the proportion (or probability) of documents in various retrieval categories be given by the following table:

	Retrieved		
Relevant	*Yes*	*No*	*Total*
Yes	p_{11}	p_{12}	p_1
No	p_{21}	p_{22}	p_2
Total	q_1	q_2	

The measure is defined as the amount of information the retrieved set provides about relevance. It is a derivative of the Shannon measure of conditional information $I(X/Y) = H(X) - H(X/Y)$, where X represents the relevant set and Y the retrieved set, namely

$$I(X \mid Y) = \sum_{i=1}^{2}\sum_{j=1}^{2} \log_2 \frac{p_{ij}}{p_i q_j}.$$

Heaps (1987) suggests a similar measure for retrieval evaluation. The information content transmitted to a user by a retrieved output is:

$$I = -n_{11}\log_e \frac{R}{N} - n_{10}\log_e\left(1 - \frac{R}{N}\right)$$

$$-(R - n_{11}) \log_e \frac{R(N - n_{11} - n_{10})}{N(R - n_{11})}$$

$$-(N - R - n_{10}) \log_e \frac{\left(1 - \frac{R}{N}\right)(N - n_{11} - n_{10})}{(N - R - n_{10})},$$

where R is the number of relevant items, N is the total number of items, n_{11} is the number of retrieved and relevant items and n_{10} is the number of retrieved and nonrelevant items.

Wilbur (1992) also uses a variant of the Shannon function to measure retrieval performance. He defines p_k as the probability of relevance to the query of the kth document retrieved using method F. Essentially, p_k represents the average precision over queries searched using method F of documents in the kth position of the retrieval order. If the retrieval method is appropriate, we should have, for $i < j$, $p_i \geq p_j$. The information about the relevant documents in the first n ranks produced in the first n retrievals by using method F, rather than random retrieval, is given by:

$$\mathrm{IF}_n = \sum_{k=1}^{n} p_k \log \left(\frac{Np_k}{\sum_{i=1}^{n} p_i} \right),$$

where N is the size of the database. The information about all relevant documents produced in the first n retrievals by using method F is given by:

$$\mathrm{IdF} = \sum_{k=1}^{n} p_k \log \left(\frac{Np_k}{\sum_{i=1}^{N} p_k} \right).$$

These formulas assume that n, the retrieval cutoff point, is less than the critical rank, defined as the point t above which the probability of finding relevant documents is less than the original uniform distribution, that is, less than random selection from the database.

De Luca and Termini (1972) extend the entropy measure from a function of probabilistic events to one of classes whose elements are described by fuzzy sets. A fuzzy set is defined as a function f from a set X to the interval [0,1]. Each outcome or message x_i in the set is assigned a value $f(x_i)$ between 0 and 1 indicating the extent to which it belongs to the set. The uncertainty function for the elements of a fuzzy set X is given by:

$$H(X,f) = -\Sigma_i f(x_i) \log_2 f(x_i).$$

This expression is similar to the Shannon entropy measure, with degree of belonging replacing probability. It is suggested that in an experiment or message transmission situation, in which x_i represents the possible messages, there are two kinds of uncertainty: (1) which element x_i of the set will occur, as measured by the Shannon entropy H(X); and (2) can the message be interpreted as belonging or not belonging to the set, as measured by H(X,f).

The total uncertainty is then the sum of these two and represents the uncertainty in predicting which message will occur and then deciding whether to accept or reject that element. Although this approach suffers from the same drawbacks as the probabilistic approach, with the added problem of estimation of the degree of belonging function, its two-stage nature suggests application in the assessment of the retrieval function. Typically, this function involves a first stage of selection or retrieval and a second stage of determination of relevance.

The de Luca and Termini approach shares another major disadvantage with the Shannon and other derived measures for our information measurement purposes: it does not take the user of the record into account in determining information. A probabilistic approach that measures the information of a user–record interaction, rather than of the record alone, has been developed by Jumarie, in two theories: a theory of relative information and a theory of subjective information. We will present the latter in greater detail, as it seems more germane to our purposes.

As we mentioned in Chapter 1, Jumarie (1990) regards all information as relative to a given observer. In order to achieve this relationship in a measure of information, he introduces what he calls semantics into the Shannon model, which, by itself, is concerned with syntax or symbols only. This extension, he believes, will permit us to measure the information received by an observer from a natural language text.

Jumarie thus defines a natural language in terms of two spaces: the syntactic space of symbols (letters, words, organized by grammar), and the semantic space of meanings described by physical and abstract entities, organized by experience. Words (or larger units, such as sentences) are associated with meanings by a lexemic correspondence that depends on the observer or user.

If $a_1, a_2, \ldots a_m$ represent a set A of possible texts or messages with probabilities $p_1, p_2, \ldots p_m$, respectively, then we can measure the uncertainty associated with the messages using the Shannon H(A) measure. If each message a_i has associated with it a number of possible meanings $a_{ij}' \in A', j = 1,2, \ldots m'$, where A′ is the set of all possible meanings, then the initial uncertainty associated with the message is increased, from H(A) to H(AA′), where

$$H(AA') = H(A) + H(A' \mid A) = H_s(A),$$

where $H(A' \mid A)$ is the conditional entropy of A′ given A, and $H_s(A)$ is the subjective entropy of A, that is, the entropy that depends on the meaning of the message to the observer.

The conditional subjective entropy $H_s(B \mid A)$ is given by

$$H_s(B \mid A) = H(B \mid A) + H(A'B' \mid AB) - H(AA')$$

and the subjective information, or transinformation provided by A about B by the difference between the initial uncertainty about B and the conditional subjective uncertainty about B given that A is known:

$$I_s(B \mid A) = H(B) - H_s(B \mid A).$$

The subjective information measure has many of the properties of the Shannon information measure. However, it is not symmetrical, that is, it is not necessarily the case that $I_s(B \mid A) = I_s(A \mid B)$. Also, the subjective information may be negative, as well as zero or positive. It will be negative if the message A created confusion, making it more difficult to determine B.

With relative information, it is assumed that the observer observes a pair of entropies $H(A,R)$ and $H(A',R)$, the syntactic and the semantic entropies, respectively. The observer may grasp all the information in the message or merely a part of it. However, this observation process does not change the total amount of information contained in the message. For the observer, the better his or her knowledge about the semantics, the better his or her knowledge about the syntactics and vice versa. This implies a certain kind of observation, called Minkowskian observation, which can be characterized by an observer-dependent parameter. Jumarie develops the theory of relative information based on this observational concept. The development is more detailed than that for subjective information; however, it is also an extension of the Shannon model, that is, probabilistically based.

Jumarie's approach is useful in considering how to measure the information associated with a user–record interaction because he assumes it is dependent on the user. It cannot be applied directly to text because, like Shannon's measure, it is based on message probabilities and, in addition, requires a knowledge of meaning probabilities for each user. How such probabilities could be obtained for large text databases or collections is unclear. However, the subjective measure does have the advantage over the Shannon measure in that it is not necessarily commutative under concatenation. The information provided by text A about text B is not necessarily the same as the information provided by text B about text A.

There have been attempts to develop a Shannon-like measure that takes information, rather than probability, as the basic concept and that, also, assigns an information value to individual messages, rather than the system as a whole. Often, interest is in the information, sometimes called local information, supplied by a particular message, and we want to specify the properties this measure must have without necessarily relating these properties to the probability of the message. Kampé de Fériet and Forte (1967) describe such an uncertainty measure, called a local measure, which has the following properties for a finite set of messages or events.

Let Ω be a finite set of outcomes (messages), X_1, X_2, . . . subsets of Ω, called events, the empty set Φ an event that never occurs, and the universal set Ω an event that always occurs. Then the information H(X) supplied by the event $X \varepsilon \Omega$ satisfies the following:

1. $H(\Omega) = 0$; $H(\Phi) = +\infty$. In other words, a certain event supplies no information and an impossible event supplies an infinite amount of information.
2. If $X_1 \subset X_2$, then $H(X_1) < H(X_2)$. In other words, subsets of events provide less information than the whole event.
3. If X_1 and X_2 are disjoint, $H(X_1 \cup X_2) = \frac{1}{2}[H(X_1) + H(X_2)]$. In other words, the information provided by one event or another occurring, when the events have no outcomes in common, is the average of the information provided by the two events individually.
4. If X_1 and X_2 are independent, $H(X_1 \cap X_2) = H(X_1) + H(X_2)$. In other words, the information provided by both events occurring when the events are independent of one another is the sum of the information provided by each event individually.

If we let $H(X) = -\log_2 p(X)$, where p(X) is the probability of event X, then the expected value of this measure is identical with the Shannon entropy function.

The problem in applying this measure to recorded information lies in the mapping from the set of records in an information system to the set of events in the model. Both the Fériet/Forte and Shannon measure assigns an uncertainty or information value to any subset of a set of outcome points. However, texts and other types of records are not naturally represented by unordered subsets of points, but by sequences or even more complex structures such as trees. The essential characteristic of text is that a sequence of texts, concatenation of texts, is also text. Concatenation is not the same as union, since it is not commutative, and subsequences are not the same as subsets, since a subsequence may occur more than once in a sequence. It is not clear, also, how the function H could be determined for the information service evaluation applications, which we described in Chapter 2.

3.2 Semantic Measures

As we have seen, the Shannon measure does not really deal with the meaning of the message. Jumarie has attempted to introduce this concept into a formal probabilistic model, but difficulties would arise in attempting to determine all the proposed meanings and their probabilities. A number of investigators have suggested measures, which might be called semantic measures, which are based on the representation of this meaning in terms of the formal structure of the text.

The best-known semantic measure is based on formal logic and was introduced by Bar-Hillel and Carnap (1953). They measure the information conveyed by a statement in what is called a language system $L(n,m)$, consisting of n individuals or entities and m primitive properties that may be associated with individuals. $L(n,m)$ consists of atomic statements and more complex statements. An atomic statement is of the form **ap** and assigns a property **p** to an individual **a.** There are mn possible atomic statements. More complex statements are built from atomic statements using the logical connectives, including negation ($-$), disjunction ($\vee$), conjunction ($\wedge$), and implication ($\rightarrow$). Complex statements may also contain variables (e.g., s), which represent any statement and the universal ($\forall$) and existential ($\exists$) qualifiers. For example, the following statement uses disjunction and the universal qualifier:

$$(\forall \mathrm{s})\ \mathrm{s} \vee - \mathrm{s}$$

and is read: for all statements s, s or not s is true. The following statement uses implication and the existential qualifier:

$$(\exists \mathrm{s})\ \mathrm{s} \rightarrow \mathbf{ap}$$

and is read: there exists at least one statement s that implies the statement **ap.** All complex statements must be well formed, that is, follow the grammatical rules of the language system.

The information carried by a statement in this system increases as the number of other statements that it implies increase. To characterize this idea formally, Bar-Hillel and Carnap define a content element as a disjunction that contains each atomic statement or its negation. The set of content elements C is thus defined by

$$\mathrm{C} = \{\mathrm{c} \mid \mathrm{c} = \vee_{ij} \sigma_{ij} \mathbf{a}_i \mathbf{p}_j\}$$

where the disjunction is over all atomic statements and σ_{ij} represents presence or absence of negation. There are 2^{mn} such disjunctions. Content elements are the weakest kind of statement as they do not imply any other content element.

For any statement s in $L(n,m)$, the content of s, c(s) is the set of all content elements implied by s. For example, if there are $n = 3$ entities and $m = 2$ properties, C contains statements of the form

$$\sigma_{11}\mathbf{a}_1\mathbf{p}_1 \vee \sigma_{12}\mathbf{a}_1\mathbf{p}_2 \vee \sigma_{21}\mathbf{a}_2\mathbf{p}_1 \vee \sigma_{22}\mathbf{a}_2\mathbf{p}_2 \vee \sigma_{31}\mathbf{a}_3\mathbf{p}_1 \vee \sigma_{32}\mathbf{a}_3\mathbf{p}_2.$$

Suppose the three entities are days of the week ($\mathbf{a}_1$ is Monday, $\mathbf{a}_2$ is

Tuesday, and $\mathbf{a}_3$ is Wednesday) and the properties relate to weather ($\mathbf{p}_1$ represents sunny and $\mathbf{p}_2$ represents freezing. Then a content element is a statement such as: sunny on Monday or not freezing on Monday or sunny on Tuesday or freezing on Tuesday or not sunny on Wednesday or freezing on Wednesday: not much of a forecast!

A forecast s such as "it will be sunny and freezing on Monday and Tuesday" implies 60 of the possible 64 content elements, since it implies all content elements in which at least one of the four signs σ_{11}, σ_{21}, σ_{12}, and σ_{22} are positive (15 of 16 possibilities) and the other two signs are positive or negative (4 possibilities). Thus, the content c(s) of the forecast s is a set containing 60 content elements, indicated by the expression $n[c(s)] = 15 \times 4 = 60$.

The semantic information measure is based on the assumption that the more content elements implied by a statement, the more information it provides. This idea is similar to an earlier one presented by MacKay (1969), in which he contrasted what he called the selective information of the Shannon measure with descriptive information. Measures of selective information are concerned with the complexity of the selection process, how unexpected the statement was. Measures of descriptive information are concerned with how many distinct features the statement has, its precision. The more distinct features the statement has, the more content elements it implies. For example, the statement "it will be sunny on Monday" implies only content elements in which the sign σ_{11} is positive, that is, 32 content elements, and so contains less information than "it will be sunny and freezing on Monday and Tuesday."

In the Bar-Hillel and Carnap approach, the amount of information I(s) provided by a statement s increases with the number of statements it implies. One such function I(s) is given by

$$I(s) = -\log_2 [1 - \text{cont}(s)],$$

where cont(s) is the proportion of the 2^{mn} content elements in C contained in c(s). Notice that this function is the same as Shannon's, with the proportion of content elements not implied by s replacing its probability. In the example above, where s is the statement "it will be sunny and freezing on Monday and Tuesday,"

$$I(s) = -\log_2 [1 - 60/64] = \log_2 16 = 4.$$

The minimum value of I(s), zero, occurs if cont(s) = 0.

If s is a content element, then −s (the negation of s), called a state description, will be a conjunction of *mn* atomic statements in which each entity and property combination appears once and only once, with and without negation. The number of state descriptions excluded by a statement measures its precision. For example, the statement "Monday will be sunny and freezing" excludes "Monday will be sunny and not freezing," "Monday will be not sunny and freezing" and "Monday will be not sunny and not freezing," whereas the statement "Monday will be sunny" excludes only the last two. It can be shown that the information provided by a statement also measures the number of state descriptions excluded by the statement, that is, its precision, again reflecting the requirements of MacKay's measure of descriptive information. If a statement s implies a content element x, then $-x$ (a state description) implies $-s$ (and so cannot be true if s is true). The larger the set of content elements x that s implies, the larger the set of state descriptions x that s excludes.

The information measure has the following properties:

1. $0 \leq I(s) \leq \infty$. (The value of the information measure is nonnegative.)
2. $I(s \wedge t) \leq I(s) + I(t)$. (The information provided by statements s and t is less than or equal to the sum of the information provided by the two statements individually.)
3. $I(s \wedge t) = I(s) + I(t)$ if and only if s and t are irrelevant to each other, that is, do not have any atomic statements or negations of atomic statements in common.
4. If s is a tautology (i.e., always logically true), $I(s) = 0$. For example, $I(s \vee -s) = 0$.
5. If s is a contradiction (i.e., always logically false), $I(s) = \infty$. For example, $I(s \wedge -s) = \infty$.

Bar-Hillel and Carnap also define a conditional semantic information measure

$$\begin{aligned} I(t/s) &= -\log_2 [1 - \mathrm{cont}(s \wedge t)]/[1 - \mathrm{cont}(s)] \\ &= I(s \wedge t) - I(s). \end{aligned}$$

$I(t/s)$ reflects the increase in information provided by s and t together over that provided by s alone.

Although the Bar-Hillel and Carnap measure of information seems more concerned with some kind of meaning, specifically propositional meaning, than the Shannon measure, it suffers from many of the same drawbacks for our purposes. It is dependent, solely, on the structure of the record, rather than the interaction of record and user. It assumes that we are dealing with a fixed, known set of entities and properties, and that all text can be put in the form of logical propositions using these sets. In order to calculate the information value of a particular statement, the set of all content elements must be completely determined. With the large collections of text found in information services, this determination would be impractical. In fact, it is questionable that it is even possible with small sets, in that, as Lakoff has argued, our understanding of text is not solely in the form of logical propositions. Nor would the user of a record likely know the set of content elements, even if they could, in principle, be determined.

Another concern is that, as Johnson-Laird (1983) has shown, people do not use formal rules of inference in moving from one statement to another. He suggests that systematic elimination or inclusion of content elements or state descriptions is beyond the capacity of working memory. Rather, people construct a cognitive model based on the statements in the text and general knowledge. They then search for alternative cognitive models, counterexamples from their memories, in order to decide whether or not to accept the statements. Johnson-Laird shows, for example, that subjects perform inferential tasks in experiments better when the statements represent real experiences for them rather than just symbols. This indicates that actual inference, unlike formal inference, involves the understanding of the subjects.

Since logical operators are commutative, informativeness of concatenated statements in this model (presumably represented by conjunctions) will be commutative. In addition, an inherent property of it is that the informativeness of a concatenation is less than or equal to the sum of the informativeness of the two statements read independently. As a result, this information measure cannot reflect interactions or synergistic effects, as when one text explains another or makes possible the comprehension of another. Thus, although it is logarithmic in form, as with the Shannon measure, it does not provide a measure that would be useful in an information services environment.

Although he does not provide a formula, Derr (1985) suggests a measure of information similar to the Bar-Hillel–Carnap one. He suggests that informativeness will vary according to: (1) the number of determinations of entities or objects that any given record contains; and (2) the specificity with which the objects are identified in the record. The following statements for example, are in order of increasing information.

Monday it rained.
Monday there was .25 cm of rain. (more specific)
Monday there was .25 cm of rain and the maximum temperature was 30°C. (more determinations)

As statements contain more determinations (and clauses) and become more specific, they exclude a larger number of alternatives, that is, state descriptions, to use the Bar-Hillel–Carnap terminology. As with their approach, the subjective element is lacking in Derr's definition.

Wells's (1961) approach to semantic information differs from that of Bar-Hillel and Carnap in that he bases his measure on informativeness, as we have defined it, rather than logical truth. By this statement we mean that he considers that informativeness is dependent on the user as well as the logical structure of the record. For Wells, one statement may be more informative than another even though they are both logically true. For example, the Pythagorean theorem contains more information than the statement "2 + 2 = 4," though both are logically true. This view of information is excluded by the Bar-Hillel and Carnap approach.

Wells suggests the following statements should be axioms (or theorems derived from the axioms) for an adequate formal explication of information. In his notation, for a statement s, IA(s) represents the informativeness of s while IC(s) represents the qualitative information content of s. The symbols $s_1, s_2, \ldots$ represent logically true statements, while $e_1, e_2, \ldots$ represent statements that may be true or false.

1. $0 \leq IA(s) \leq \infty$. Informativeness is nonnegative.
2. $(\exists s_1, s_2)\ IA(s_1) < IA(s_2)$. True statements may differ in amount of informativeness.
3. $(\exists s_1, s_2)\ IA(s_1 \wedge s_2) > IA(s_1) + IA(s_2) - IA(s_1 \vee s_2)$. The informativeness of a conjunction may be more than the informativeness of the two parts.
4. $(\exists s_1, s_2)\ (s_1 \rightarrow s_2) \wedge IA(s_2) > IA(s_1)$. Where one statement implies a second, the second may be more informative than the first.
5. $(\forall s_1, s_2)\ IA(s_1 \wedge s_2) \geq IA(s_1) + IA(s_2) - IA(s_1 \vee s_2)$. Conjunction can never diminish informativeness of two true statements.
6. $(\exists s_1, s_2)\ IA(s_1 \vee -s_1) < IA(s_2 \vee -s_2)$. True statements of the sort "to be or not to be" or "does or does not P = NP," that is, questions, may have different informativeness values.
7. $(\exists e_1, e_2)\ IA(e_1 = e_1) < IA(e_2 = e_2)$. Concepts or "vacuous" identities can have different information values. For example, the concept of "employment equity" may be felt to be more informative than the concept "pay equity."
8. $(\exists s_1, s_2)\ IC(s_1) \subset IC(s_2) \wedge IA(s_1) > IA(s_2)$. This axiom essentially denies the Bar-Hillel and Carnap measure, in that it says that statements with a smaller information content may be more informative than those with a larger information content.
9. $(\exists s_1, s_2)\ s_1 \leftrightarrow s_2$ and $IA(s_1) < IA(s_2)$. Logically equivalent statements may be unequal in informativeness. For example, "today is April 8" and "today is my birthday" are logically equivalent, but the latter may contain more information for me.
10. $(\exists s_1, s_2)\ IC(s_1 \neq IC(s_2)$ and $IA(s_1) = IA(s_2)$. Two true statements can be qualitatively different, but have the same informativeness.
11. $(\exists s_1, s_2, s_3)\ IC(s_1) \neq IC(s_2)$ and $IC(s_1) \neq IC(s_3)$and $IC(s_2) \neq IC(s_3)$ and $IA(s_1) > IA(s_2) + IA(s_3)$. This axiom amplifies Axiom 2 by allowing fairly wide differences in amount of information.

A drawback to the axioms is that for the most part they are concerned only with logically true statements. However, if we interpret the axioms in terms, also, of statements that may be true or false, they seem reasonable for a measure of informativeness as we have defined it.

Wells calls his measure a subjective measure of information and suggests that it must be assessed via human judges. He appears to believe, however, that there is an informativeness value to a statement that is independent of the reader of the statement and that reader assessments are simply estimates of this value. He suggests that interreader agreement may be increased by:

1. allowing judges to confer and revise their informativeness judgements;
2. checking on the within-judge consistency, that is, transitivity; and
3. dividing judges into schools of thought such that there is agreement within a school.

Wells' axioms are very useful in clarifying the nature of a subjective measure of information, that is, a measure dependent on the user of the record. Unfortunately, they represent only a beginning, since Wells did not develop an actual measure from them. Also, they do not deal with text in general, but, as with Bar-Hillel and Carnap, solely with logical statements. In particular, they do not recognize that concatenation of statements is not the same as conjunction and may not be commutative.

Hoffman (1980; 1982) has presented a semantic model that is not based on the predicate calculus formalism but rather on semantic nets. He suggests the information content (IC) of a text may be determined by first representing the text as a graph of nodes and edges and then calculating

$$IC = \Sigma C_{j-i} \times IU_{j-i},$$

where C is the connectivity of an information unit, defined as two nodes connected together (j–i), and IU is the number of units with this connectivity value. Connectivity is defined as the total number of edges connected to the two nodes of the unit (exclusive of their internal connecting edge). The problem with this approach is isolating the individual facts and their connections. The reliability of the extraction of facts and connections was not tested. In addition, it fails to satisfy the requirements of user dependence, noncommutativity, and logarithmic scale.

3.3

Statistical and Decision-Theoretic Measures

Statistical measures of information determine the amount of information sample evidence provides about a hypothesis concerning a population or, more precisely, the parameters of the population. For example, we might be interested in determining the average amount of time a user of an information service spends with a book or at the online catalog, or the percentage of people in a community who use an information service. They can be developed in a straightforward way from the Shannon probabilistic measure, using a Bayesian approach (for greater detail, see Guiasu, 1977).

The Bayesian approach assumes that the parameter itself has a probability distribution, called the prior distribution, the sample evidence has a probability distribution dependent on the parameter, and the evidence is used to revise the prior distribution of the parameter to obtain a posterior distribution. The latter may then be used as a basis for estimation or decision making. The approach assumes that we know the form of the prior and sample evidence probability distributions. It can be applied to parameters that assume only discrete (integer) values or to parameters that assume a continuum of values. In the latter case, the prior and probability distributions will be density function and the techniques of integral calculus need to be applied to determine probabilities.

Let θ be the parameter of the probability distribution of a discrete random variable X, with probability function $p_1(X|\theta)$. For example, θ might represent the average number of accesses per record per month in a database. Let $p_0(\theta)$ be the prior probability function for θ. (For simplicity, we shall assume that θ is discrete, rather than continuous.) The prior probability function is based on our past knowledge or our beliefs about the parameter of interest. If only the prior function is known, then the uncertainty regarding θ is given by

$$H_0(\theta) = -\sum_{j=1}^{m} p_0(\theta_j) \log_2 p_0(\theta_j).$$

If nothing is known about θ except that it has a finite number, say, m possible values, then the prior uncertainty is usually taken to be $\log_2 m$.

Let $\mathbf{X} = (X_1, X_2, \ldots X_n)$ represent a random sample of n observations of X, taken to obtain information about θ. For example, $\mathbf{X}$ might represent observations of number of accesses per month of n records. This information is then used to revise the distribution of θ. The joint distribution of the sample observations, given θ, is the product

$$p_1(X|\theta) = \prod_{i=1}^{n} p_1(X_i|\theta),$$

the posterior probability for θ is

$$p_2(\theta|X) = \frac{p_1(X|\theta)p_0(\theta)}{\sum_{j=1}^{m} p_1(X|\theta_j)\, p_0(\theta_j)},$$

and the posterior uncertainty, given the sample **X**, is

$$H_1(\theta|X) = -\sum_{j=1}^{m} p_2(\theta_j|X) \log_2 (\theta_j \mid X).$$

This expression gives the uncertainty about θ following sampling in which **X** is observed.

The expected uncertainty about θ averaged over all possible samples, i.e., values of **X**, is then

$$H_2 (\theta,X) = -\sum_x \sum_j p_1 (X|\theta_j) \, p_0 (\theta_j) \log_2 p_2 (\theta_j|X)$$

If θ assumes a continuum rather than a discrete set of values, the summations in the above expressions are replaced by integrals.

Then, following Guiasu, we may denote by

$$I (\theta,\mathbf{X}) = H_0 (\theta) - H_2(\theta,\mathbf{X})$$

the amount of information we may expect a sample to contain about an unknown parameter. This expression represents the average decrease in uncertainty about the parameter resulting from the observations in the sample. If θ and **X** are independent, $I (\theta,\mathbf{X}) = 0$.

As an example of this kind of analysis, suppose that the number of relevant items θ in a large database is unknown but is thought to be described by the prior probability function

$$p_o(\theta) = a/2^{\theta + 1},$$

where a is a constant, such that

$$\Sigma_\theta p_0(\theta) = 1.$$

Then the prior uncertainty about θ is given by

$$H_0 (\theta) = a \, \Sigma_\theta(\theta + 1)/2^{\theta + 1},$$

where the summation is over the integers from 0 to the total number of items in the database. For large databases, the summation can be taken to be infinite. In this case, a will be one and $H_0(\theta)$ approximately two.

Now, suppose that in an initial search strategy a single document is retrieved. Let $X = 1$ if the document is relevant to the query and $X = 0$ if the document is nonrelevant. Suppose, also, that the sample distribution, conditional on θ, is given by

$$p_1(0 \mid \theta) = 1/2^\theta, \; p_1(1 \mid \theta) = 1 - 1/2^\theta.$$

Then we have, using the posterior probability formula,

$$p_2(\theta \mid 0) = 3/2^{2\theta+2}, \; p_2(\theta \mid 1) = 3(1 - \tfrac{1}{2}^\theta)/2^{\theta+1},$$

and

$$H_2(\theta,X) = -\sum_{\theta=0}^{\infty} (\tfrac{1}{2})^{2\theta+1}\log_2 3(\tfrac{1}{2})^{2\theta+1}$$

$$-\sum_{\theta=0}^{\infty} [1 - (\tfrac{1}{2})^{\theta}]\,(\tfrac{1}{2})^{\theta+1}\log_2 3[1 - (\tfrac{1}{2})^{\theta}]\,(\tfrac{1}{2})^{\theta]+1}.$$

If we approximate $\log_2[1 - \frac{1}{2}^{\theta}]$ by $\frac{1}{2}^{\theta}/\log_e 2$, we get

$$H_2(\theta,x) = 1.44$$

and so

$$I(\theta,x) = 2 - 1.44 = .56.$$

Thus, on the average, a sample of a single document will provide us with .56 bits of information regarding the value of θ.

Truly realistic examples of this information function are difficult to find because they depend on a knowledge of the prior distribution of the parameter and the sampling distribution, functions that are frequently not available in information services environments.

Information measures may also be used to determine the amount of information samples provide in hypothesis testing. Good (1983) has defined a similar Bayesian measure $I(H \mid E)$, which he calls explicativity and which represents the amount of information concerning a hypothesis H provided by evidence E. The measure can be adapted to the comparison of two hypotheses H_1 and H_2. Let $P(E \mid H_1)$ and $P(E \mid H_2)$ denote the probability of the data E assuming, respectively, models H_1 and H_2. Let $P(H_1)$ and $P(H_2)$ denote the initial probabilities of the two models. As in all Bayesian approaches, these probabilities can be interpreted as physical (relative frequencies) or subjective (degrees of belief). The explicativity of a model H for evidence or date E is given by:

$$I(E \cdot H) = (1 - \tau)\,[\log P(E/H) - \log P(E)] + \tau \log P(H),\ 0 \leq \tau \leq 1.$$

The amount by which the explicativity of one model H_1 exceeds that of another H_2 is given by

$$\begin{aligned} I(E:H_1/H_2) &= I(E:H_1) - I(E:H_2) \\ &= [(1 - \tau)][\log P(E/H_1) - \log P(E/H_2)] \\ &\quad + \tau[\log P(H_1) - \log P(H_2)]. \end{aligned}$$

The factor τ represents the relative weight to be assigned to the model and so can be used to represent the analyst's expectations or beliefs about the model. The factor $(1 - \tau)$ then represents the relative weight to be assigned to the sample evidence. A value of $\tau = 0$ corresponds to letting the evidence speak for itself. A value of $\tau = 1$ corresponds to ignoring the sample evidence. Tague-Sutcliffe (1992a) has applied this measure to the problem of assessing the information provided by bibliometric models.

A measure of the information that the sample provides about a parameter that is non-Bayesian and hence does not require a knowledge of the prior distribution of the parameter has been provided by Fisher (1938). Let X be a random variable whose probability distribution depends on a parameter θ (assumed here to be continuous). Fisher defines the amount of information provided by a single observation of X about the parameter as follows:

$$\begin{aligned} I(\theta \mid X) &= E\{d/d\theta\,[\log_e p(X \mid \theta)]\}^2, \\ &= \Sigma_x\{d/d\theta\,[\log_e p(X \mid \theta)]\}^2 p(X \mid \theta), \end{aligned}$$

where E represents the expected value of the squared function over all values of X, and $d/d\theta$ represents a derivative with respect to θ. For continuous distributions of X, the sum is replaced by a definite integral.

If T is an unbiased estimator of θ from a random sample of size n and V(T) is the variance of T, then, as Fisher shows,

$$I(\theta) \geq 1/nV(T).$$

Thus, the smaller the variance of a sample estimator, the more information it contains.

As an example of the Fisher function, suppose the number of times a book circulates in a year is assumed to have a Poisson distribution with mean (and variance) μ, that is,

$$p(X \mid \mu) = e^{-\mu}\mu^{x}/X!.$$

To estimate μ, a sample of n books is taken and the number of circulations of each book is observed. Then

$$\log_e p(X \mid \mu) = -\mu + X\log_e\mu - \log X!$$

and

$$d/d\mu\,[\log p(X \mid \mu)] = (X - \mu)/\mu.$$

Then

$$I(\mu \mid X) = \frac{\sum_{X=0}^{\infty} (X - \mu)^2 p(X \mid \mu)}{\mu^2} = \frac{1}{\mu} = \frac{1}{nV(X)}.$$

In other words, the information provided by the sample mean is n times the variation of the sample mean.

For hypothesis testing, Kullback (1959) defines the mean information

$I(p_1 \mid p_2)$ for discrimination in favor of one hypothesized distribution p_1 over another p_2 as the expected value of the logarithm of the likelihood ratio $p_1(X)/p_2(X)$:

$$I(p_1 \mid p_2) = \Sigma_X p_1(X)\,[\log_e p_1(X) - \log_e p_2(X)],$$

where $p_1(X)$ and $p_2(X)$ are the joint probabilities of the sample under the two hypotheses and the sum is overall sample value sets.

Similarly, the mean information $I(p_2 \mid p_1)$ for discrimination in favor of p_2 over p_1 is defined by

$$I(p_2 \mid p_1) = \Sigma_X p_2(X)\,[\log_e p_2(X) - \log_e p_1(X)].$$

The divergence J(1,2) between p_1 and p_2, that is, the distance between the two models, is measured by $I(p_1 \mid p_2) + I(p_2 \mid p_1)$. This quantity will be zero if the two distributions are the same.

For example, if we were testing the hypothesis that the average number of times books in a library collection are circulating this year is 1, rather than 2, assuming, as before, that book circulations have a Poisson distribution, the average information for discrimination in favor of model 1 over model 2, of model 2 over model 1, and the divergence are:

$$\begin{aligned}
I(p_1 \mid p_2) &= \sum_{X=0}^{\infty} \frac{e^{-1}}{X!}[\log_e \frac{e^{-1}}{X!} - \log_e \frac{e^{-2}}{X!}] \\
&= 1 - \log_e 2, \\
I(p_2 \mid p_1) &= \sum_{X=0}^{\infty} \frac{e^{-2}}{X!}[\log_e \frac{e^{-2}}{X!} - \log_e \frac{e^{-1}}{X!}] \\
&= 2\log_e - 1, \\
J(1,2) &= \log_e 2.
\end{aligned}$$

Utility theory is a natural extension of Bayesian statistics to the problem of decision making. A utility theoretic approach to information is taken by Marschak (1971). He equates information handling with symbol manipulation and defines an information system as a sequence of transformations of symbols onto symbols. Each transformation or process P is defined as a quintuple

$$P = < Z, A, \eta, \gamma, \tau >,$$

where Z is a set of inputs or events, A is a set of outputs or actions, η is a transformation matrix, representing the conditional probability $p(A = a \mid Z = z)$, γ is a cost function on Z, and τ is a time-delay function on Z. The decision maker is given a probability distribution π_z on the set of inputs or events and a utility function $w[a, z, \gamma(z), \tau(z)]$ associated with output or action a and input or event z, taking into account costs and delays assocītated with these inputs. The decision maker will choose information system P over information system P′ if and only if $U_{\pi w}(P) > U_{\pi w}(P')$, where

$$U_{\pi w}(P) = \Sigma_a \Sigma_z \pi_z w[a,z,\gamma(z),\tau(z)].$$

In other words, utilities are averaged over the inputs and actions or outputs of an information system to determine its utility. The utility function for an input/output pair (z,a) may be expressed as a difference between costs and benefits, that is,

$$w[a,z,\gamma(z),\tau(z)] = \beta(a,z)d^{\tau(z)} - \gamma(z),$$

where $\beta(a,z)$ is the benefit of output a from input z and d is a discount constant, $0 \leq d \leq 1$. Benefits are discounted because they occur later than the costs. Marschak suggests that d represents impatience and the obsolescence of inputs to the decision maker.

Marschak applies this model to two kinds of symbol processing chains, or information systems. In statistical inquiries, there are two processes in the chain: experiments or inquiries, in which inputs are events and outputs are observations, and strategies or decisions, in which inputs are observations and outputs are actions. In message transmission, there are four processes in the chain: storing, encoding, transmission, and decoding.

As we shall see in Chapter 4, Marschak's idea that a delay discounts the amount of information provided by a message is a useful one in an information services environment. However, Marschak's utility-theoretic approach to information shares with other statistical approaches the limitation of being based on message probabilities, not on the effect messages produce on the reader.

A simpler decision-theoretic approach is provided by Yovitz *et al.* (1981), and Yovits and Kleyle (1993), who define information as data of value in decision making. A decision maker is faced with a number of possible courses of action and outcomes of these actions. The decision maker obtains information, via feedback and external sources, and selects what appears to be the best course of action. The effectiveness of the decision maker is determined by his or her "probability spectrum" over the courses of action. An expert decision maker will assign a probability of one to the course of action with the greatest expected value. An inexperienced decision maker will choose courses of action with equal probabilities. Yovitz's information measure is determined by the mean square variation of the decision makers' probabilities over the courses of action and the number of courses of action being considered. The formula, in what Yovitz calls binary choice units, is given as

$$i = 2\sum_i p(a_i)^2,$$

where $p(a_i)$ is the probability the decision maker will choose the ith course of action. The measure is at a maximum when the probability is one for a single course of action and at a minimum value when probabilities of all courses of action are the same. Yovitz suggests that the probabilities can be determined as average values, in particular decision-making tasks, of the choices of groups of decision makers judged to be of equal effectiveness.

The Yovitz measure is actually a linear, rather than logarithmic, form of the Shannon probability measure, with courses of action replacing messages. It would be difficult to use as a measure of the information provided by user–record interactions, since the course of action probabilities used in the information measure must be determined by averaging action choices over groups.

A variety of information measures have been described in this section on statistical and decision-theoretic measures. In all cases, these have been based on various prior, posterior, and sample probability distributions. As with the probabilistic measures, they are appropriate only in limited situations, where such distributions will be known. In some situations, the record is a random sample taken for the purpose of hypothesis testing or estimation. As Kullback (1959) notes: "Whenever we make statistical observations or design and conduct statistical experiments we seek information." Statistical information measures are useful in telling us how much we can infer from the sample about models or populations. However, they do not appear to be extendable to more general kinds of text. Decision-theoretic measures require utilities associated with a number of courses of action and outcomes, in addition to the probabilities, and so are even more difficult to implement. Both statistical and decision-theoretical measures focus on average, rather than individual, information values.

3.4 Algorithmic Measures

Kolmogorov (1968) and Chaitin (1974) developed measures of information that can be applied to specific records or text independently of such characteristics of the total set of records as its probabilistic, logical, or statistical structure. $I(X \mid Y)$, in this approach, is the quantity of information required for constructing a text X, where text is viewed as a string of symbols, when the text Y is known. $I(X)$ is the quantity required when nothing is known, that is, when Y is the null text. $I(X)$ is called the algorithmic information content or complexity of X.

For uniformity, it is assumed in this approach that the text can be expressed as a binary sequence, as it would be, for example, in computer storage. The quantity of information I(X) in a text is the number of instructions in the smallest program for computing or producing the text. As Chaitin says: "The complexity of a binary string is the information needed to define it, that is to say, the number of bits of information that must be given to a computer in order to calculate it, or, in other words, the size in bits of the shortest program for calculating it."

For example, if the length of a string is 20 binary digits (e.g., 10110011011110011110), a program of 20 output instructions will be proportional in size to the length of the string and will obviously produce it. However, the string 01010101010101010101 can be produced by a program consisting of two output instructions and a repeat instruction.

The joint information I(X, Y) of two tests is defined to be the size of the smallest program to calculate X and Y simultaneously. The relative or conditional information I(X, Y) of X given Y is defined to be the size of the smallest program to calculate X beginning from a minimal program for Y.

Of the 2^n possible binary coded texts of length *n*, those texts are called algorithmically random whose complexity is approximately *n*. The greater the difference between I(X) and the length of X, the less random X is. Most texts will be random. This is because the number of programs of length *n* is proportional to 2^n. For $k < n$, there are only 2^k programs of length k and these programs can produce at most 2^k different texts. Thus, the number of texts produced by programs of length greater than k will be at least 2^{n-k}, a large number for small values of k. For example, there are $2^{20} = 2048$ texts of length 20. However, no more than $2^5 = 32$ of these will be produced by programs of 5 instructions.

Thus, most texts will have an algorithmic information content close to their length in bits. This function is not a logarithmic one as is Shannon's; however, there is a relationship between the Shannon and the algorithmic measures of information. The less random a text, the less surprising and hence, the less its probabilistic information content.

Chaitin suggests that the algorithmic information measure may be applied in scientific methodology to measure the simplicity of a model as inversely proportional to the length of the program that constitutes it. If the number of instructions in the program is approximately the same as the number of observations, then the model is too *ad hoc* to be useful in comprehension or prediction. This interpretation seems related to Good's explicativity measure, described in Section 3.3, which measures the amount of information the model provides about the data. However, in Chaitin, length of a program replaces probability as the basic concept.

As with the other measures of information described earlier, complexity measures a property of text alone, not user–text interactions, and so does not satisfy our first requirement for measure of information. As early as 1965, Schreider argued that a statement containing more information for a person does not necessarily contain more binary symbols. As an example, he pointed out that a statement on the discovery of a new chemical element might require fewer symbols to present than measurements of properties of existing elements, yet contains more information. To calculate it, one must determine the size of the minimal program that will produce the text, an undertaking that involves a determination of any patterns (i.e., nonrandomness) in the string. Exactly how this determination will be carried out is not clear for a general situation, though it may be done in computational settings as part of an algorithm design process. Unlike most of the other measures that we have reviewed, complexity is not logarithmic. However, it is nonadditive in that the length of a program to produce a concatenation of two strings may take advantage of similarities between the two. Similarly, it is a nonsymmetric function, in that it is possible that $I(X \mid Y) \neq I(X \mid Y)$, and so can be used to represent the order dependence of the informativeness of some text concatenations.

3.5 Summary

In considering earlier measures of information, it is clear that most investigators have assumed that this property depends solely on the record and not on the user. Some also assume that it is not only ordinal but additive, so that, for example, reading a record 20 times provides 20 times as much information as does reading a record once. All assume that the text has been put into some canonical form, probabilistic, logical, linguistic, or computational. Such a transformation would be extremely difficult and time consuming to implement for documents of any length and databases of any size. Indeed, it is questionable that it is possible. The measures of informativeness are thus based on more restrictive definitions of information than we proposed initially and cannot be applied to all information service environments, that is, with organizations and systems whose aim is to provide information in many different forms to respond to many different user needs. We shall now attempt to develop a measure that will address these deficiencies.

3.6 Review Problems

3.6.1 In an information retrieval experiment, ten documents are retrieved in ranked order by two different retrieval methods. The following numbers of total and relevant items were determined at each point in the ranked output:

Number Retrieved	*Number Relevant and Retrieved*	
	Method 1	*Method 2*
1	1	1
2	1	2
3	2	3
4	3	4
5	3	4
6	4	4
7	4	4
8	4	4
9	4	4
10	5	4

Assuming a total of ten relevant documents in the 100,000-document database, calculate and compare the Guazzo, Heaps, and Wilbur measures of the effectiveness of the retrieval by the two methods. Which effectiveness measure seems best to you, and why?

3.6.2 A prize is to be awarded to one of four finalists {a, b, c, d} in a competition. Use the Bar-Hillel and Carnap semantic measure to determine the amount of information in the following statements:

1. *a did not win the award*
2. *neither a nor b nor c won the award*

3.6.3 Do you agree that statistical measures of information are not generalizable to all information-providing situations? To which functions of an information service might they be applied?

4

An Ordinal Measure of User–Record Informativeness

We shall now develop a general measure of informativeness that can be used for evaluation and decision making in information services and that will avoid some of the limitations, for this purpose, of the measures we described in Chapter 3. We shall develop a formal model that is applicable to the assessment of an information service at the individual user, the individual record, and the community service levels.

In assessing the amount of information resulting from the interaction of a user and a record, we need, as we indicated earlier, to distinguish all of the information provided to a user by a record from the information that relates to some information gap that the user is experiencing or some problem that she or he wishes to solve. The problem might be of a general nature, learning about a new subject, or of a specific nature, answering an immediate concern. The unconstrained environment when no information gap is involved (e.g., reading an article selected at random) means that the user may find it difficult to compare the information provided by two records and that, therefore, it may not be possible to develop even an ordinal measure. However, with the second kind of measurement, when the understanding is being related to the user's information need, we may hope for a greater comparability of records and the existence of an ordinal measure. We therefore propose to address the measurement of information from this perspective. In other words, we will consider the basic event to which an informativeness value can be attached to be the interaction between a user with a need for information and a record.

This restriction makes sense in terms of information service environments, since most users of such services come to them because they have some kind of information need. The information a user obtains from a record will be determined by the need or interest and by what the user does not already know relative to this need or interest, by the size of the user's gap in understanding.

We will begin by developing an information measure for the interaction of a single user and a record. If informativeness is simply ordinal, and not additive, it can be measured in only a relative rather than an absolute way. In other words, we can say that record x is more informative than record y for user u, but not that record x has z more units of information for user u than does record y. Ordinal measurement means we cannot *a priori* assign absolute values to the informativeness of one record, independently of that of other records in a sequence of records relating to the information need. Also, any monotonic function of the original information measure will serve as well. However, by making additional specifications for the function, such as its general shape and range of values, we will be able to develop a unique measure that can be applied in information service environments to a variety of evaluation processes.

In developing the model for the measurement of information at the individual user level, we will assume that the purpose of the information service is to provide records from the available databases or collections to the user in an order that will resolve the user's information need in the shortest possible time. Such a sequence will be called an optimal sequence. Some of this model has been previously presented in Tague and Schultz (1989) and Tague-Sutcliffe (1992a and 1994).

Mathematically, a general measure of informativeness is represented by the triple $<T,U,I>$, composed of a set T of records in the database or collection available to an information service, a set U of potential uses of the service by those in the community with an information need, and an information function $I: T \times U \rightarrow \Re$ from the set $T \times U$ of pairs of records and uses to the real numbers. In other words, I(t,u) associates an informativeness value with each interaction of a record t and a user u.

The database or collection can be considered a sequence of symbols from some alphabet (e.g., text) and each record in T a meaningful subsequence of the total sequence. The amount of text or other symbol sequences in a record may vary over databases or over views of the same database. For example, one view of the database might be as a sequence of journal volumes, another as a sequence of journal articles, and a third as a sequence of screens of text representing hypertext nodes from the articles. Each element of U represents a user or potential user with an information need. Thus, U can also be interpreted as a set of individual information needs. An element of the cross-product $T \times U$ represents a use, a reading or other perusal of the text, graphics, and so on of a record in T by a user in U.

4.1 Measuring User–Record Preferences

The informativeness function I(t,u), $t \in T$, $u \in U$, assigns an informativeness value to these interactions of users with needs and records at a particular point in time. It is assumed to satisfy a set of twelve axioms; these will be presented as we develop the measure. The initial development involves three axioms and shows how we may define a preference ordering on the set of records relative to their informativeness for a user's information need.

Axiom 1 For each information need u of a potential user of an information service, there exists a set of zero or more records $T^{\star}(u) \subset T$, which he or she can identify as informative. For records $t \in T^{\star}(u)$, $I(t,u) > 0$. For records $t \notin T^{\star}(u)$, $I(t,u) = 0$.

This axiom says that a user can distinguish informative from noninformative records. These are records that change the user's understanding of the problem or interest that brought the user to the information service. Informative records have an informativeness value greater than zero for the user. Noninformative records have an informativeness value of zero for the user.

Notice that we are not assuming here that the user is making this judgment from a surrogate, but that he or she is looking at the record itself. In such a case, it is unlikely that the user would not be able to distinguish informative from noninformative records. In practice, if the user is in doubt, he or she should assign the record to the informative set. We will later distinguish degrees of informativeness. First, though, we address the problem of two equivalent informative sets.

Axiom 2 The records in $T^{\star}(u)$ may be grouped into one or more subsets $T^{(i)\star}(u) \subset T^{\star}(u)$, where each subset provides the same information to the user. These subsets are not necessarily disjoint. $T^{(i)\star}(u)$ will be called an informative set for u.

This axiom says that there may be more than one way of satisfying the user, more than one set of records that provides the needed information. For example, if the need is for a word definition, there may be entries from five dictionaries in the collection that equally well provide this definition. Then $T^{\star}(u)$ contains all five entries and $T^{(i)\star}(u)$ the single entry from the ith dictionary, $i = 1,5$. On the other hand, if the information need involves previous research published on a problem, some of the publications may be repetitive and so may be included in one set and not in the other, while others provide original information and so must be in all. The important points about the informative sets is that the user need see only one of them.

Axiom 3 An informativeness relation $>$ is defined on the set of informative records $T^{\star}(u)$ as follows. Given a user u and two records t_1 and t_2, one and only one of the following statements is true:

- *t_1 is more informative than t_2 for user u ($t_1 > t_2$);*
- *t_1 is equally informative with t_2 for user u ($t_1 \approx t_2$);*
- *t_2 is more informative than t_1 for user u ($t_2 > t_1$);*
- *t_1 and t_2 cannot be compared as to informativeness by user u ($t_1 \sim t_2$).*

This axiom means that, for some pairs of records, the user can order the records with respect to informativeness or find them equally informative. With other record pairs, however, as, for example, with records dealing with different aspects of a query, the user is unable to make a comparison as to their relative informativeness.

An informativeness measure must take into account the user preference judgments described in Axiom 3. When all records are comparable and when the preferences form a strict weak order, we can find an ordinal measure that describes these preferences, as we saw in Chapter 2. However, when all records are not comparable or when preferences do not form a strict weak order, we must modify the approach described there. We do this by first showing how to structure an informative set $T^\star(u)$ into a minimal set of informative chains $\mathbf{C}^\star(u) = \{C^\star_i(u) | i = 1, p)\}$ for the set on the basis of the user preference judgments. From these chains, a single chain of informative records will be developed that can be used as the basis for an ordinal informativeness measure.

Recall that a chain is a sequence of edges, that is, $C^\star_i(u) = < E_{i1}, E_{i2} \ldots E_{iq(i)}$. In an informative chain, each edge is a subset of equally informative elements of an informative set $T^\star(u)$ and the ordering of the edges within the chain corresponds to the user's informativeness preferences, with the most informative records first and the least informative records last. A set of informative chains for an informative set is minimal if omitting any chain means that some comparable records in the set will not be together in the same chain.

The ranking of the edges in the informative chains, that is, the edge index j of edge E_{ij}, can form the basis for an ordinal informativeness function for the records within the chain. If there is a single informative chain in the set $\mathbf{C}^\star(\mathbf{u})$, then an ordinal informativeness function can be developed directly from the edge index. However, because the user may not be able to compare all records, there may be more than one chain in the minimal set and we must determine a way of ranking records that takes into account their positions in all of these chains. We shall now develop such a method.

The chains in $\mathbf{C}^\star(\mathbf{u})$ are structured so as to satisfy the following six properties:

Property 1 If $t \in E_{ij}$, $t' \in E_{ik}$, t and t′ are comparable, that is, either $t > t'$ or $t' > t$ or $t \approx t'$.

This property means that each informative chain contains comparable records only.

Property 2 If $t \in E_{ij}$, $t' \in E_{ij}$, then t and t′ are equally informative, $t \approx t'$.

This property means that records in the same edge of a chain are equally informative.

Property 3 If $t \in E_{ij}$, $t' \in E_{ik}$, $j < k$, then t is more informative than t′, that is, $t > t'$.

This property means that records in earlier edges in the chain (i.e., with smaller values of the subscript *j*) are more informative than records in later edges in the chain (i.e., with larger values of the subscript *j*).

Property 4 Within the union of the edges of a single chain, the relation > satisfies the requirements of a strict weak order, that is, it is asymmetric and negatively transitive.

This property means that records in the same chain can be described by an ordinal utility function.

Property 5 For any record t and for any two comparable records t, t′ ε T*(u), there exists at least one chain containing t and one chain containing both t and t′.

This property means that all records are in at least one edge and all comparable records are together in at least one chain.

Property 6 If any chain is removed from **C*(u),** either there will be at least one t ε T*(u) that is not contained in a chain in **C*(u)** or there will be at least one comparable pair t, t′ ε T*(u) that are not together in a chain in **C*(u).**

This property means that **C*(u)** is the smallest possible set of informative chains.

The sets of comparable records are tolerance sets and, following Schreider's suggestion (see Chapter 2, Section 2.1.1), are seen as representing "canonical" features, that is, explicit or implicit features or aspects of the user's information need. Each chain consists of one of these tolerance sets, ranked in descending order according to the user's informativeness preferences. If the user can compare all records as to informativeness, there will be only one informative chain. However, if some records cannot be compared as to informativeness, additional chains will be formed as necessary to include all informative records.

Property 4 states that, within sets of comparable records, the user's preferences obey the requirements for a strict weak order. The requirement of negative transitivity may be difficult to realize. If the user displays a lack of negative transitivity in his or her preferences, then he or she will be asked to reconsider the preference assignments. If the problem cannot be resolved, then, as we shall describe later, a default informative chain, with all informative records in a single edge, will be used.

This procedure for creating the informative chains involves, first, determining the chain containing the record that is preferred to the largest number of other records. A subset is formed containing all records comparable to this one and mutually comparable. To produce the chain, records in the subset are ordered by user preference. If incomparable records remain, a second chain is begun with the remaining record that is preferred to the largest number of other records. Records comparable to the latter are added to this additional chain. The procedure is continued until no records remain that have not been included within a chain. An example may clarify the process.

Example 4.1 Let the user's informativeness preferences be as follows, for a set of seven records, $t_1, t_2, t_3, t_4, t_5, t_6, t_7$:

$$t_1 > t_2,\ t_1 > t_3,\ t_1 > t_4,\ t_1 > t_5,\ t_1 > t_6,\ t_1 \sim t_7$$
$$t_2 \approx t_3,\ t_2 > t_4,\ t_2 > t_5,\ t_2 \sim t_6,\ t_2 < t_7$$
$$t_3 \approx t_4,\ t_3 > t_5,\ t_3 \sim t_6,\ t_3 \approx t_7$$
$$t_4 > t_5,\ t_4 \sim t_6,\ t_4 \sim t_7$$
$$t_5 \sim t_6,\ t_5 \sim t_7$$
$$t_6 \sim t_7$$

These preferences can be represented by a 7 × 7 matrix PREFER in which

$$\text{PREFER(i,j)} = \begin{cases} 1 \text{ if } t_i > t_j \\ -1 \text{ if } t_i < t_j \\ 0 \text{ if } t_i \approx t_j \\ 9 \text{ if } t_i \sim t_j \end{cases}$$

and where the values $N(t_i)$ shown on the right represent the number of other records to which t_i is preferred, that is, the number of ones in the row.

PREFER(*i*,*j*)

i \ *j*	*1*	*2*	*3*	*4*	*5*	*6*	7	$N(t_i)$
1	0	1	1	1	1	1	9	5
2	−1	0	0	1	1	9	−1	2
3	−1	0	0	0	1	9	0	1
4	−1	−1	0	0	1	9	9	1
5	−1	−1	−1	−1	0	9	9	0
6	−1	9	9	9	9	0	9	0
7	9	1	0	9	9	9	0	1

The first comparable subset $T_1^\star$, containing t_1, the record with the largest value of $N(t)$, is

$$T_1^\star = \{t_1, t_2, t_3, t_4, t_5\},$$

since t_2, t_3, t_4, and t_5 are all comparable with t_1 and also mutually comparable. The records t_6 and t_7 are not contained in $T_1^\star$, since t_6 is not comparable with t_2, t_3, t_4, and t_5 and t_7 is not comparable with t_1, t_4, and t_5. The next comparable subset $T_2^\star$ contains the record t_7, since $N(t_7) > N(t_6)$, and all records that are comparable with it and that are mutually comparable:

$$T_2^\star = \{t_2, t_3, t_7\}.$$

The final comparable subset contains the record that is comparable with the remaining record t_6:

$T_2{\star} = \{t_1, t_6\}$.

The value of the function $N_i(t)$ (the number of records to which t is preferred in $T_i{\star}$) for each record t in each of the three subsets T_i is given below. A blank indicates that a record is not a member of the subset.

	$N_i(t_j)$						
	j						
i	*1*	*2*	*3*	*4*	*5*	*6*	*7*
1	4	2	1	1	0		
2		0	0				1
3	1					0	

In assessing whether $\langle t_1{\star}, >\rangle$ satisfies the requirements of a strict weak order, it is found that $N_1(t_2) > N_1(t_3)$ but $t_2 \approx t_3$. The reason for the inconsistency is that $t_2 \approx t_3$ and $t_3 \approx t_4$, but $t_2 > t_4$. The user revises preferences so that $t_3 > t_4$, keeping both records in the subset.

Similarly, with $\langle T_2{\star}, >\rangle$ it is found that $N(t_7) > N(t_3)$ but $t_7 \approx t_3$. The reason for the inconsistency is that $t_7 \approx t_3$ and $t_3 \approx t_2$, but $t_7 > t_2$. The user revises preferences so that $t_7 \sim t_3$, thus eliminating t_3 from the subset.

The three chains are then formed by putting records with equal values of $N_i(t)$ in the same edge and arranging edges by descending values of $N_i(t)$. This procedure gives us:

$$C_1{\star}(u) = \langle\{t_1\}, \{t_2, t_3\}, \{t_4\}, \{t_5\}\rangle$$
$$C_2{\star}(u) = \langle\{t_7\}, \{t_2\}\rangle$$
$$C_3{\star}(u) = \langle\{t_1\}, \{t_6\}\rangle.$$

The procedure for creating the informative chains can be formalized as follows:

Step 1 Calculate the function $N(t)$ for all $t \in T{\star}(u)$, the set of informative records, where $N(t)$ is the number of records t' such that $t > t'$. Let $t^{(1)}$ represent the most informative record, that is, a record such that $N(t^{(1)}) \geq N(t)$ for all $t \in T{\star}(u)$. Then determine the set $T_1{\star}$, which contains all records that are comparable with $t^{(1)}$ and with each other.

Step 2 Determine if any records or comparable pairs of records have not been included in $T_1{\star}$. If records remain, determine the set $T_2{\star}$, which contains all records that are comparable with $t^{(2)}$, where $t^{(2)}$ represents a record that does not appear in $T_1{\star}$ and where $N(t^{(2)})$th $\geq N(t)$ for all t in this remaining set.

Step 3 Repeat Step 2, creating additional sets of comparable records until there are no records that have not been assigned to a set $T_i{\star}$, $i = 1, p$, of comparable records.

Step 4 For each set $T_i{\star}$, determine if the user performance relation $>$

satisfies the requirement of a strict weak order by determining, for each pair t, t′ $\in T_i^\star$, if the following relationship is satisfied:

$$t > t' \text{ if and only if } N_i(t) > N_i(t'),$$

where $N_i(t)$ is the number of records t″ ε $T_i^\star$ such that t > t″. If a pair does not satisfy this relationship, it does not satisfy the requirement of negative transitivity with at least one other record. Determine triples (t, t′, t″) for which the negative transitivity requirement does not hold and have the user reassess preferences and comparabilities so that, if possible, negative transitivity is satisfied. If this is not possible, create two separate chains, one with t and the other with t′.

Step 5 Let E'_{ij} be the subset of records t ε $T_i^\star$ such that $N(t) = j$. Renumber the subsets E'_{ij} to obtain the edges E_{ij}, $j = 1$ to q, where q is the number of nonempty subsets E'_{ij} and where the initial ordering by the $N_i(t)$ is reversed, so that E_{i1} has the most informative records. In other words, if t_j ε E_{ij} and t_k ε E_{ik}, $t_j > t_k$ if and only if $j > k$. Then $C_i^\star(u) = \langle E_{i1}, E_{i2}, \ldots E_{iq(i)}\rangle$ satisfies the requirements for an informative chain listed above.

An algorithm for determining the informative chains, given a set of user preferences, is provided in Appendix 4.1 at the end of this chapter. The algorithm for finding the comparable sets is similar to algorithms for finding complete link clusters.

We have seen how one or more informative chains for a user can be developed. Our next problem is to determine an informativeness function for the records in all the informative chains. From the result given in Chapter 2, Section 2.1.1, we know that the function $N(t)$, the number of records t′ such that t > t′, or any monotonically increasing function of it, will be an ordinal utility function for the records within a single chain, since these records form a strict weak order. We would like, however, to develop an informativeness function that would permit us to make comparisons of informativeness across chains, not just within chains. To do this, we must develop a preference ordering for all the informative records, not just the records within a single informative chain. By Property 6, all informative chains are necessary to describe the informativeness relationships of all of records in the data with respect to user queries. Can the position of a record in the informative chains form the basis for an ordinal measure of informativeness for all records when there is more than one chain?

Without further structure, the answer to this question is No, because the value $N(t)$ may not be unique, if t appears in more than one informative chain. In the example, $N_1(t_1) = 4$, but $N_2(t_1) = 1$. Similarly, $N_1(t_2) = 0$, but $N_3(t_2) = 1$. We must have some way of determining a unique informativeness value for records that appear in more than one informative chain. To do this, we must be able to compare all pairs of records in the informative chains for a query, not just those that appear together in a single chain.

One approach which suggests itself is the following:

Set $t > t'$ if and only if there exists at least one informative chain $C^\star(u)$ in which $t \in E_j$ and $t' \in E_k$ with $j > k$. Otherwise set $t \approx t'$.

Will this approach provide a preference relation for which an ordinal measure exists, that is, does it define a strict weak order? Again, the answer to this question is No, because the relation $\langle T^\star, > \rangle$ does not satisfy the property of negative transitivity.

It is easy to construct examples to show that the relation $>$ as we have just defined it is not negatively transitive. Recall that this property means that, if not $(t > t')$ and not $(t' > t'')$, then not $(t > t'')$. Suppose that there are three records and two informative chains structured as follows:

$$C^\star_1(u) = \langle \{t_1\}, \{t_2\} \rangle$$
$$C^\star_2(u) = \langle \{t_3\}, \{t_1\} \rangle.$$

Then, using the approach described above, $t_1 > t_2$, $t_2 \approx t_3$, and $t_3 > t_1$. Thus, not $(t_3 > t_2)$ and not $t_2 > t_1$, but $t_3 > t_1$, and so negative transitivity is not satisfied.

We have suggested that the chains, in a sense, represent explicit or implicit aspects or features of the user's information need. If these aspects can be ranked by the user as to importance in the information need, then a single chain can be defined that will be a strict weak order and therefore an ordinal informativeness function will exist. A proof of this assertion is given in Appendix 4.2 at the end of this chapter.

The procedure for determining the single informative chain, to be called the ideal chain, is as follows:

1. Extend the *i*th chain with an edge $E_{iq(i)+1}$, where $q(i)$ represents the number of edges in the original chain. The edge $E_{iq(i)+1}$ contains those records $t \in T^\star(u)$ that were not included in the *i*th chain originally. It is assumed that, for the aspect of the query represented by the chain $C^\star_i(u)$, no record is preferred to t for $t \in E_{iq(i)+1}$. We also assume that the aspects are ranked in ascending order by the users, so that the aspect represented by $C^\star_i(u)$ is more important than the aspect represented by $C^\star_j(u)$ if and only if $i > j$.

2. Define a preference ordering of the records of $T^\star(u)$ as follows: For any $t, t' \in T^\star(u)$, $t > t'$ if and only if

- there exists at least one chain $C^\star_r(u)$ in which $t > t'$, that is, in which, if $t \in E_{rj}$ and $t' \in E_{rk}$, then $k > j$, and
- for all other chains $C^\star_i(u)$, $i \neq r$, containing t and t', either not $(t' >_i t)$ or if $(t' >_i t)$, then $i > r$.

3. Let $N(t)$ be the number of records t' such that $t > t'$ under this preference ordering. Then $N(t)$ is an ordinal utility function defined on $T^\star(u)$.

4. Construct a single informative chain, which we shall call the ideal chain C★(u), as follows: Let the edge E'_i be the subset of records t such that $N(t) = i$. If there are q nonempty edges E'_i, renumber these in descending order of value of $N(t)$, from 1 to q to obtain the ideal chain

$$C\star(u) = \langle E_1, E_2, \ldots E_q \rangle.$$

Then C★(u) is a single chain that is ordered by descending informativeness values.

Now we'll continue with Example 4.1.

Determination of the overall informativeness chain or ideal chain, based on a ranking of the chains in the set **C★(u),** will be illustrated using the set of three informative chains derived in this example. These chains, extended with the incomparable records in the final edge of each chain, are:

$$C_1\star = \langle \{t_1\}, \{t_2,t_3\}, \{t_4\}, \{t_5\}, \{t_6,t_7\} \rangle$$
$$C_2\star = \langle \{t_7\}, \{t_2\}, \{t_1, t_3, t_4, t_5, t_6\} \rangle$$
$$C_3\star = \langle \{t_1\}, \{t_6\}, \{t_2, t_3, t_4, t_5, t_7\} \rangle.$$

Let us suppose that the subscripts indicate the relative importance of the three aspects of the query represented by the chains, that is, $C_3\star$ represents the most important aspect, $C_2\star$ the next most importance aspect, and $C_1\star$ the least important aspect. Then the overall preference relation > is as follows:

t_1 is preferred to t_2, t_3, t_4, t_5, t_6, t_7,
t_2 is preferred to t_3, t_4, t_5,
t_3 is preferred to t_4, t_5,
t_4 is preferred to t_5,
t_6 is preferred to t_2, t_3, t_4, t_5, t_7, and
t_7 is preferred to t_2, t_3, t_4, t_5.

The values of the ordinal utility function $N(t)$ are:

i	$N(t_i)$
1	6
2	3
3	2
4	1
5	0
6	5
7	4

Thus, the overall chain is

$$C\star(u) = \langle \{t_1\}, \{t_6\}, \{t_7\}, \{t_2\}, \{t_3\}, \{t_4\}, \{t_5\} \rangle.$$

We have shown that an ordinal informativeness function exists for the interactions of users and records if either of two conditions hold for the set **C★(u)** of informative chains:

1. There is a single informative chain. This situation will occur when the user is able to compare all records as to informativeness, and the preference order resulting from the comparisons is a strict weak order. We say that the information need, in this situation, is a simple one, with one aspect or feature corresponding to the single informative chain.
2. There is more than one informative chain; however, the chains can be ranked. This situation will occur when the user is unable to compare some records or the preference order resulting from the comparisons is not a strict weak order. We say that the information need in this situation is a complex one with several, say, *p*, aspects or features corresponding to the *p* informative chains, and the several aspects can be ranked as to their significance or importance relative to the overall information need.

We call this single chain C★(u) the ideal chain for user u.

Suppose that neither of the two conditions listed above holds. Can we still determine an ideal chain for the user? We have seen that if the user cannot provide a preference ordering that is negatively transitive or if the user cannot rank the several aspects of a query, a single chain that reflects the user's preferences does not exist. However, one may still define a function that will be zero for noninformative records and a constant value greater than zero for informative records. This function at least reflects the user's decision about what is informative. In essence, the separation of informative from noninformative records creates the lowest level of preference ordering, an ideal chain with a single edge. This chain represents a kind of combining of the aspects of the information need into a single catchall category. Individual records within the edge will all have the same informativeness value. This value will be consistent with the values determined by the measure we will now develop.

4.2 Standardizing the Informativeness Measure

We shall now define an ordinal informativeness function, that is, a function that preserves the user's preferences among records as represented by the ideal chain. This function will assign an informativeness value to each record t ε T based on its edge index e★(t) in the ideal chain C★(u) $= <E_i$ $E_2, \ldots E_q >$. The edge index is defined as follows: for t ε E_i, e★(t) $= i$. Note that as the edge index of records increases, their informativeness decreases.

Since the edge index is an ordinal measure, any monotonically decreasing function of the edge index will be an informativeness measure. Among the many functions, we will choose the one that satisfies four additional axioms of our system. These axioms, Axioms 4, 5, 6, and 7, are, we believe, appropriate to an information services environment. They require: (1) that informativeness values of individual records lie between zero and one; (2) that a concatenated sequence of records corresponding to the ideal chain (to be called an ideal sequence) have an informativeness value of one for an individual information need; (3) that the informativeness of a subsequence of the ideal sequence be related logarithmically to the amount of material or number of records in the sequence; and (4) that informativeness of sequential text be independent of the extent to which it is divided into records.

Axiom 4 $0 \leq (t,u) \leq 1$.

These limits permit us to standardize the informativeness of records so that comparisons of informativeness for different uses will be possible. The lower limit means that records cannot have negative informativeness. We have already specified, in Axiom 1, that noninformative records have zero informativeness, that is, if $t \in T\text{-}T^\star(u)$, $I(t,u) = 0$. The upper limit means that no use can have an informativeness value greater than one. A use here will be defined as the perusal by the user of a sequence of records at some point in time, in an attempt to satisfy his or her information need.

Axiom 5 Let $\mathbf{t^\star(u)}$ represent the following concatenation of records:

$$\mathbf{t^\star(u)} = t_{11}t_{12} \ldots t_{1n(1)}t_{21} \ldots t_{qn(q)},$$

where $n(i)$ is the number of records in the ith edge E_i of the ideal chain and the subsequence $t_{i1,} \ldots .t_{in(j)}$ represents a sequence of the records in E_i in any order. $\mathbf{t^\star(u)}$ will be called an ideal sequence for u. The $I\ (\mathbf{t^\star(u)},u) = 1$.

An ideal sequence $\mathbf{t^\star(u)}$ is the ideal chain restructured as a sequence of records. Since sequences of concatenations of records are also records, we can assign informativeness values to them, something we cannot do with the ideal chain, since it may not be a comletely determined sequence of records (some edges may contain more than one record). This axiom says that the informativeness value of any sequence that is consistent with the ordering of the edges in the informative chain is one. There may be more than one ideal sequence, since the ordering of records within the same edge is irrelevant. From Axiom 2, we conclude that if any records are removed from the ideal sequence, its informativeness value will be less than one.

Axiom 5 essentially determines what one unit of informativeness represents. To say that a sequence consistent with the ideal chain has an informativeness of one means that we are counting each information need in the community as equivalent in terms of the amount of information needed to satisfy it. This standardization is needed is so that we can compare different ways of satisfying users or the extent to which one user is satisfied compared to another. Later on, in Section 5.3, we will look at a modification of this approach, to permit differential weighting of user needs.

Axiom 6 Let n be the number of records in the ideal sequence $\mathbf{t}^\star(\mathbf{u})$ and let $\mathbf{t}^{k\star}(\mathbf{u})$ be a subsequence containing the k leftmost edges of the ideal chain $C^\star(u)$, that is, a sequence of the form

$$\mathbf{t}^{k\star}(\mathbf{u}) = t_{11}t_{12} \ldots t_{1n(1)}t_{21} \ldots t_{k1} \ldots t_{kn(k)}.$$

Then $I[\mathbf{t}^{k\star}(\mathbf{u}),u]$ is an increasing function of the logarithm of $\Sigma_i n(i)$, the number of records in the subsequence.

This axiom corresponds to the law of diminishing returns for information searching, described earlier. The more records searched, the sparser the density of information per record.

Axiom 7 t_1 is said to be a subrecord of t_2 if both t_1 and t_2 are records, that is, sequences of symbols that are potentially meaningful to users, and if

$$t_2 = a_1a_2, \ldots a_n, \text{ then}$$
$$t_1 = a_ia_{i+1}, \ldots a_{i+m}, \; 1 \le i \le n - m, \; m \le n - 1.$$

Let $t_1, t_2, \ldots t_m$ represent a set of disjoint, that is, nonoverlapping subrecords of t such that

$$t = t_it_2 \ldots t_m = \Sigma_j t_j.$$

We shall call such a set of subrecords a subsequence partition of t. Then

$$I(t,u) = I(\Sigma_j t_j,u).$$

In other words, partitioning a record into smaller units, for example, volumes into chapters and chapters into paragraphs, does not affect its overall informativeness.

We wish to develop a measure of the informativeness of the individual records in the sequence $\mathbf{t}^\star(\mathbf{u})$, that is, of records in the ideal chain, which satisifies these four additional axioms. First, however, we will develop a measure of the informativeness of subchains of the informative chain.

The following function is proposed as a measure of the informativeness of $\mathbf{t}^\star(\mathbf{u})$, that is, the records sequence containing all nodes in the leftmost k edges of the ideal chain $C^\star(u)$:

$$I[t^{k\star}(u)] = \log_2[\sum_{i=1}^{k} \frac{n(i)}{n} + 1] = \log_2[\sum_{i=1}^{k} \frac{n(i) + n}{n}], \tag{4.1}$$

where $n(i)$ is the number of records in the ith edge in the ideal chain and n is the total number of records in the chain. This measure satisfies Axiom

6, in that it is an increasing function of the logarithm of the number of records in the subsequence. It also satisifies Axioms 4 and 5, since its maximum value will be one, achieved when the sequence contains all n records in the ideal chain, and its minimal value will be 0, achieved when there are no records in the sequence.

The function in Equation (4.1) satisifies Axiom 7 as well. If each record in $\mathbf{t}^\star(\mathbf{u})$ is partitioned into r subrecords, giving $\mathbf{t}'^\star(\mathbf{u})$, then both the total number of records and the number of records in the first k edges would be multiplied by r, but the function $I(\mathbf{t}_{\star k}{}^\star(\mathbf{u}))$ would remain unchanged, since

$$I[t^{k'}\star(u)] = \log_2[\sum_{i=1}^{k} \frac{rn(i)}{rn} + 1] = I[t^{k}\star(u)].$$

Thus, reducing or increasing the granularity of the division of a database into records in a consistent fashion does not change the informativeness values.

Now, let us define a measure of the informativeness of the individual records in the ideal chain. If a record t is not in the ideal chain, then $I(t,u) = 0$, as specified in Axiom 1. Otherwise, if $t_k \, \varepsilon \, E_k$, we let

$$\begin{aligned} I(t_k,u) &= \frac{1}{n(k)}\{I[t^{k}\star(u)] - I[t^{k-1}\star(u)]\} = \frac{1}{n(k)}\log_2[\frac{\sum_{i=1}^{k} n(i) + n}{\sum_{i=1}^{k-1} n(i) + n}] \\ &= \frac{1}{n(k)}\log_2[1 + \frac{n(k)}{\sum_{i=1}^{k-1} n(i) + n}]. \end{aligned} \tag{4.2}$$

Essentially, this function is derived by assigning to the kth edge E_k an informativeness $I[\mathbf{t}^{k}\star(u)] - I[\mathbf{t}^{k-1}\star(u)]$ and then dividing this amount equally among the $n(k)$ records in E_k.

$I(t_k,u)$ defines an informativeness measure on the records in an ideal chain. From Axiom 1 we know that records not in the ideal chain have an informativeness value of zero. $I(t,u)$, thus defined, is an ordinal measure. We show this result as follows.

Suppose that the edge index j for t_j is less than the edge index k for t_k, that is, that $t_j \, \varepsilon \, E_j > t_k \varepsilon \, E_k$. Then from Equation (4.2)

$$I(t_j,u) = \frac{1}{n(j)}\log_2[1 + \frac{n(j)}{\sum_{i=1}^{j-1} n(i) + n}]$$

and

$$I(t_k,u) = \frac{1}{n(k)}\log_2[1 + \frac{n(k)]}{\sum_{i=1}^{k-1} n(i) + n}.$$

To prove that $I(t_j,u) > I(t_k,u)$ we use the mathematical inequality $x/(1 + x) < \log_e(1 + x) < x$, for $x > 0$, which follows from the series expansion for e^x. We thus have

$$I(t_j,u) > \frac{\dfrac{n(j)}{n(j)\log_e 2[\sum_{i=1}^{j-1} n(i) + n]}}{1 + \dfrac{n(j)}{\sum_{i=1}^{j-1} n(i) + n}} = \frac{1}{\log_e 2[\sum_{i=1}^{j} n(i) + n]}$$

and

$$I(t_k,u) < \frac{1}{(\log_e 2)n(k)} \frac{n(k)}{\sum_{i=1}^{k-1} n(i) + n} \leq \frac{1}{(\log_e 2)\,[\sum_{i=1}^{j} n(i) + n]}$$

$$< I(t_j,u).$$

Conversely, one can show using the same mathematical inequality, that if $I(t_j,u) > I(t_k,u)$, then $j < k$ and so $t_j > t_k$. Also, if t_k and t_k, are both records in E_k, then by definition $t_k \approx t_k'$ and $I(t_k,u) = I(t_k',u)$.

Since, for any informative record t, $I(t,u) > 0$, and from Axiom 1, for any noninformative record t', $I(t',u) = 0$, it will be the case that for any two records t and t' in T, if $t > t'$, then $I(t,u) > I(t',u)$. Thus, $I(t,u)$ is an ordinal measure of the informativeness of a single record in an ideal sequence, given its order in the sequence.

Essentially, the function $I(t,u)$ divides the total informativeness of an edge, given by $I(\mathbf{t^k(u)},u)$-$I(\mathbf{t^{k-1}(u)},u)$ equally among the records in the edge. If the informative chain is a strict ranking, that is, if each edge in the informative chain contains only one record, then for $t_k \varepsilon E_k(u)$,

$$I(t_k,u) = \log_2[1 + \frac{1}{k - 1 + n}]. \tag{4.3}$$

The function we have just defined resembles the Shannon probability-based measure (Section 3.1.1). In fact, Equation (4.3) can be interpreted as a Shannon uncertainty value $-\log_e p_k$, where p_k represents the probability that, after we have examined the first *k* records, we have already obtained the information remaining in the database. This probability is given by

$$p_k = \frac{1}{1 + \dfrac{1}{k - 1 + n}} = 1 - \frac{1}{k + n}.$$

Now we will continue with Example 4.1. If, as in this example, there are seven edges in the chain, each containing a single record, the above function gives the following informativeness values for the records in the informative set T★(u):

i	$I(t_i,u)$
7	.19
2	.17
1	.15
6	.14
3	.13
4	.12
5	.12

If it had proved not to be possible to develop a single informative chain that would take preferences into account, then all seven informative records would form a single edge in the informative chain, each record t with an informativeness value I(t,u) = 1/7th = .14.

4.3 Summary

In this chapter, we have developed an ordinal measure for the informativeness of a record to a user with an information need or interest. In developing this measure, we assume that the user can distinguish informative from noninformative records and can compare at least some, though not necessarily all, pairs of records as to informativeness. We do not assume that he or she can specify numeric informativeness values. The informativeness measure is based on the concept of an ideal chain, a sequence of sets of informative records in decreasing informativeness order, all of which are needed to satisfy the user's information need. It would be possible to define many ordinal information measures on the records in the ideal chain. The one presented here obeys the additional assumptions of a logarithmic relation to position in the ideal chain and independence of record granularity. In addition, it is normalized to vary between zero, for a noninformative record, and one, for a record that completely satisfies the user's information need.

In Chapter 5 we show how the concept of an ideal chain can be used in the evaluation of information retrieval systems, that is, systems that facilitate user access to a "trail" of records that may help answer the user's query. The practical problems of applying the proposed informativeness measure and, in particular, of estimating parameters of the ideal chain, will be addressed in Chapter 6.

4.4 Review Problems

4.4.1 Given the following set of user preferences, determine the informativeness of each item by following these steps:

1. determine the matrix PREFER showing the preference relationship (1, −1, 0, or 9) for each pair of records and the function $N(\mathrm{t})$ for each record t,
2. determine the set of informative chains,
3. assume that the informative chains represent aspects of a need that can be ranked by the user and determine a single ideal chain, and
4. determine the informatives value of each record using Equation (4.2).

Preferences:

$t_1 = t_2,\ t_1 = t_3,\ t_1 > t_4,\ t_1 > t_5,\ t_1 > t_6,\ t_1 \sim t_7,\ t_1 \sim t_8$
$t_2 = t_3,\ t_2 > t_4,\ t_2 > t_5,\ t_2 > t_6$
$t_3 > t_4,\ t_3 > t_5,\ t_3 > t_6$
$t_4 > t_5,\ t_4 > t_6,\ t_4 \sim t_7,\ t_4 \sim t_8$
$t_5 > t_6,\ t_5 \sim t_7,\ t_5 \sim t_8$
$t_7 > t_2,\ t_7 > t_3,\ t_7 > t_6,\ t_7 = t_8$
$t_8 > t_2,\ t_8 > t_3,\ t_8 > t_6$

4.2.2 Suppose that the preferences were as follows:

$t_1 = t_2,\ t_1 = t_3,\ t_1 > t_4,\ t_1 > t_5,\ t_1 > t_6,\ t_1 > t_7,\ t_1 \sim t_8$
$t_2 = t_3,\ t_2 > t_4,\ t_2 > t_5,\ t_2 > t_6$
$t_3 > t_4,\ t_3 > t_5,\ t_3 > t_6$
$t_4 > t_5,\ t_4 > t_6,\ t_4 \sim t_7,\ t_4 \sim t_8$
$t_5 > t_6,\ t_5 \sim t_7,\ t_5 \sim t_8$
$t_7 > t_2,\ t_7 > t_3,\ t_7 > t_6,\ t_7 = t_8$
$t_8 > t_2,\ t_8 > t_3,\ t_8 > t_6$

What changes would occur in the answers to **4.4.1** (1–4), above?

4.4.3 Do you think it is realistic to assume that the user can identify the set of informative records? Under what conditions might this be difficult?

Appendix A4.1
Algorithm to Determine the Informative Chains

```
**Input N and array PREFER
*N is the number of records in the informative set.
*The input array PREFER is defined as follows:
     PREFER(I,J)=1 if the Ith record is more
                     informative than the Jth record,
                =0 if the Ith and Jth records are
                     equally informative,
                =-1 if the Jth record is more
                     informative than the Ith record,
                =9 if the Ith and Jth records are
                   incomparable.
INPUT n
INPUT ARRAY PREFER
**Determine array NUM
*NUM(I) is the number of records T such that the Ith
record T(I) is more informative than T.
*Q1 is an index that determines if NUM has to be
recalculated because of user revisions to preferences
Q1=1
REPEAT TO LABEL (2) UNTIL Q1=0
Q1=0
ARRAY NUM = ZERO
FOR I=1 TO N
   FOR J=I TO N
      IF PREFER (I,J)=1 THEN NUM(I)=NUM(I)+1
   NEXT J
NEXT I
**Determine pairs for which NUM is not an ordinal
function
*NON contains the nontransitive triples if NUM is not
ordinal
*M is the number of such nontransitive triples
M=0
FOR J=1 TO N
   FOR K=1 TO N
      IF {PREFER(J,K)=1 AND N(J)>N(K)}
         OR {PREFER(J,K)=-1 and N(K)>N(J)}
         OR {PREFER(J,K)=0 AND N(J)=N(K)}
         OR PREFER (J,K)=9
```

```
        THEN
            GO TO LABEL(1)
        ELSE
            FOR H=1 TO N
            IF {PREFER(J,K)=1} AND J<>H AND K<>H
                AND {PREFER(J,H)=-1 OR PREFER(J,H)=0}
                AND {PREFER(H,K)=-1 OR PREFER(H,K)=0}
            THEN
                M=M+1
                NON(M,1)=J:NON(M,2)=K:NON(M,3)=H
            ENDIF
            NEXT H
        ENDIF
LABEL(1) NEXT K
NEXT J
**Revise preferences to satisfy negative transitivity
IF M>0
THEN
    Q1=1
    PRINT ''PREFERENCES FOR THE FOLLOWING RECORDS ARE
    NOT CONSISTENT. PLEASE REVISE''
    FOR J=1 TO M
        FOR K=1 TO 3
            A=NON(J,K)
            S=K MOD (3)+1
            B=NON(J,S)
            PRINT A,B,PREFER(A,B)
        NEXT K
        FOR K=1 TO 3
            A=NON(J,K)
            S=K MOD (3)+1
            B=NON(J,S)
            PRINT ''PREFERENCE FOR.''; A; ''VS ''; B
            INPUT PREFER (A,B)
            IF PREFER(A,B)=1 THEN PREFER(B,A)=-1
            IF PREFER(A,B)=-1 THEN PREFER(B,A)=1
            IF PREFER(A,B)=0 THEN PREFER(B,A)=0
            IF PREFER(A,B)=9 THEN PREFER(B,A)=9
        NEXT K
    NEXT J
ENDIF
LABEL (2) CONTINUE
**Calculate the array OUTT
```

```
*The array OUTT(I,J) is calculated as follows:
   OUTT(I,J)=1 if the Ith and Jth records are
          comparable and have yet to be assigned to a
          comparable set,
             0 otherwise.
FOR I=1 TO N
   FOR J=I TO N
      IF PREFER(I,J)=1 THEN OUTT(I,J)=1: NUM(I)=
            NUM(I)+1
      IF PREFER(I,J)=0 THEN OUTT(I,J)=1
      IF PREFER(I,J)=-1 THEN OUTT(I,J)=1
      IF PREFER(I,J)=9 THEN OUTT(I,J)=0
   NEXT J
NEXT I
**Sort NUM in descending order.
*ID(I) is the original number of the Ith sorted record
FOR K=1 TO N
   ID(K)=K
NEXT K
FOR K=N TO 2 STEP -1
   FOR J=K-1 TO 1 STEP -1
      IF NUM(J+1)>NUM(J)
      THEN
         TEMP1=NUM(J): TEMP2=ID(J)
         NUM(J)=NUM(J+1): ID(J)=ID(J+1)
         NUM(J+1)=TEMP1: ID(J+1)=TEMP2
      ENDIF
   NEXT J
NEXT K
**Determine comparable sets
*The matrix COMPARE will be calculated as follows:
   COMPARE(I,J)=1 if the Jth record is in the Ith
           comparable set,
               =0 if the Jth record is not in the
           Ith comparable set.
*P is the number of the comparable set currently
being created.
*Determine the first comparable set, containing the
record ID(1).
P=1
K1=ID(1)
COMPARE(P,K)=1
OUTT(K1,K1)=0
```

```
FOR J=2 TO N
   K2=ID(J)
   IF PREFER (K1,K2)=9
   THEN
      TEST=0
   ELSE
      TEST=1
      FOR K=1 TO J-1
         K3=ID(K)
         IF COMPARE(P,K3)=1 AND PREFER(K3,K2)=9
         THEN TEST=0
      NEXT K
   ENDIF
   IF TEST=1
   THEN
      COMPARE(P,K2)=1
      FOR K=1 TO J
         K3=ID(K)
         IF COMPARE(P,K3)=1 THEN OUTT(K3,K2)=0:
         OUTT(K2,K3)=0
      NEXT K
   ELSE
      COMPARE(P,K2)=0
   ENDIF
NEXT J
**Iteratively determine if all pairs have been
  assigned to a comparable set. If not, create
  another comparable set.
FOR I=1 TO N
   K1=ID(I)
   FOR J=1 TO I
      K2=ID(J)
      IF OUTT(K1,K2)=1
      THEN
         P=P+1
         COMPARE(P,K1)=1: COMPARE(P,K2)=1
         OUTT(K1,K2)=0: OUTT(K2,K1)=0
         FOR H=1 TO N
            K3=ID(H)
            IF PREFER(K1,K3)=9 OR PREFER(K2,K3)=9
            THEN
               TEST=0
            ELSE
```

```
                    TEST=1
                    FOR K=1 TO H-1
                    IF COMPARE(P,K)=1 AND PREFER(K3,H)=9
                    THEN TEST=0
                    NEXT K
                 ENDIF
                 IF TEST=1
                 THEN
                    COMPARE(P,K3)=1
                    FOR K=1 TO J
                       K4=ID(K)
                       IF COMPARE(P,K4)=1 THEN OUTT(K3,K4)
                       =0:
OUTT(K4,K3)=0
                    NEXT K
                 ELSE
                    COMPARE(P,K3)=0
                 ENDIF
         NEXT H
         ENDIF
      NEXT J
   NEXT I
**Determine chains
*The output matrix EDGE is defined as follows:
   EDGE(I,J)=K, K>0, if the Jth record is in the Kth
            edge of the Ith chain,
            =0 if the Jth record is not in the Ith
            chain.
FOR I=1 TO P
*Redetermine array NUM for the Ith chain
   FOR J=1 TO N
   NUM(J)=0
   IF COMPARE(I,J)=0
   THEN
      NUM(J)=-1
   ELSE
      FOR K=1 TO N
         IF COMPARE(I,K)=1 AND PREFER(J,K)=1
         THEN
            NUM(J)=NUM(J)+1
         ENDIF
      NEXT K
```

```
   ENDIF
   NEXT J
*Sort array NUM in descending order
*ID(I) is the original number of the Ith sorted record
   FOR K=N TO 2 STEP -1
      FOR J=K-1 STEP -1
      IF NUM(J+1)>NUM(J)
      THEN
         TEMP1=NUM(J): TEMP2=ID(J)
         NUM(J)=NUM(J+1): ID(J)=ID(J+1)
         NUM(J+1)=TEMP1: ID(J+1)=TEMP2
      ENDIF
      NEXT J
   NEXT K
*Assign records to edges in Ith chain based on value
of NUM
   NUM(N+1)=-1
   R=0
   FOR J=N TO 1 STEP -1
      IF NUM(J)≠NUM(J+1) THEN R=R+1
      EDGE{I,ID(J)}=R
   NEXT J
NEXT I
END
```

Appendix A4.2

Proof of the Existence of an Ideal Chain When Query Aspects Are Ranked

To Prove: Given a set of q informative chains $C^\star(u) = \{C_i(u) \mid i = 1,q\}$, where each chain consists of a sequence of edges, that is,

$$C^\star_i(u) = \langle E_{i1}, E_{i2}, \ldots E_{iq(i)} \rangle,$$

where $q(i)$ is the number of edges in the ith chain, and where the chains represent aspects that can be ranked as to their importance in the query, an ordinal measure can be defined on the set of all records that appear in at least one chain in $C^\star(u)$, that is, on the set of informative records $T^\star(u)$.

To develop the proof for this assertion, we extend the ith chain with an edge $E_{iq(i)+1}$, where $q(i)$ represents the number of edges in the chain. The edge $E_{iq(i)+1}$ contains those records $t \in T^\star(u)$, which were not included in the ith chain originally. It is assumed that, for the aspect of the query represented by the chain $C^\star_i(u)$, $I(t,u) = 0$ for $t \in E_{iq(i)+1}$. We also assume that the aspects are ranked in ascending order by the users, so that the aspect represented by $C^\star_i(u)$ is more important than the aspect represented by $C^\star_j(u)$ if and only if $i > j$. We then define the overall informativeness ranking as follows.

For any $t,t' \in T^\star(u)$, $t > t'$ if and only if

1. there exists at least one chain $C^\star_r(u)$ in which $t >_r t'$,
2. for all other chains $C^\star_i(u)$, $i \neq r$, either not $(t' >_i t)$ or, if $(t' >_i t)$ then $i > r$.

To prove: $<T^\star(u), >>$ is a strict weak order, that is, asymmetric and negatively transitive.

Asymmetry

To prove: if $t > t'$, then not $(t' > t)$.

Assume the contrary, that is, that both $t > t'$ and $t' > t$. Then there exists a chain $C^\star_r(u)$ such that $t > t'$ and there is no chain $C^\star_i(u)$, $i > r$, such that $t' >_i t$, by definition of $t > t'$. However, we cannot then have $t' > t$, since by definition of $t' > t$, there does exist a chain $C^\star_i(u)$, $i > r$, such that $t' >_i t$. Thus we arrive at a contradiction and so we conclude that if $t > t'$ then not $(t' > t)$.

Negative Transitivity

To prove: if not $(t > t')$ and not $(t' > t'')$ then not $(t > t'')$.

Not $(t > t')$ implies either:

$t' >_i t$ or $t' \approx_i t$ for all chains $C^\star_i(u)$ *(Condition 1)*

or

if there exists a chain $C^\star_r(u)$ such that $t >_r t'$, there also exists a chain $C^\star_s(u)$ such that $s > r$ and $t' >_s t$. *(Condition 2)*

Not $t' > t''$ implies either:

$t'' >_i t'$ or $t'' \approx_i t'$ for all chains $C^\star_i(u)$ *(Condition 3)*

or

if there exists a chain $C^\star_v(u)$ such that $t' >_v t''$, there also exists a chain $C^\star_w(u)$ such that $w > v$ and $t'' >_w t'$. *(Condition 4)*

We will have one and only one of the following condition combinations:

Conditions (1) and (3)
Conditions (1) and (4)
Conditions (2) and (3)
Conditions (2) and (4)

We shall show that, in each case, we have the desired conclusion, namely not (t $>$ t″). By definition, this relationship holds if either:

t″ $>_i$ t or t″ $\approx_i$ t for all chains $C\star_i$(u) (*Condition 5*)
or
if there exists a chain $C\star_x$(u) such that t $>_x$ t″, there also exists a chain $C\star_y$(u) such that $y > x$ and t″ $>_y$ t. (*Condition 6*)

Conditions (1) and (3)
For all chains $C\star_i$(u) we have

(t′ $>_i$ t or t′ $\approx_i$ t) and (t″ $>_i$ t, or t″ $\approx_i$ t′).

Therefore, from the transitivity of the $>_i$ and the $\approx_i$ relations, Condition (5) holds, that is, t″ $>_i$ t or t″ $\approx_i$ t for all chains $C\star_i$(u).

Conditions (1) and (4)
For all chains $C\star_i$(u) we have

t′ $>_i$ t or t′ $\approx_i$ t.

For $i = v$ we have

t′ $>_v$ t″ and (t′ $>_v$ t or t′ $\approx_v$ t)

and so we may have t $>_v$ t″. However, for $w > v$ we have

t″ $>_w$ t′ and (t′ $>_w$ t or t′ $\approx_w$ t).

Thus, by the transitivity of the $>_i$ and $\approx_i$ relations, t″ $>_w$ t. Thus, there exists a chain $C_w\star$(u) such that $w > v$ and t″ $>_w$ t, that is, Condition (6) holds with $x = v$ and $y = w$.

Conditions (2) and (3)
The argument is similar here to that for the combination of Conditions (1) and (4) above. Condition (6) holds with $x = r$ and $y = s$.

Conditions (2) and (4)
Without loss of generality, we may assume that $C\star_r$(u) is the highest ranking chain such that t $>_i$ t′, so that

t′ $>_i$ t or t′ $\approx_i$ t, $i > r$.

Similarly, without loss of generality, we may assume that $C\star_v$(u) is the highest ranking chain such that t′ $>_i$ t″, so that

t″ $>_i$ t′ or t″ $\approx_i$ t′, $i > v$.

We also have, for some $s > r$, $t' >_s t$ and for some $w > v$, $t'' >_w t'$. If $w \geq s$, then

$$(t' >_w t \text{ or } t' \approx_w t) \text{ and } t'' >_w t',$$

and therefore $t'' >_w t$. Similarly, if $s \geq w$, $t'' >_s t$. Thus, there exists a chain $C^\star_y(u)$ in which $t'' >_y t$, where $y > r$ and $y > v$.

Thus, in either case, Condition (6) is satisfied with $y = s$ or $y = w$, and the proof is complete.

The single informative chain, the ideal chain, is determined using the following procedure:

1. Define a preference ordering of the records of $T^\star(u)$ as follows: For any $t,t' \in T^\star(u)$, $t > t'$ if and only if

- there exists at least one chain $C^\star_r(u)$ in which $t >_r t'$,
- for all other chains $C^\star_i(u)$, $i \neq r$, either not $(t' >_i t)$ or, if $(t' >_i t)$ then $i < r$.

2. Let $N(t)$ be the number of records t' such that $t > t'$. Then $N(t)$ is an ordinal utility function defined on $T^\star(u)$.

5

Aggregation of the User–Record Informativeness Measure

We have developed an informativeness measure for a single user–record interaction based on a unit informativeness value for a sequence corresponding to the ideal record chain. In this section, we look at the problem of aggregating these informativeness values in some fashion so that (1) the informativeness of a sequence of records that an information service presents to a user, called a [user] retrieval trail; (2) the informativeness of a sequences of uses of a single record over time, called a [record] use trail; and (3) the informativeness of all the user–record interactions that an information service provides for its community, called a service delivery, can all be evaluated. In order to develop measures for these situations, we introduce five additional axioms: Axioms 8, 9, and 10 relate to retrieval trails; Axiom 11 relates to use trails; and Axiom 12 relates to service delivery.

The informativeness of a sequence of user–record interactions may not be a simple sum of the informativeness values of the individual interactions because of a time factor. A record provides maximum information to a user at a certain point in time. If there is a delay, its informativeness may be diluted. For example, an information service may provide the user with noninformative records before informative ones, thus lessening the impact of the informative ones. Or one record may be more understandable if another is read first, but this introductory record is not provided by the service or provided at a later point. Delivery of the informative records may be delayed because there is a problem in obtaining the record and, when finally received, the record may be less informative to the user because the nature of the information problem has changed. Conversely, records may be delivered before the user can understand their significance and so are less informative. As records age, their informativeness may diminish and they may become less relevant to the information needs of the community. Because of this delay, a record may not contribute to the user's understanding; it may not provide as much information as it might have done had it been presented to the user at an earlier point in time.

Thus, a delay in providing a record may discount its informativeness. In the measures of informativeness that we will develop, the discounting effect of a delay will be represented by a delay discount factor (D), a value between zero and one, which will reduce the original informativeness value of the record for the user. The idea of discounting information for delays was originally presented by Marshak (see Chapter 3, Section 3.5), though in different contexts (communication channels and statistical decision making, rather than information services). We shall now develop this approach to information measure aggregation for the three situations, retrieval trails, use trails, and service deliveries, described above.

5.1 Retrieval Trails

Let **t** represent a sequence of records $\mathbf{t} = t_1t_2, \ldots t_m$ provided by an information service in response to a user's request for information (u). We shall call **t** a retrieval trail and represent its informativeness by the function I(**t**,u). Then I(**t**,u) will be a function of the informativeness of the individual records in **t** and the order in which they are presented to the user. It may be necessary for informative records to be read in a specified order to achieve maximal informativeness. In addition, noninformative records in the retrieval trail reduce the informativeness because of the delay they cause for the user.

The effect of concatenation (combining) and the order of concatenation on the informativeness of two records is formalized in Axiom 8.

Axiom 8 It will not necessarily be the case that $I(t_1t_2,u) = I(t_2t_1,u)$.

This axiom says that the informativeness of two records may depend on the order in which they are read. We have already identified situations when this might be the case, for example, if explanations in one record are necessary to an understanding of another record. Thus, by extension, with any set of records (e.g., a set of retrieved records), the informativeness of the set will depend on the sequence in which they are presented.

What is the optimal sequence, the best order for the user to visit the records in a database? We might expect that the user will want to access the informative records of the database in order of decreasing informativeness and not access any of the noninformative records. However, sometimes the user will prefer to access a record rated as less informative first, if the less informative record, say, t′, interacts with the more informative record, say, t, in such a way that the concatenation t′t is more informative than the concatenation tt′, that is, $t't > tt'$. Such a case might occur, for example, if t′ defined terms used in t, or t′ gave a simplified explanation of some complex analysis in t. Thus, in addition to assuming the existence of an ideal chain C★(u), in which informative record subsets are ranked by the user's preferences regarding their informativeness, we assume the existence of an optimal retrieval chain C★★(u), in which retrieved record subsets are ranked by the user's preferences regarding retrieval order.

The retrieval trail informativeness measure I(**t**,u) is a function of the extent to which the elements of edges of C★(u) are in **t** and the extent to which the order of the records of **t** corresponds to their order in C★★(u). The more the actual order diverges from the preferred order, the greater the user's delay in getting his or her desired information and so the more the information is discounted.

Noninformative items in the retrieval trail also contribute to the user's delay. It is assumed that noninformative items in the retrieval trail are always assigned to the last edge of the optimal retrieval chain C★★(u). What might be called the stopping point in the optimal retrieval chain lies between the penultimate edge and the final edge of C★★(u), whereas the stopping point in the retrieved chain lies at the end of the retrieved set. The fact that the noninformative records occur before the stopping point in the actual retrieval trail and the fact that the informative records in the trail are out of order both contribute to the delay the user experiences in getting needed information.

These ideas are formalized in Axiom 9.

Axiom 9 The informativeness of a retrieval trail $\mathbf{t} = t_1t_2, \ldots t_m$, provided by an information service in response to a user need, will be represented by the function I(**t**,u), which is a product of two factors

$$I(\mathbf{t},u) = I_0[\mathbf{t},C^\star(u)]\ D_0[t,C^{\star\star}(u)], \tag{5.1}$$

where $I_0[\mathbf{t},C^\star(u)]$, the user's initial informativeness, is the sum of the informativeness values of the informative records in **t,** as determined by their position in the ideal chain C★(u), and $D_0[\mathbf{t},C^{\star\star}(u)]$ is the retrieval delay discount factor, which discounts the initial informativeness by an amount that penalizes the service for divergence from the optimal retrieval chain C★★(u).

From equation (4.2) we have, for the first factor, the initial informativeness,

$$I_0[t,C^\star(u)] = \sum_{i=1}^{m} I(t_i,u), \tag{5.2}$$

where

$$I(t_i,u) = \frac{1}{n[e^\star(t_i)]}\log_2\left[\frac{\sum_{j=1}^{e^\star(t_i)} n(j) + n}{\sum_{j=1}^{e^\star(t_i)-1} n(j) + n}\right]$$

if t_i is informative, and $I(t_i,u) = 0$ if t_i is noninformative. The value $e^\star(t_i)$ is the edge index for retrieved record t_i in the ideal chain $C^\star(u)$ (i.e., if $t_i \in E_j$, $e^\star(t_i) = j$). The value $n(j)$ is the number of records in the jth edge of the ideal chain, $n = \Sigma_j n(j)$ is the number of records in the ideal chain, and m is the number of records in the retrieval trail.

The form of the delay discount function $D_0[\mathbf{t},C^{\star\star}(u)]$ reflects the priorities and policies of the information service relating to the kind of retrieval trail they should be providing to their users. This function is determined by the following four-part axiom.

Axiom 10.1 $0 \leq D_0[\mathbf{t},C^{\star\star}(u)] \leq 1$.

A discount of 0 results from a retrieval delay so great that the information in the retrieved records loses its value. A discount of 1 indicates there was no delay. As the delay increases, the discount decreases from 1 to 0.

To describe the optimal retrieval chain $C^{\star\star}(u)$, we define an edge index $e^{\star\star}(t)$ for any record $t \in T$ as follows: if t is in the ith edge of the optimal retrieval chain, $e^{\star\star}(t) = i$. All noninformative items are put in the last edge, $E^{\star\star}_{q'}(u)$, of the optimal retrieval chain. A retrieval trail is said to be a sequence consistent with the optimal retrieval chain $C^{\star\star}(u)$ if it is a sequence in which t precedes t′ if $e^{\star\star}(t) < e^{\star\star}(t')$.

Axiom 10.2 Let t be a retrieval trail containing all the informative records in an order consistent with the optimal retrieval chain $C^{\star\star}(u)$. Then $D_0[\mathbf{t},C^{\star\star}(u)] = 1$.

The delay discount for the informativeness of retrieval trails other than the optimal one is a function of two variables, as indicated by the last two parts of Axiom 10.

Axiom 10.3 $D_0[\mathbf{t},C^{\star\star}(u)]$ is a decreasing function of the number of transpositions needed to permute the retrieval trail to a sequence consistent with $C^{\star\star}(u)$.

Axiom 10.4 $D_0[\mathbf{t},C^\star(u)]$ is a decreasing function of the number of noninformative records in **t**.

What is a reasonable form for the delay discount factor $D_0[\mathbf{t},C^{\star\star}(u)]$ for an information service? In general, the delay discount function should reflect the service standards of an information-providing organization. From the axiom, the factor will be one when there are no noninformative items and all informative items are retrieved in the proper sequence. The more out of order the sequence and the more noninformative items it contains, the greater should be the extent of the delay and the smaller should be the value of $D_0[\mathbf{t},C^\star(u)]$. It may be reduced to zero when the extent of the delay is so great that the retrieval trail has probably lost its informativeness for the user.

Of the many possible functions that could satisfy these requirements, we look at two forms that have the virtue of simplicity and that represent the two approaches to discounting that seem most likely to reflect the concerns of the user communities served by an information service. Let $0 \leq X \leq 1$ represent the extent of the delay and b be a constant. Then the two functions are the linear function D_0' [**t**,C★★(u)] and the exponential function D_0''[**t**,C★★(u)]:

D_0'[**t**,C★★(u)] = 1 − bX for $0 \leq X \leq 1/b$; 0 otherwise;
D_0''[**t**,C★★(u)] = b^{-X}, $b > 1$.

With both functional forms, the discount factor is one (i.e., no discount) if there is no delay ($X = 0$). The linear function is appropriate for situations where, in general, users have a limited time in which to examine records and will not look through large numbers of noninformative records to find informative ones. Beyond a certain percentage of noninformative records the retrieval trail discount becomes 0. With the exponential function, there is no number of noninformative records for which the retrieval trail loses all informativeness; the maximum discount will reduce informativeness by a factor of 1/b.

The delay extent X is a function that varies between zero and one and is calculated as a weighted sum of two terms, each of which also vary between zero and one:

$$X = wX_1 + (1 - w)X_2, \; 0 \leq w \leq 1 \tag{5.3}$$

X_1 is the extent to which the informative items are retrieved in nonoptimal order and X_2 is the extent to which retrieved items are noninformative. X_1 is a linear transformation of the rank correlation coefficient R between the optimal order, as described by the chain C★★(**t**,u) and the retrieval trail **t**. R is normalized so that it increases from 0 to 1 as the trail becomes more disordered, rather than decreasing from 1 to −1. X_2 is simply the proportion of retrieved items that are noninformative. More specifically, we have

$$R = \frac{\sum_{i=1}^{m} i r^{\star\star}(t_i) - m(m+1)^2/4}{\sqrt{m(m^2-1)/12[\sum_{i=1}^{m} r^{\star\star}(t_i)^2 - m(m+1)^2/4]}};$$

$$X_1 = \frac{1 - R}{2}, \; X_2 = \frac{m(q')}{m}. \tag{5.4}$$

In these expressions for X_1 and X_2, m *is* the total number of retrieved records in the retrieval trail, $m(i)$ is the number of records retrieved in the ith edge of the optimal retrieval chain, and q' is the number of edges in the optimal chain. Thus, $m(q')$, the number of records in the last edge of the optimal retrieval chain, will be the number of retrieved noninformative records. The expression $r^{\star\star}(t_i)$ represents the rank of t_i in the optimal retrieval chain $C^{\star\star}(\mathbf{t},u)$. If t_i is in the edge number $e^{\star\star}(t_i)$ of the optimal chain, then its rank is the average rank for all records in this edge, namely

$$r^{\star\star}(t_i) = \sum_{j=1}^{e^{\star\star}(t_i)-1} m(j) + \frac{m[e^{\star\star}(t_i)]}{2}.$$

X_1 will have its maximum value of one when the actual and the optimal retrieval orders correspond. X_1 will have its minimum value of zero when the actual retrieval order is the opposite to the optimal one.

To determine the form of the delay discount function and the values of the parameters b and w, the information service needs to answer three questions:

1. If a retrieval trail has no noninformative items, but the informative items are retrieved in an order opposite to the optimal one, by what percentage should the informativeness of the search be reduced? Let this percentage, expressed as a proportion between 0 and 1, be represented by b_1.
2. If the order of the trail is correct, with noninformative ones at the end, is there an upper limit to the proportion of the items in the trail that can be noninformative, that is, a limit beyond which most users will not search, so that the informativeness of the search becomes 0? If the answer is Yes, let this proportion be b_2.
3. If there is no upper limit, as specified under point 2, for what proportion b_3 of noninformative items should the informativeness of the trail be reduced by one-half?

If the answer to the question in point 2 is Yes, the delay discount function is linear. It reflects a situation in which there is an upper limit to the amount of material users will examine. If the answer to the question in point 2 is No, the delay discount function is exponential. It reflects a situation in which the retrieval trail gradually declines in informativeness with increasing numbers, but never totally loses its informativeness value.

When the delay discount function is linear, that is, when

$$D[t,C^{\star\star}(u)] = 1 - b[w(1 - r)/2 + (1 - w)m(q')/m],$$

for $w(1 - R)/2 + (1 - w)m(q')m \leq 1$ and 0 otherwise, then the parameters w and b are given by:

$$w = \frac{b_2 - b_1 b_2}{b_2 - b_1 b_2 + 1}$$

$$b = \frac{1 - b_1}{w}. \qquad (5.5)$$

When the delay discount function is exponential, that is, when

$$D_0[t,C^{\star\star}(u)] = b^{w(1-R)/2+(1-w)m(q')/m},$$

the parameters w and b are given by:

$$w = \frac{b_3 \log_e b_1}{b_3 \log_e b_1 - \log_e 2}$$

$$\log_e b = \frac{\log_e 2}{b_3(1 - w)}. \tag{5.6}$$

Example 5.1 Suppose that the ideal chain consists of seven items at seven unique informativeness levels, as in the earlier example, that is, that

$$C^\star(u) = <\{t_{11}\}, \{t_4\}, \{t_1\}, \{t_{12}\}, \{t_5\}, \{t_8\}, \{t_9\}>$$
$$= <E^\star_1, E^\star_2, E^\star_3, E^\star_4, E^\star_5, E^\star_6, E^\star_7,$$

that the actual retrieval trail is

$$\mathbf{t} = t_1\, t_2\, t_3\, t_4\, t_5\, t_6\, t_7\, t_8\, t_9\, t_{10},$$

and that the optimal retrieval chain is

$$C^{\star\star}(u) = <\{t_4\}, \{t_1\}, \{t_5\}, \{t_9\}, \{t_8\}, \{t_2, t_3, t_6, t_7, t_{10}\}>$$
$$= <E^{\star\star}_1, E^{\star\star}_2, E^{\star\star}_3, E^{\star\star}_4, E^{\star\star}_5, E^{\star\star}_6>.$$

Then the number of informative records $m^\star = 7$, the number of retrieved records $m = 10$, the number of edges in the ideal chain $q = 7$, and the number of edges in the optimal retrieval chain $q' = 6$. The values, for each record t in the retrieval chain, of the actual retrieval rank, the optimal retrieval chain edge index e★★(t), the optimal retrieval rank r★★(t), the ideal chain edge index e★(t), and the initial informativeness I(t,u) are all shown in the table below:

Actual retrieval rank [*i*]	*Optimal retrieval chain edge index* [$e^{\star\star}(t_i)$]	*Optimal retrieval rank* [$r^{\star\star}(t_i)$]	*Ideal chain edge index* [$e^\star(t_i)$]	*Initial informativeness* [$I(t_i)$]
1	2	3	3	$\log_2(10/9)$
2	6	8	—	0
3	6	8	—	0
4	1	1	2	$\log_2(9/8)$
5	3	3	5	$\log_2(12/11)$
6	6	8	—	0
7	6	8	—	0
8	5	5	6	$\log_2(13/12)$
9	4	4	7	$\log_2(14/13)$
10	6	8	—	0

Since in the ideal chain informative records are ranked with no ties, Equation (3.3) can be used to determine the initial informativeness of each informative record. Substituting actual values we get

$$I(t,u) = \log_2[1 + 1/[6 + e^\star(t)].$$

Then from Equation (5.2),

$$I_0[\mathbf{t},u] = \log_2[(10/9)(9/8)(12/11)(13/12)(14/13] = .67.$$

Substituting in Equation (5.4) for the rank correlation coefficient R, we get

$$R = \frac{1(2) + 2(8) + 3(8) + 4(1) + 5(3) + 6(8) + 7(8) + 8(5) + 9(4) + 10(8) - 10(11)^2/4}{\sqrt{10(99)/12[1 + 4 + 9 + 16 + 25 + 5(64) - 10(11)^2/4]}}$$
$$= 24.$$

and so $X_1 = (1 - .24)/2 = .38.$

$$X_2 = 5/10 = .5$$

As an example of a linear delay discount, suppose that the service decided a set of informative items in an order opposite to the optimal one should have an informativeness of 90% of the initial informativeness and that no more than 80% of items retrieved should be noninformative. Then, in Equation (5.5), $b_1 = .9$ and $b_2 = .8$, and, substituting, $w = .07$ and $b = 1.35$. The delay discount is then

$$D_0[\mathbf{t},C^{\star\star}(u)] = 1 - 1.35[.07(.38) + .93(.5)] = .37$$

and the informativeness of the retrieval trail is

$$I[\mathbf{t},u] = .67(.37) = .25.$$

As an example of an exponential delay discount, suppose that, again, the service decided that a set of informative items in an order opposite to the optimal one should have an informativeness of 90% of the initial informativeness and that, in addition, the informativeness should be reduced by one-half if 80% of the items were noninformative. The, in Equation (5.6), $b_1 = .9$ and $b_3 = .8$, and, substituting, $w = .14$ and $b = 2.23$. The delay discount is then

$$D_0[\mathbf{t},C^{\star\star}(u)] = 2.23^{-[.14(.38)+.86(.5)]} = .68$$

and the informativeness of the retrieval trail is

$$I[\mathbf{t},u] = .67(.68) = .46.$$

Example 5.2 To provide some sense of how the function $I[\mathbf{t},u]$ varies for different retrieval trails involving seven informative items, Table 5.1 shows the values of $I_0[\mathbf{t},u]$, X (assuming $w = 1/3$), m (the total number of records retrieved), and $I[\mathbf{t},u]$ assuming an exponential delay discount function with

Table 5.1
Informativeness of Retrieval Trails for Ideal Chains of Seven Records

Ideal edge	Retrieval rank	Ideal edge	Retrieval rank
Trail (1)		Trail (4)	
1	1	1	100
2	2	2	99
3	3	3	98
4	4	4	97
5	5	5	96
6	6	6	95
7	7	7	94
$I_0[\mathbf{t},u] = 1.0$ $X = 0$ $m = 7$		$I_0[\mathbf{t},u] = 1.0$ $X = .8604$ $m = 100$	
$I[\mathbf{t},u] = 1.0$		$I[\mathbf{t},u] = .5508$	
Trail (2)		Trail (5)	
1	7	1	0
2	6	2	0
3	5	3	0
4	4	4	0
5	3	5	0
6	2	6	0
7	1	7	0
$I_0[\mathbf{t},u] = 1.0$ $X = .33$ $m = 7$		$I_0[\mathbf{t},u] = 1.0$ $X = 0$ $m = 7$	
$I[\mathbf{t},u] = .79$		$I[\mathbf{t},u] = 0$	
Trail (3)		Trail (6)	
1	94	1	0
2	95	2	0
3	96	3	0
4	97	4	0
5	98	5	0
6	99	6	0
7	100	7	1
$I_0[\mathbf{t},u] = 1.0$ $X = .8601$ $m = 100$		$I_0[\mathbf{t},u] = .11$ $X = .64$ $m = 7$	
$I[\mathbf{t},u] = .5509$		$I[\mathbf{t},u] = .07$	
Trail (7)		Trail (8)	
1	1	1	1
2	2	1	2
2	3	1	3
3	4	1	4
4	5	1	5
5	6	1	6
5	7	1	7
$I_0[\mathbf{t},u] = 1.0$ $X = 0$ $m = 7$		$I_0[\mathbf{t},u] = 1.0$ $X = 0$ $m = 7$	
$I[\mathbf{t},u] = 1.0$		$I[\mathbf{t},u] = 1.0$	

b = 2, for various retrieval trails, informative chains, and optimal retrieval chains for a set of seven informative records and various numbers of noninformative records. The first column, labeled "Ideal edge," shows the edge index for each item in the ideal chain, and the second column, labeled "Retrieval rank," shows the position in the retrieval trail for the same record. A retrieval rank of 0 indicates a nonretrieved informative item. The optimal retrieval chain is assumed to be consistent with the ideal chain.

In Trail (1), the ordering is optimal and all informative records and no noninformative records are retrieved; thus, X = 0, and I(**t**,u) = 1. In Trail (2), again, all informative and no noninformative records are retrieved, but the ordering is opposite to the optimal one; thus X = 1/3. Trails (3) and (4) show, respectively, the best and worst orderings of the informative items but with the addition of 93 noninformative items at the beginning of the retrieval trail. The contribution of X_2 to X thus increases substantially, essentially masking the effect of the informative item ordering differences between the two trails. Trail (5) has no informative items and hence zero informativeness. Trail (6) has a single retrieved information item, the least informative one. Trail (7) is a trail with ties in some of the informative edges. In Trail (8), all informative records have the same informativeness and all are retrieved.

Example 5.3 To illustrate this approach to the measurement of the informativeness of a retrieval trail with some real data, we will now present the results from a small retrieval experiment. The experiment was part of an evaluation of a "learning" interface, which was intended to encourage library and information science students at the author's school to move from menu-based to command-based use of the school's OPAC. Students in an administration course used the experimental interface to an enhanced OPAC (containing table of contents data) to collect materials to assist in writing reports on a number of assigned topics. All students were given the same set of assigned topics; however, they were expected to find their own background materials in the library.

All items listed in the bibliography of a student's report were considered to be informative items. Students were asked to rank these according to informativeness. Some, but not all, of the informative items were found in the OPAC search. Logs were kept of all searches by the students on the OPAC and from these the sequence of nodes (catalog items) was determined for each search.

Informativeness values were calculated using the informativeness function, Equation (4.2), applied to the retrieval ranks determined from the transaction logs and the informativeness ranks determined from the student bibliographies. The optimal retrieval chain is assumed to be a subchain of the informative chain because at the time of data collection, no information was gathered about the preferred retrieval ordering of the records. Of course, it is possible that the student would have improved performance on the assignment with a different bibliography. This question of the *value* of information and its relation to informativeness or *amount* of information is one that needs further study and we shall refer to it again. An exponential delay discount function with w = 1/3 and b = 2 was used, as in the previous example.

In Table 5.2, the results of searches by four students are shown for each of four assigned topics: Topic (1), motivation; topic (2), the difficult boss; topic (3), performance appraisal; and topic (4), training and discipline.

Informative items are identified by the surname of the first author. The actual and optimal retrieval ranks are listed for each item, together with the initial informativeness (I_0), the delay extent (X), and the discounted informativeness (I) for each research. As in the previous example, a 0 retrieval rank indicates an informative item not found in the OPAC search.

It will be seen that, despite the fact the "query," that is, the assignment, was the same, the informative chains are very different from student to student. Both the informative chain and the informativeness value of the search is clearly dependent on the user with this type of query. A standard Mann-Whitney test was used to compare searches carried out using the two interfaces, but no significant difference was found. (A more detailed discussion of this type of testing will be found in Chapter 6.)

The range of informativeness values is from .37 to .62, a reasonable degree of variation given that the searchers were all at approximately the same level of experience with the OPAC and were searching for material for the same set of four different assignments. Higher scores are associated with retrieval of larger numbers of informative items near the beginning of the trail and fewer numbers of noninformative items in the trail. Lower scores are associated with retrieval of larger numbers of noninformative items and delayed retrieval or nonretrieval of informative items.

One interesting aspect of these searches is the variation in the titles that the students found informative and in the number retrieved for the same assignment. In many cases, the same items were found in the OPAC search, but different selections were made of the ones to use in the assignment. Clearly, there were large individual differences in students' understandings in their interaction with both the catalog records and the books themselves. Although the assignment was the same, the information problem was different for each of them.

Is this approach to the measurement of the informatives of a retrieval trail realistic? In other words, can information service users assess the informativeness of pairs of records, or rank records, in this fashion? To answer this question, we need to use the approach with actual users and find out whether or not they can make such pairwise comparisons. In the trials just

Table 5.2
Informativeness Scores for Sixteen OPAC Searchers

Topic number	Student number	Informative items	Ranks		Informativeness		
			Retrieval	Optimal	I_0	X	I
1	1	Hecht	0	3	.83	.76	.49
		Scanlon	5	3			
		Stevens	22	1			
		Stone	20	2			
		Stueart	42	3			
		Total retrieved: 52					
	2	Gellerman	1	2	1.00	.78	.58
		Ponder	27	3			
		Sisk	31	1			
		Stueart	42	4			
		Total retrieved: 56					
	3	Gellerman	5	2	1.00	.71	.61
		Scanlon	1	1			
		Stueart	3	3			
		Total retrieved: 41					
	4	Batten	20	3	1.00	.77	.59
		Eddy	40	2			
		Gellerman	14	4			
		Stueart	17	1			
		Van Dersel	31	5			
		Total retrieved: 96					
2	1	Kies	10	4	.89	.65	.57
		Marchant	0	6			
		McClure	9	3			
		Naughton	22	2			
		Reynolds	6	5			
		Stevens	3	1			
		Stueart	21	3			
		Total retrieved: 24					
	2	Martin	5	1	.89	.79	.46
		Riggs	18	2			
		Stueart	67	3			
		Wilson	0	3			
		Total retrieved: 180					
	3	Davis	12	2	.84	.78	.49
		Euster	5	1			
		French	76	3			
		Koontz	0	4			
		Vaughn	27	4			
		Total retrieved:134					
	4	Armstrong	6	6	.62	.76	.37
		Duda	10	1			
		Evans	0	6			
		Jones	0	4			
		Plate	0	2			

(*continues*)

Table 5.2 (*Continued*)

Topic number	Student number	Informative items	Ranks		Informativeness		
			Retrieval	Optimal	I_0	X	I
		Rogers	20	6			
		Stueart	14	3			
		Stewart	37	5			
		Total retrieved: 108					
3	1	Chen	20	1	1.00	.77	.59
		Stueart	4	1			
		Total retrieved: 39					
	2	Emery	0	1	.75	.80	.43
		Jenkins	16	1			
		Kitchener	43	1			
		Stueart	40	1			
		Total retrieved: 62					
	3	Rawles	19	1	1.00	.79	.58
		Stueart	23	2			
		Total retrieved: 83					
	4	AMA	29	5	1.00	.69	.62
		Armstorng	22	3			
		Cummings	3	8			
		Johnson	2	2			
		Littlefield	28	9			
		Meidan	1	1			
		Odiorne	36	1			
		Raia	4	7			
		Shaffer	27	4			
		Total retrieved: 76					
4	1	Shaffer	35	1	1.00	.81	.57
		Stueart	31	2			
		Total retrieved: 63					
	2	CUPE	0	3	.66	.72	.40
		Cummings	10	1			
		Shaffer	5	2			
		Stahl	9	4			
		Stueart	0	5			
		Total retrieved: 11					
	3	Armstrong	13	1	.67	.81	.38
		Stueart	0	1			
		White	68	1			
		Total retrieved: 95					
	4	AMA	65	5	1.00	.77	.59
		Cummings	39	6			
		Durey	4	2			
		Littlefield	56	4			
		Odiorne	31	1			
		Raia	3	3			
		Shaffer	63	7			
		Total retrieved: 76					

described with library and information science students, they appeared to have little difficulty in making such judgments.

To collect evidence regarding the validity of the proposed measure of retrieval informativeness itself, another independent assessment of the value of the retrieval needs to be carried out with the user community for the service and compared with the value of the calculated measure. Since informativeness is an ordinal measure, validation involves comparing the rankings of the proposed informativeness measure with rankings of user perceptions of relative informativeness over a set of searches.

A trial of this validation process was carried out with a group of five users at the author's School of Library and Information Science. The validation process again involved a series of searches of the school's online catalog for material to help with student assignments. Four of the student users carried out three searches each and one user five searches over the period of a term. Transaction logs were made of their searches and, in addition, students were asked to provide a listing of the monographs actually

Table 5.3
Informativeness Ranking for Seventeen OPAC Searches

Student and search number	Number informative	Number retrieved	Informativeness	I-Rank[a]	U-Rank[b]
S1.1	5	53	.28	1	1
1.2	5	31	.21	2	2
1.3	5	21	.19	3	3
S2.1	4	50	.57	2	1
2.2	2	18	.61	1	2
2.3	4	7	.41	3	3
S3.1	3	7	.62	1	1
3.2	10	28	.50	2	2
3.3	4	13	0	3	3
S4.1	1	17	.55	2	1
4.2	2	44	.59	1	2
4.3	6	199	.32	3	3
S5.1	5	20	.59	1	1
5.2	2	18	.58	2	2
5.3	5	24	.48	3	3
5.4	4	23	.46	5	4
5.5	5	35	.47	4	5

[a] I-rank is the informativeness of the retrieval as determined by the informativeness measure.
[b] U-rank is the informativeness of the retrieval as judged by the user relative to her or his other searches.

used for each assignment and a ranking of these items as to informativeness. This information was used to determine the informativeness of each search, based on the assumption that the ranked items in the listing represented the ideal chain and the items in the transaction logs the retrieval trail. The students were then asked to rank the three searches or five searches by their informativeness relative to the assignment. The results are given in Table 5.3. Discrepancies of the informativeness measure from user perceptions of informativeness appear to arise primarily with small retrieval sets, specifically with the second searches of students 2 and 4, and when measured informativeness values are close. Even so, the overall rank correlation between the values of the informativeness measure and the user perception informativeness rankings was 82%.

5.1.1 Relationship of Informativeness to Other Retrieval Evaluation Measures

Tague-Sutcliffe (1992c) reviews the most commonly used measures of retrieval performance. The best known of these are recall, precision, and fallout defined as follows: recall is the proportion of relevant documents retrieved, precision is the proportion of retrieved documents that are relevant, and fallout is the proportion of nonrelevant documents retrieved. The concept of relevance is similar to informativeness, although it, too, has many different meanings and so needs to be defined in any context in which it is used. In particular, a distinction is sometimes made between relevance, representing "aboutness" of the item to the query, and pertinence, representing usefulness of the item to the user. Informativeness, the amount of information, where information is what the user understands from the record, has aspects of both. In general, the more an item is about the query, the more information it will provide, but this informativeness will also be dependent on the relationship of the information to the user's need.

The measure of informativeness just presented is related to recall and precision. If all of n informative items are equally informative, the informativeness of each is simply $1/n$ and so if m_1 of them are retrieved, m_1/n, or the recall, is the initial informativeness, $I_0(t,u)$ of the retrieval. If the user assigns a weight of $w = 0$ to the X_1 term, representing retrieval order, in the delay extent function X (Equation 3.6), then X is equivalent to $1\text{-}m_1/m$, where m_1/m is the precision. Thus, if we use a linear delay discount function $D(t,u) = 1 - X$, then the delay discount value and the precision are the same. Thus, recall is simply a special case of initial informativeness and precision a special case of delay discount.

A number of writers have suggested measures that combine recall and precision into an overall retrieval performance measure. Van Rijsbergen (1979) suggested the E measures, defined as follows:

$$E = 1 - \frac{1}{\alpha P^{-1}(1 - \alpha)R^{-1}},$$

where R and P are recall and precision, respectively, and α is a parameter reflecting the relative importance of recall and precision for the user. Shaw (1986) suggested the MZ metric, defined as follows:

$$D = 1 - \frac{1}{P^{-1} + R^{-1} - 1}.$$

Bollmann and Cherniavsky (1981) show that any measure of the form

$$F_{\alpha,\beta} = 1 - \frac{\alpha a}{\alpha a + \beta(b + c)}, \alpha,\beta > 0$$

is an ordinal measure equivalent to either the Van Rijsbergen or the Shaw measures.

The approach in our development is a multiplicative one, rather than additive, as in the Van Rijsbergen and Shaw approaches. A *lack* of precision is used to discount the informativeness, represented by the recall.

5.2 Use Trails

One problem faced by informative services is the determination over time of the total informativeness of a record in the collection or database to users of the service. Such a sequence of uses of a record will be called a record use trail. These uses will vary in number over time and individual uses will vary in informativeness values. Some records may decline in informativeness over time, even become obsolete. Others may retain their informativeness, and for still others the informativeness values may fluctuate up and down. It is important to be able to detect these patterns of past informativeness in order to predict future informativeness of the item.

In the past, managers of information services have employed the number of times a record in the collection was used (or frequency of circulation) as a measure of its value to the user community. The most fully developed model of frequency of use is the gamma-Poisson of Burrell (1985), which assumes that the number of loans of a record is a Poisson process with initial rate (called desirability), which varies from record to record according to a gamma distribution and which decreases exponentially over time. The overall frequency of circulation of a collection and the frequency conditional on circulation in the immediately preceding time interval will both then have a negative binomial distribution. The conditional distribution can then be used to predict future use.

Another measure of the value of a record to the user community is the total time users spend reading, viewing, or consulting the record, the contact or exposure time. Beheshti (1989) studied this measure and found that the distribution of contact times, in minutes, over book uses in a university library collection followed a two-parameter gamma distribution. A third measure, suggested originally by Trueswell (1975), is the last circulation or use date, that is, the length of time a record has been unused. This measure is inversely related to the value of the record to the user community.

The number of uses of a record and the length of time that a user is in contact with a record reflect, to some extent, how informative, that is, how desirable to the user community, that record is. The length of time a record has been unused reflects, to some extent, its lack of informativeness. The advantage of these measures over informativeness is that they are easier to obtain and they are independent of the values assigned by the user to other items in the user's ideal chain. To determine informativeness, we must ask the user to provide us with both the ideal chain of informative items and the optimal retrieval chain of retrieved items. To determine frequency of circulation we need determine only whether or not the user used the item. To determine contact time, we need determine only how long the user used the item. To determine time since last use, we need determine only the times at which the record is used.

In the model to be presented in this section, we use two of these other measures, number of uses and contact time, to estimate informativeness when it is difficult to obtain exact values of this measure. A similar model could be developed using time since last use and contact time. The basic assumption of the model is that informativeness, averaged over the uses of a record, serves as a parameter of the distributions of frequency of use and contact time for the record. Informativeness thus may be used to integrate these earlier approaches to record evaluation. If all users are equally significant to the information service, the summed contact time of all users of a record will then be proportional to its total and average informativeness to the community. We will now develop the frequency models for number of uses and contact times, which will permit us to make predictions of the future informativeness of a record.

Consider the uses of a record over a period of time, divided into a number (u) of time intervals. Initially, we define three variables:

1. The *informativeness* α_{ij} of the record for the *j*th user in the *i*th unit time interval, where $0 \leq \alpha_{ij} \leq 1$;
2. The *contact time* Z_{ij} between the record and its *j*th user in the *i*th time interval, where $Z_{ij} \geq 0$;
3. The *number of users* N_i of the record in the *i*th time interval.

We also let $\nu_i = E[\alpha_{ij}]$ represent the expected informativeness of the record over all users in the ith time interval. This parameter is similar to Burrell's desirability, mentioned at the beginning of this section.

In Axiom 11, three assumptions are made about these variables.

Axiom 11.1 The expected number of users of a record in the ith time interval is proportional to its expected informativeness, that is,

$$E[N_i] = \beta\nu_i,$$

where β is the constant of proportionality.

Axiom 11.2 The expected contact time of a record in the ith time interval is proportional to its expected number of users and hence to its expected informativeness, that is,

$$E[Z_{ij}] = \gamma\beta\nu_i,$$

where γ is a constant of proportionality.

Axiom 11.3 The contact times Z_{ij} of users of a record in the ith interval have a gamma distribution with parameters $\beta\nu_i$ and γ, that is, the density function for Z_{ij} is given by

$$f(z) = \frac{z^{\beta\nu_i - 1} e^{-z/\gamma}}{\gamma^{\beta\nu_i}\Gamma(\beta\nu_i)},$$

where ν_i is the expected informativeness, β represents aspects of the user community other than informativeness (e.g., demand, demographic characteristics), and γ represents aspects of the record other than informativeness (e.g., availability, difficulty of reading). It is assumed that both β and γ remain constant over the time period under consideration.

From the known properties of the gamma distribution (Johnson and Kotz, 1970), the expected value of the contact times in the ith time period is given by $E[Z_{ij}] = \nu_i\beta\gamma$ and the variance is given by $V[Z_{ij}] = \nu_i\beta\gamma^2$. Thus, the parameter γ satisfies the relation

$$V[Z_{ij}] = \gamma\beta E[Z_{ij}].$$

Given observations of contact times Z_{ij} in time intervals $i = 1,2, \ldots u$, we can obtain the sample mean M_i and sample variance S_i^2 for each interval. Then the least squares estimate of γ will be given by

$$\gamma = \frac{\sum_{i=1}^{u} M_i S_i^2}{\sum_{i=1}^{u} M_i^2}. \tag{5.7}$$

For purposes of use trail evaluation, our interest is not so much in the individual contact times in an interval, the Z_{ij}, but in the total contact time of all users in the interval, since this reflects the total informativeness of the record to the user community at that time. We let Y_i represent the total contact time of all users of the record in the *i*th time interval, that is,

$$Y_i = \sum_{j=1}^{N_i} Z_{ij}.$$

Then from the known properties of the gamma distribution, conditional on the number of users $N_i = n_i$, the total contact time Y_i in the *i*th time interval will have a gamma distribution with parameters $n_i\beta\nu_i$ and γ. The expected value of Y_i, conditional on n_i, will be $E[Y_i \mid n_i] = \gamma n_i\beta\nu_i$ and we recall that the expected value of N_i is $\beta\nu_i$.

From these two expressions for expected values we may derive the unconditional expectation of the total contact time in a time interval, that is, not dependent on a known value of the number of users. This expected value is derived as follows:

$$E[Y_i] = E_{N_i}[Y_i \mid N_i = n_i] = \sum_{n=0}^{\infty} E[Y_i \mid n]P[N_i = n],$$

$$= \gamma\beta\nu_i \sum_{n=0}^{\infty} nP[N_i = n] = \gamma\beta^2\nu_i^2.$$

Models for use trails often assume obsolescence, that is, that use declines with age. If a record declines in expected informativeness over time, we may represent the ν_i as a function of ν_1, the initial expected informativeness, and $0 \le \theta \le 1$, the aging factor. Burrell suggests the form

$$\nu_i = \nu_1\theta^{i-1}. \tag{5.8}$$

If informativeness declines over time according to this equation, $E[Y_i \mid n_i] = \gamma n_i\beta\nu_1\theta^{i-1}$, $E[N_i] = \beta\nu_1\theta^{i-1}$, and the unconditional expected value for total contact time Y_i in the *i*th time interval will be given by

$$E[Y_i] = \gamma\beta^2\nu_1^2\theta^{2(i-1)} = \delta\,\varepsilon^{i-1}, \tag{5.9}$$

where $\delta = \gamma\beta^2\nu_1{}^2$ and $\varepsilon = \theta^2$.

Given a history of total contact times over a period of u time intervals, $Y_1, Y_2, \ldots Y_u$, we may estimate δ and ε using a loglinear least squares procedure, since from the expression for $E[Y_i]$ in Equation (5.9) we may write

$$\log_e E[Y_i] = \log_e\delta + (i - 1)\log_e\varepsilon.$$

Least squares estimates may thus be determined for the logarithms of δ and ε, namely

$$\log_e(\varepsilon) = \frac{\sum_{i=1}^{u}(i-1)\log_e Y_i - \sum_{i=1}^{u}\log_e Y_i \sum_{i=1}^{u}(i-1)/u}{\sum_{i=1}^{u}(i-1)^2 - [\sum_{i=1}^{u}(i-1)]^2/u}$$

$$\log_3\delta = \sum_{i=1}^{u}\log_e Y_i/u - \log_e\varepsilon\sum_{i=1}^{u}(i-1)/u.$$

Our interest in estimating the total contact time function is so that we can estimate total future contact time. If expected informativeness declines according to Equation (5.9), this quantity can be determined, as we shall now show.

Let $S_{[u,h]}$ represent the total contact time of all users in the period from interval u +1 to interval u + h inclusive, that is, the total contact time with the item in the h time intervals after time u, or

$$S_{[u,h]} = \sum_{i=u+1}^{u+h} Y_i.$$

The expected value of this function may be used to predict the expected total future contact time for an item after some u-length period of use. Suppose that the contact times are known for the intervals $i = 1$ to $i = u$. As we have just seen, these values can be used to estimate the parameters δ and ε, assuming expected informativeness declines according to Equation (5.8). The expected value of $S_{[u,h]}$ will be

$$E[S_{[u,h]}] = \sum_{i=u+1}^{u+h} E[Y_i] = \sum_{i=u+1}^{u+h} \delta\varepsilon^{i-1} = \frac{\delta\varepsilon^{u-1}(1-\varepsilon^h)}{1-\varepsilon},$$

where, as before, $\delta = \gamma\beta^2\nu_1{}^2$ and $\varepsilon = \theta^2$.

As h increases without limit (in order to estimate total future contact time with the item), the expected value of the future sum becomes

$$E[S_{u,\infty]}] = \frac{\delta\varepsilon^{u-1}}{1-\varepsilon}.$$

This quantity then represents the expected total future contact time for the record. In order to determine how the actual values of the total future contact time may vary about this expected value, we need, also, to determine the variance of $S_{[u,h]}$. If we assume that the individual user contact time Z_{ij} are independent within the ith time interval, we may use the same reasoning to determine the variance of their sum Y_i as we did to determine their expected value $E[Y_i]$. The resulting variance $V[Y_i]$ is given by

$$V[Y_i] = \gamma^2\beta^2\nu_1^2\theta^{2(i-1)} = \gamma\delta\varepsilon^{i-1}.$$

To determine the variance of the summed total future contact time after interval u, we let h increase without limit, as before, and obtain

$$V[S_{[S,\infty]}] = \frac{\gamma\delta\varepsilon^{u-1}}{1 - \varepsilon}.$$

As indicated earlier, we may obtain a least squares estimate of γ from the means and variances in each time interval using Equation (5.7).

Since $S_{[u,\infty]}$ is the sum of a large number of independent variables, it will be approximately normally distributed, with the designated mean and variance. Thus, a 95% confidence interval for $S_{[u,\infty]}$ is given by

$$\frac{\delta\varepsilon^2}{1 - \varepsilon} \pm 1.96\sqrt{\frac{\gamma\delta\varepsilon^2}{1 - \varepsilon}}.$$

An example of these determinations is presented in Table 5.4 and 5.5 and illustrated in Figure 5.1. Contact times and numbers of users are shown for a journal issue over a period of eight time intervals (months) in Table 5.4, together with the mean and standard deviation of the contact times in the indicated month. Observed and expected total contact time in each month are shown in Table 5.5, together with the mean and standard deviation of the future total contact time. Figure 5.1 shows the observed monthly total contact time, the expected monthly total contact time, and the mean and standard deviation of the predicted future contact time, based on the model, for each of the eight months.

Table 5.4
Monthly Contact Times

Month	Number of users	Contact times	Monthly	
			Mean	SD
(i)	(n_i)	(z_{ij})		
1	8	100 75 50 50 45 30 25 10	48.13	718.36
2	6	85 40 35 30 15 10	35.83	595.14
3	4	30 25 10 10	18.75	79.69
4	3	25 15 10	16.67	38.89
5	2	15 10	12.50	6.25
6	2	10 10	10.00	0.00
7	1	10	10.00	0.00
8	1	5	5.00	0.00

Table 5.5
Prediction of Future Contact Times

	Total contact time in months		Total predicted contact time after *i*th month	
Month (i)	Observed Y_i	Expected $E[Y_i]$	Mean $E[S_{[1,\infty]}]$	SD $\{V[S_{[1,\infty]}]\}^{1/2}$
1	385	333.69	741.53	100.87
2	215	183.53	407.84	74.80
3	75	100.94	224.31	55.48
4	50	55.52	123.37	41.14
5	25	30.53	67.85	30.51
6	20	16.79	37.32	22.63
7	10	9.24	20.53	16.78
8	5	5.08	11.29	12.45

Note: $\gamma = 13.72$; $\delta = 333.69$; $\varepsilon = .55$; $E[Y_i] = 333.69\ (.55)^{i-1}$; $E[S_{[1,\infty]}] = 741.54\ (.55)^{i-1}$; $V[S_{[i,\infty]}] = 10178.06(.55)^{i-1}$.

5.3 Service Delivery

We shall now consider the problem of determining the informativeness to a community of the service delivery of an information service over a period of time. This informativeness is a function of the extent to which

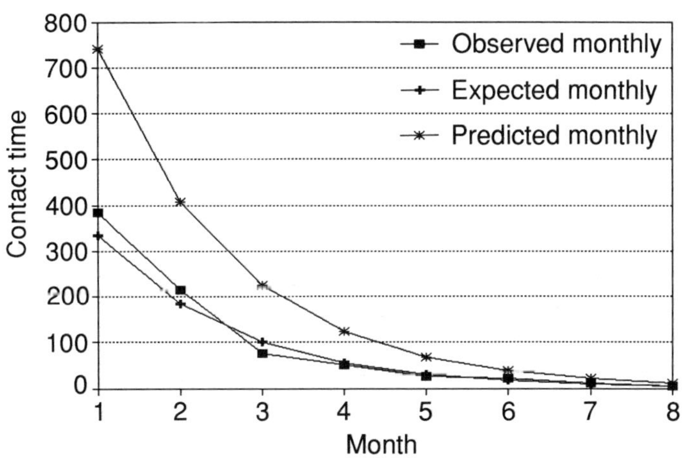

Figure 5.1
Observed monthly total contact time, expected monthly total contact time, and predicted future contact time, based on the gamma function model, for eight months' use of a journal issue in a library.

the information needs of the community are met by the user–record interactions that occur and by their timeliness, that is, by the order in which they occur.

To formalize this approach to the evaluation of service delivery, we present the following axiom.

Axiom 12 For any time period during which an informative service serves a user community, there exists an optimal or ideal service (super) chain of the form

$$C\star = \langle C_1\star, C_2\star, \ldots C_v\star \rangle,$$

where $C_i\star$ represents the set of ideal chains $C\star(u)$ that should be provided to the user community in the *i*th time interval of the period and ν is the total number of time intervals under consideration. By "should be provided," we mean that, from the point of view of the service's mission to the user community, the records in the ideal chain $C\star(u)$ should be presented in the *i*th time interval to the user u in an order consistent with the user's optimal retrieval chain. It can usually be assumed that all services that actually occur are represented by ideal chains in the optimal service sequence, though not necessarily in the time interval in which they do occur. In other words, no services are censored. In special circumstances it might be necessary to depart from this principle, for example, when release of the record is illegal or unethical or a violation of confidentiality.

Let C be a chain representing the actual user–record interactions that the information service has provided to the community, that is,

$$C = \langle T_1, T_2, \ldots T_v \rangle,$$

where T_i contains all of the retrieval trails, all of the user–record interaction sequences, which occurred in the *i*th time interval. Then the overall informativeness $I(C,C\star)$ of the information service is given by the sum of the discounted informativeness values for each service, where the discount represents delay due both to nonoptimal retrieval sequence and to service nonavailability, that is, to delays in the providing of service. Specifically,

$$I(C,C\star) = \sum_{i=1}^{v} \sum_{j=1}^{n'(i)} I_0(t_{ij},u_{ij})D(t_{ij},u_{ij}) = \sum_{i=1}^{v} \sum_{j=1}^{n'(i)} I_0(s_{ij})D(s_{ij}), \qquad (5.10)$$

where $n'(i)$ is the number of user needs that are satisfied in the *i*th time period; t_{ij} is the retrieval trail provided by the service in response to u_{ij}, the *j*th user need arising in the *i*th time period; $s_{ij} = (t_{ij},u_{ij})$; $I_0(s_{ij})$ is the initial informativeness of retrieval trail t_{ij} provided to user u_{ij} as given by Equation (5.2); and $D(s_{ij})$ is the delay discount function for needs arising in the *i*th time period. If no response is made by the service, then $I_0(s_{ij}) = 0$.

The rationale for using a sum of informativeness values is that we are adding individual informativeness values each of which represents the degree (between 0 and 1) to which the information service has satisfied a user need. Although the original user preferences defined on the set of records produced an ordinal measure, by applying the operations of summation, normalization, and discounting we have obtained an interval measure on the set of user needs because the unit (the range of informativeness) is the same for all users.

The delay discount $D(s_{ij})$ is a function of the extent of the delay experienced by a user of the service. For any user, the delay extent is the sum of the delay resulting from imperfect retrieval, as given by Equation (5.4), and the delay resulting from imperfect service (the retrieved records were not provided in the time period in which they were first needed). As in the preceding paragraph, let s_{ij} represent the service provided in response to the *j*th information need arising in the *i*th time period, let $0 \leq X(s_{ij}) \leq 1$ represent the retrieval delay for this service, as given by Equation (5.4), and $v(s_{ij})$ the time period when the service was actually provided. For an individual service s_{ij}, the delivery delay $0 \leq Y(s_{ij}) \leq 1$ is

$$Y(s_{ij}) = [v(s_{ij}) - i]/v,$$

where v is the total number of time intervals under consideration. Then the extent $0 \leq Z(s_{ij}) \leq 1$ of the delay per individual service is obtained by averaging $X(_{ij})$ and $Y(s_{ij})$, that is,

$$z(s_{ij}) = \frac{X(s_{ij}) + Y(s_{ij})}{2}.$$

As with the retrieval delay discount discussed earlier, two relatively simple functions for delay discount are the linear and the exponential:

$$D(s_{ij}) = 1 - bZ(s_{ij}), 0 \leq Z(s_{ij}) \leq \frac{1}{b'} \leq \frac{1}{b}; \text{ 0 otherwise}$$

$$D(s_{ij}) = b^{-Z(s_{ij})}, 0 \leq Z(s_{ij}) \leq 1, b > 1.$$

In the linear form, the maximum delay discount is zero. In the exponential form, the maximum delay discount is 1/b. If we do not wish to discount delays, we set b = 0 for the linear function or b = 1 for the exponential function. The constant b′ in the linear form permits us to have a discount function that will reduce to zero before the delay extent reaches 1/b. For example, if we wish delays of up to $Z(s_{ij}) = 1/2$ not to be discounted and delays greater than $Z(s_{ij}) = 1/2$ to reduce the informativeness to zero, we could set b = 1 and b′ = 1/2, so that $D(s_{ij}) = 1 - Z(s_{ij})$ if $Z(s_{ij})$ was less than or equal to 1/2 and zero otherwise. It is up to the information service to determine a functional form and the values of the parameter or parameters appropriate to its user community.

The linear and exponential delay discount functions just presented assume that the same scaling, that is, the same values of the constant b and the constant b′ will be used for all users. However, this may not be the case; different users may require different discounts and a single user may wish to scale the retrieval and delivery delay discount differently. To allow for this flexibility, we could use a more general delay discount function, in which the parameter b, and also b′ in the case of a linear function, would depend on the user or the user group. Specifically, we would then have:

$$D(s_{ij}) = 1 - b_{ij}Z(s_{ij}), 0 \leq Z(s_{ij}) \leq \frac{1}{b'_{ij}} \leq \frac{1}{b_{ij}};\ 0 \text{ otherwise}$$

for the linear function, and

$$D(s_{ij}) = b_{ij}{}^{-Z(s_{ij})}, 0 \leq Z(s_{ij}) \leq 1, b_{ij} > 1$$

for the exponential function.

For some services different kinds of needs have different priorities. In this case, the management of the information service will rank the services that should occur in each time period as to priority and then assign priority weights. Let s_{ijk} represent the kth service in the jth priority class in the ith time interval, where priority classes are numbered from 1 to p in order of decreasing priority, and let $n'(ij)$ represent the number of services in the jth priority class in the ith time interval. Then the delay extent function $Z(s_{ijk})$ can be weighted by priority and the total informativeness becomes:

$$I(C,C^\star) = \sum_{i=1}^{v}\sum_{j=1}^{p}\sum_{k=1}^{n'(ij)} w_j I_o(s_{ijk}) D(s_{ijk}),$$

where the priority weights $w_j > 0$ sum to one over the p priority classes and where the priority weight is any function such that $w_j > w_k$ if $j < k$. For example, we could define w_j as follows:

$$w_j = (1/2)^j/(1 - 1/2^p).$$

The overall informativeness for a service will vary between 0 and n, the number of needs that arise in the period under study. Although we do not need to know this total number n (only the number of needs n' that are brought to the service) in order to calculate the total informativeness in the designated period, we do need its value in order to assess the meaning of the calculated total informativeness, how good or bad the service is. The maximum total informativeness value n will occur if and only if all needs are satisfied in the time interval in which they arise by an optimal retrieval trail containing all and only informative records. The minimum value will occur if no informative records are retrieved for any user need or if users are provided with some informative records but the delay is so great their informativeness is discounted to zero.

The overall informativeness of an information service in some time period is thus a function of the informativeness of the records in the retrieval trails provided by the service, the order in which informative records are presented in these trails, the number of noninformative records presented, and the extent to which these retrieval trails occur close to the time at which the need arises. In other words, the overall informativeness measures the extent to which all desirable uses of records actually occur and occur in the most timely fashion.

We will now present an example of the calculation of the total informativeness, using the data presented earlier.

Example 5.4 In the OPAC study described in the last section, sixteen searches were carried out by students in order to locate information for their assignments. Ideally, the searches should have been carried out a week before each assignment, in order to be of maximum benefit to the user. For some of the users, however, the OPAC was not available when they came to carry out their search in that week because of system problems and the search had to be carried out later. Thus, the total informativeness of the OPAC to the users whole searches were described in Table 5.2 was not as great as it could have been.

Specifically, the four topics described in the previous example should have been searched, respectively, in weeks 1,2,3, and 4. Table 5.6 shows

Table 5.6
Informativeness of OPAC Service for Four Assignments

	Week			Delay extent		
User	Assign.	Search	Initial inform.	Retrieval	Delivery	Discouted inform.
1	1	1	0.83	0.76	0.00	0.64
2	1	1	1.00	0.78	0.00	0.76
3	1	1	1.00	0.78	0.00	0.76
4	1	1	1.00	0.77	0.00	0.77
1	2	2	0.89	0.65	0.00	0.71
2	2	2	0.89	0.80	0.00	0.67
3	2	3	0.84	0.78	0.20	0.60
4	2	2	0.62	0.76	0.00	0.48
1	3	4	1.00	0.79	0.20	0.71
2	3	4	0.75	0.80	0.20	0.53
3	3	4	1.00	0.79	0.20	0.71
4	3	5	1.00	0.69	0.40	0.69
1	4	4	1.00	0.81	0.00	0.76
2	4	5	0.67	0.71	0.20	0.49
3	4	4	0.67	0.81	0.00	0.51
4	4	5	1.00	0.77	0.20	0.71
	Total informativeness I(C,C*)					10.49
	Maximum possible informativeness					16.00
	Average informativeness					0.66

the variation between the assignment week, when the search should have been done, the actual search week, and the resulting values for the service informativeness for this particular set of user needs. Table 5.6 also shows the initial informativeness values $I_0(s_{ij})$, the retrieval delay extent values $X(s_{ij})$, and the delivery delay extent $Y(s_{ij})$ for each of the sixteen searches carried out in the four-week period under study. An exponential delay discount function with $b = 2$ is used to determine the final informativeness value $I(C,C^\star)$ for the service relating to this group of users.

The major difficulty in assessing service delivery lies in the determination of *n,* the number of user needs in the community over the specified time period. This number may not be known in large-scale evaluations, because some needs will never be brought to the service. However, it may be estimated by a sampling of needs identified by a group of expert judges, people knowledgeable about the information needs of the community. These experts might include representatives of community groups, both formal and informal, and external consultants. Ideally, the expert group should *not* include administrators of the service being evaluated.

In an evaluation procedure based on sample evidence, the sample would have three subsets:

1. a sample of the actual services for information needs that were brought to the service and satisfied, at least in part;
2. a sample of information needs that were brought to the service and lie within its goals, but were not satisfied;
3. a sample from the user community of information needs that, for whatever reason, were not brought to the service but lie within its goals.

For the first subset, we need to determine the initial informativeness, the optimal retrieval chain, the actual retrieval trail, and the delivery delay for each user need in the subset. For all three subsets, we need to determine the relative size of this group of needs (served and satisfied, served and not satisfied, unserved) in the population. Appropriate estimation techniques for all these variables will be considered in Chapter 6.

Is $I(C,C^\star)$ an ordinal utility function? To answer this question, we need to look at the values it assigns to different service configurations and determine if, indeed, it ranks different services in a way that corresponds to knowledgeable intuitions. We have developed an informativeness measure whose value increases with:

- the number of informative records provided to a user,
- the informativeness values of the provided records,
- the number of information needs satisfied,

and decreases with:

- the number of noninformative records provided,
- the extent of the discrepancies of the provided order from the optimal retrieval order for the user,
- the delay in providing service.

These attributes are all reasonable ones for a measure of informativeness. However, the relative values this measure assigns to different services depend also on its particular mathematical form. The validity of this form and of the arguments presented in its support cannot be assessed by internal arguments. We need to have the panel of experts validate this measure by comparing its rankings of information services with the intuitive assessments of the experts of the rankings of a set of different information services. This validation would follow the same procedure as that described earlier for a validation of the measure of individual retrieval trail informativeness assessments, namely a comparison, via a rank correlation measure, of the two approaches.

5.4 Summary

In this chapter we have developed an axiomatic structure for measuring the informativeness of a user–record interaction in an information services environment. The measure is: context sensitive in that it depends on previous user–record interactions; ordinal level in that it is based on user preference judgments; time dependent in that delays discount is value; and logarithmic in form, to represent the declining density of information. We have then considered how this measure can be aggregated to determine:

1. the informativeness of a retrieval trail, a sequence of records presented to a user with a specified information need;
2. the informativeness of a record use trail, a sequence of uses of a record by members of the user community;
3. the total and average informativeness provided by an information service to a user community over a specified time period.

The last two chapters have been theoretical and mathematical, and the reader may well wonder whether their developments have any relevance to practical evaluation. In Chapter 6 we will turn from theory to practice and show how the mathematics can be put to use, how the proposed measures can be used to answer most of the questions raised by users, funders, administrators, and others about the value of information services and their four component functions: collection, description, retrieval, and packaging of records. We will develop procedures for estimating informativeness and comparing the informativeness of different functional approaches. Thus, we turn from the problems of theory development to the equally important ones of sampling design, data collection, and statistical analysis.

5.5 Review Problems

5.5.1 Suppose that the ideal chain for a user is

$$C^\star(u) = \langle \{t_7, t_8, t_9\}, \{t_4\}, \{t_1, t_5\}, \{t_{10}\} \rangle,$$

that the actual retrieval trail is

$$\mathbf{t} = \langle t_1, t_2, t_3, t_4, t_5, t_6, t_7, t_8, t_9, t_{10} \rangle,$$

and that the optimal retrieval chain is

$$C^{\star\star}(u) = \langle \{t_4\}, \{t_7, t_8\}, \{t_1, t_5\}, \{t_2, t_3, t_6\} \rangle.$$

Suppose that the information service wishes to discount delays so that if the retrieval trail were

$$\mathbf{t} \langle t_5, t_1, t_8, t_7, t_4 \rangle ,$$

that is, if there were no noninformative items and the order was opposite to optimal, the delay discount would be .95. As well, suppose that there is no upper limit to the proportion of noninformative items that will be tolerated, but that if that proportion is .99, the informativeness will be discounted by one-half.

Determine the initial informativeness, the delay extent, the delay discount function, and the final informativeness value for this retrieval trail.

5.5.2 What would be the effect, in Problem 5.5.1, of retrieving another 100 records of which all were noninformative except the last, which was t_9?

5.5.3 Assuming an informative item represents a relevant item, calculate the recall and precision for the retrievals described in Problems 5.5.1 and 5.5.2. Compare these values with the initial and final informativeness values.

5.5.4 Given the following set of number of accesses and average contact time in minutes per access for a database of online abstracts of material published in some field in the year 1980, determine the functions for the expected value and the variance of the future contact time for the 1980 abstracts in the following years. Use these functions to determine a 95% confidence interval for the expected total future contact time for the 1980 abstracts after 1992.

		Contact Time Per Abstract	
Year	*Number of Accesses*	*Mean*	*SD*
1981	249	15.2	5.1
1982	181	15.0	5.1
1983	152	13.9	4.8
1984	125	14.3	4.3
1985	110	12.9	4.5
1986	89	12.5	4.4
1987	65	12.8	3.1
1988	52	11.3	3.2
1989	46	10.1	3.0
1990	39	8.3	2.5
1991	33	7.9	2.5
1992	31	6.2	2.1

5.5.5 A legal information retrieval service obtains feedback from the ten users of its databases at a large law firm over a five-day period. The initial informativeness, retrieval delay, and service delay for each user's retrieval is as follows:

		Extent of Delays	
User Number	*Initial Informativeness*	*Retrieval*	*Service (in days)*
1	.78	.25	0
2	.54	.43	1
3	.66	.22	0
4	.80	0	2
5	.93	.67	1
6	.24	.39	0
7	.68	.27	0
8	.21	.38	3
9	.48	.13	0
10	.93	.46	1

Find the total informativeness of the service to the law firm over this period assuming combined retrieval and service delays of greater than .9 are unacceptable, that is, reduce the amount of information to zero, but are not otherwise discounted.

5.5.6 Do you agree that some service delays can reduce the informativeness of a retrieval to zero? Describe some circumstances under which such a discounting might be appropriate.

6

Evaluation of Information Services

In Chapter 1 we defined information services as agencies that supply the information we require in order to function in our society, but which we cannot obtain from our immediate environment. These services exist in many forms, from libraries to online database vendors to information management units within organizations. They provide information within a widely or narrowly defined area of concern and may aim to serve a general or a specialized community. We suggested that evaluation of the effectiveness of its services is essential for an information agency competing, typically, for limited funds available to the community it is designed to serve.

What, exactly, do we mean by evaluation? Powell (1992, following Knightly, 1979) suggests that there are four approaches to information service evaluation: (1) effort evaluation (i.e., measurement of inputs); (2) process evaluation (i.e., measurement of processing efficiency); (3) effectiveness evaluation (i.e., measurement of outputs); and (4) impact evaluation (i.e., measurement of benefits).

Informativeness measurement is a kind of effectiveness evaluation. It looks at how much information is output to the user community in total and on the average. In this book, we do not go beyond effectiveness evaluation to impact evaluation, though this question, of the benefit or value of the information obtained from an information service, is, as Powell says, a very important one. The assessment of information value is a difficult problem and would need another book of this length to address. The reasons for this difficulty were presented in Chapter 1: the impact of information may occur over a long period of time, as reflected in a variable such as productivity, and may go beyond the initial user to other members of the community.

Many factors affect the effectiveness of an information service to its community of users: what records are in the database or collection; how knowledge is represented in the database or catalog; how records are retrieved; and how information from a retrieval is packaged for the user. However, in the final analysis, what matters is how well the information needs of the user community have been satisfied. Other factors are simply a means to this end. It is the thesis of this book that the best measure of this satisfaction level is the informativeness measure proposed in Chapter 5.

In practical terms, how can we actually use the informativeness measure in an evaluation? Measures such as total and average informativeness, which require user and expert input, usually cannot be determined for all of the information needs in the community, for reasons of limited resources and availability of users and experts. Thus, informativeness values must be estimated from samples and so we will look at the problems of sampling, data collection, and data analysis design. Thus, in this chapter, the measure we have proposed will be used to determine the effectiveness of the four functions of an information service using various techniques of statistical inference. It will be compared with other measures that have been suggested for the evaluation of these tasks. Many of these other measures will be seen to lack two key strengths of the informativeness measure, namely:

1. It evaluates an information service on the basis of how well it satisfies the needs of its user community, rather than on how many records or users it processes.
2. It provides an integrated approach to the measurement of the effectiveness of the four individual functions (collection, description, retrieval, and packaging) and the overall effectiveness of the service.

Effectiveness evaluation using the informativeness measure has a number of dimensions. Sometimes we simply want to estimate, in a reliable and valid manner, the total or average informativeness of a service over some period of time. More often, though, we want to compare one service approach with another or look at trends in a service over several time periods or compare service provided to different user groups. Sometimes we want to carry out an experiment, where we manipulate one or more of the functions of a service, trying out different approaches to collection, description, retrieval, or packaging in order to determine which one provides the optimal informativeness for the community.

We will first look at how the total and average informativeness values for an information service, as presented in Chapter 5, can be estimated from a sample of user needs. We will then present an inferential statistical framework for using the informativeness measure to make comparisons involving any of the four information service functions. Each of these four functions will be examined from the following points of view:

1. What questions are typically asked about the value of this function in an information service?
2. What measures have been suggested by earlier investigators for the evaluation of this function?

3. How can the proposed informativeness measure be used to answer evaluation questions about this function?

4. What is the relationship of the proposed informativeness measure to these earlier measures?

6.1 Determination of Overall Informativeness

To determine the overall total informativeness $\mathrm{I}(\mathbf{C},\mathbf{C}^\star)$ of an information service and the average informativeness

$$\mu = \mathrm{I}(\mathbf{C},\mathbf{C}^\star)/n,$$

where n is the total number of user needs in an information service community over some period of time, we need to collect the following information about the user needs actually brought to the service:

1. the set of records that are accessible through the service and that are informative for the user with respect to his or her need and their relative informativeness (the ideal chain);
2. the sequence of records actually retrieved for the user (the retrieval trail);
3. the user's preferred perusal order of the retrieved records (the optimal retrieval chain); and
4. the delay in providing service.

In order to estimate the average informativeness we need, as well, to determine the number of user needs that were not served in the community in the period of interest, since total informativeness, though summed over served needs, is averaged over both served and unserved needs.

To collect this information we must, first of all, define what we mean by a single or unit user need. One user may have a need for the address of a company, the next user for a manual for fixing her automobile, the next user for a summary of all court cases involving software copyright infringements, the next user for any recent studies of complex adaptive systems. Are all of these single (unit) information needs? Clearly, they will require differing amounts of user time and system resources to satisfy.

The view we shall take is that of Dervin (1980), Belkin (1980), and others, called the sense-making approach. Users are seen as involved in a decision-making or problem-solving or curiosity-fed process. They are stopped in this process by a gap or anomaly and seek information in order to overcome it. In the time line method proposed by Dervin, an investigator tries to identify and categorize critical events in this process in the lives of individuals in the community served by the service. Each such critical event is considered to be a user need. Thus, each gap or anomaly that brings a user to the service represents an information need. Needs of individuals that are not brought to the service from the community but that could be handled by the service are more difficult to determine. However, these too can be assessed, on a sample basis, primarily via interview and journal-keeping techniques.

We have earlier (Tague-Sutcliffe, 1992a) described needs, at least for some user communities, as falling into four categories, which are distinguished by the precision with which the question is defined (the specificity), the expected length of the answer sequence (the size), and the extent to which the answer will vary from person to person (the substitutability). These three properties might be considered as three dimensions of user needs as pictured in Figure 6.1. The four categories of questions, which are distinguished by their positions on the three dimensions, are as follows:

• **Facts** A precise fact is requested, usually in answer to a question beginning with "who," "what," "when," "which," "where," "how much," or "how many." In libraries, these are called quick reference questions. Expected answers will normally be a single record and will vary little from one user to another.

• **Methods** A method or way of doing something is requested (how-to-do-it questions). Such questions are usually moderately well defined. Expected answers will consist of a small number of records, possibly only one, giving sets of instructions. A moderate variation in the ideal chain can be expected

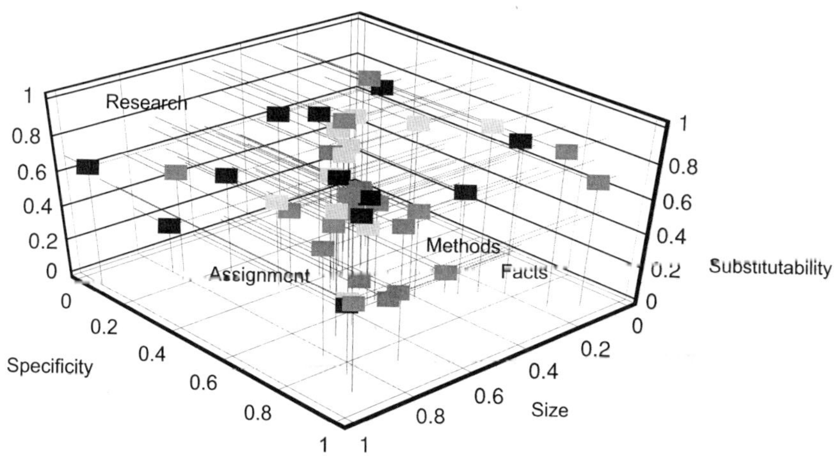

Figure 6.1
The three dimensions of user needs.

from one user to another, even though seemingly they have the same questions, since the experience and prior knowledge they bring to the task will vary.

• **Assignments** The user, typically a student, is required to collect and synthesize what he or she knows about some more or less precisely defined topic. Answers will consist of texts about the assigned topic. More than one text will be the norm, but the expected answer need not include all texts on the assigned topic. Variation in the ideal chain can be expected from one user to another, as we saw in the example in Chapter 5.

• **Research** A literature search is to be carried out for a research project that may involve several investigators. The problem will be described in terms of the entities, variables, and relationships to be studied, and these may themselves vary depending on the investigator stating the problem. The answer is required to include all items in the database or collection that involve prior investigations of this problem, wholly or in part. However, some user-dependent variation can be expected in decisions about what records are informative with respect to the research and so should be included in the ideal chain.

A fifth category could be added:

• **Overview** Records in the database or collection are to be summarized, either through statistical manipulations, graphical techniques, or verbal summarization, to provide the user with an overview of some subject or situation. The length of the answer in this case will be shorter than the original ideal chain; in fact, it will be a new record. Some variation in user expectations for this new record can be expected.

All of these represent unit information needs for the individual user. We will now consider how to collect information about these unit information needs for purposes of estimating total informativeness and average informativeness per user need of the service over a designated period of time.

In Chapter 5, we identified three components of an evaluation sample:

1. a sample of the actual services for information needs that were brought to the service and satisfied, at least in part (serviced, satisfied needs);
2. a sample of information needs that were brought to the service and lie within its goals, but were not satisfied (serviced, unsatisfied needs); and
3. a sample from the user community of information needs that, for whatever reason, were not brought to the service but lie within its goals (unserviced needs).

With a small and compact user community, such as the employees of a company information service, and a small database such as the current records of the company, it may be possible to collect the required information, that is, the ideal chain, the actual retrieval trail, and the ideal retrieval chain for all serviced needs and make a tally of unserviced needs for the entire period of time under study. However, usually sampling techniques will be needed because of the size of the user community and the difficulty of obtaining information about unserviced needs.

To determine the unserviced needs, a panel of knowledgeable people from the community are asked to suggest classes of potential users whose needs are not being serviced. For example, via such a panel, a public library may find low income groups or small businesses are not bringing relevant information problems to their reference service. A corporate information center may find the needs of clerical, as opposed to professional and managerial, personnel are not being met by the information management system. An online information service may find that potential users are not using the service because they do not have a local network connection.

To determine the average informativeness, using the measure developed in Chapter 5, we need to identify the total period of time over which the service will be evaluated and then divide this period into a number of equal-length service intervals. By a service interval we mean a time interval during which service would normally be provided, for example, an hour, a day, and so on. If a need is not served during that period, a service delay is assumed to occur. The length of the intervals will depend on the urgency of the information needs in the community. If most needs must be satisfied within a day (as, e.g., by an information service for financial analysts), then one-day intervals should be used. If most needs must be satisfied within a week, for example, by an information service for university students and faculty, then intervals of a week will be appropriate. The total length of the period should be such that a reasonable number of representative uses will be included and such that most service delays, except for uses occurring at the end of the period, can be calculated.

A random sample of members of the user community (past users and nonusers) are then asked to keep a journal identifying: the information needs that arose during the period; when they arose; what service, if any, was provided; and when it was completed. The sample should contain representatives of all groups in the community identified by the expert panel. There are a number of ways this sample can be taken.

When diverse groups must be represented, a stratified sample may be appropriate. In this case, groups are sampled in proportion to their size in the community, though it may be necessary to overrepresent very small groups so that they can be included. If a list of all members of the user community, for example, all subscribers to an online vendor service, or all students, faculty, and staff on a university campus, is available, then a systematic random sample may be taken using this list. A systematic sample means that every *n*th name on the list is selected after a random start. The periodicity, *n,* is selected so that the number of names on the list divided by *n* approximates the desired sample size.

For large user communities where a listing of all members may not be available, such as those for a public library, it may be useful to use an area sample, in which defined areas such as city blocks or census enumeration areas are sampled in the first stage, and a simple random or systematic sample of householders is taken in the second stage.

For some service environments, a time slice sample may be useful. One or more random time periods are sampled and data collected about all user needs in these periods or a random sample of the needs, if the number is large. This approach is valid if it can be assumed that the service does not change much from one time period to another. For example, a commercial online medical information service with a known customer base might be evaluated in this fashion using a one-month time slice, but not a university undergraduate library service, where use of the service tends to be seasonal.

The sample size should be large enough that large-sample statistical techniques can be used, that is, those based on the central limit theorem. The informal limit is a sample size of at least thirty. More specific sample sizes can be determined to obtain estimates with stated error limits, as we shall describe later in this section. Once the sample of users and potential users have been selected, it will be necessary to contact them and convince them to participate in the study, unless participation is some kind of work or academic assignment. Although appeals to general welfare of the community can be made, it is often useful to offer a remuneration or other inducement to participation. At the least, participants should be reimbursed in some way for time spent on the evaluation.

The recommended method for obtaining the required information about needs and services is via journals kept by participants for the specified time interval of the evaluation study. The reliability of diary or journal keeping can be improved by interviews with the participants at the end of the journal-keeping interval, to be sure they have recalled all information needs. If the journal keeping method is not feasible, a cross-sectional interview approach may also be used to estimate the number of needs that arose during the evaluation period. At one or more points in time during the period, a sample of members of the community are contacted, face-to-face or by telephone, and asked to describe an information need that arose during a short preceding time interval (e.g., day, two hours) and whether or not they used the service for this need. The preceding time interval must be short, to ensure that the subject's recollections are reasonably accurate.

The journal method can be used to obtain information about whether the information need was brought to the service and, if so, the results of the service. The interview approach, however, since it is *post facto,* may not provide reliable information on the results of the service because of the delay in seeking this information.

The information that must be obtained about each serviced need and that should be collected in "real time" is:

1. the set of informative items in the collection for the user and the informativeness ranking of each (i.e., the informative chain);
2. the optimal retrieval rank for those informative items actually retrieved (i.e., the optimal retrieval chain);
3. the delay in providing the retrieved items; and
4. the items retrieved by the service for the user (the retrieval trail).

The set of informative items in the collection may not be known in total. If the user is satisfied with the retrieval trail, that is, feels that her or his need has been met, then the ideal chain is simply the set of informative items in the retrieval chain ordered by the user as to informativeness. If the user is not satisfied, or is unsure, then there may be items that would satisfy her or him in the nonretrieved part of the database or collection. In this case, the set of informative items may be approximated by doing several broad searches on the topic, from different points of view such as keywords, class codes, and citations, or by having several intermediaries develop independent search strategies. The user then assesses the informativeness of all items in these broader searches. However, this and similar methods of estimation will usually *underestimate* the number of items in the ideal chain for the high recall literature search type of need described earlier. If the user is not satisfied despite all efforts to find informative items, then a single "not found" informative item can be postulated in the first edge of the ideal chain.

In an interactive electronic full-text environment, the user should be able to "mark" informative items as she or he follows a retrieval trail. In a more paper-oriented environment, the user will enter this information on a form listing the retrieval trail items. In both cases, the user should be provided with explicit instructions about entering this and other evaluative information. An example of instructions that could be distributed in either electronic or printed form is given in Table 6.1.

Table 6.1
Information Service Informativeness Estimation Data Collection Form

Instructions to the User:

We will be presenting you with a sequence of records that our service believes may be useful in filling your need for information. Please examine these records in order and, for each record, indicate whether it was informative, that is, whether it helped to satisfy your need. If, at any point in the sequence, you do not wish to examine further records, please mark this point with an "END" notation. If you do terminate before the end of the sequence, please indicate the reason for the termination in the space provided.

You will then be presented with the set of records that you have chosen as informative.

Table 6.1 *(Continued)*

Please indicate whether any are more informative than others, by assigning informativeness rank 1 to the most informative records, informativeness rank 2 to the next most informative records, and so on (ties in ranking are permitted).

Also, for the informative records, please indicate the order in which you would prefer to read them, by assigning rank 1 to the records you would prefer to read first, rank 2 to the records you would prefer to read next, and so on (ties in ranking are permitted). This reading order may be the same as or different from the informativeness order.

Record ID	Informative (Y/N)	Informativeness order (1,2, . . .)	Preferred reading order (1,2, . . .)
Heaps78			
Abramson65			
Klein89			
Fraenkel76			
Choueka85			
Herdan66			
Votter87			
Bookstein90			
Knuth85			
Nelson91			
Moffatt92			
Huffman52			

Reason for terminating examination of records:

_____ I reached the end of the list

_____ I obtained the information I needed

_____ I did not feel it worth my time to continue

Do you know of records in the database that were not retrieved and that would have been informative for you? (Y/N)

If yes, identify the records:

____

____

____

Given a sample of serviced and unserviced needs, the procedure for estimating the average informativeness of the service for the user community is then as follows:

1. From the forms for the sample of n' users, determine the initial informativeness $I_0(s_{ij})$, the delay extent $Z(s_{ij})$, and the discounted informativeness $I(s_{ij})$ of the service s_{ij} provided to the jth user in the ith time interval, using the formulas developed in Chapter 5. These are as follows:

For $I_0(s_{ij})$:

$$I_0[s_{ij}] = \sum_{k=1}^{m_{ij}} I(t_{ijk}, u_{ij})$$

where

$$I(t_{ijk}, u_{ij}) = \frac{1}{m_{ij}{}^{\star}[e^{\star}(t_{ijk})]} \log_2 \left[\frac{\sum_{h=1}^{e^{\star}(t_{ijk})} m_{ij}{}^{\star}(h) + m_{ij}}{\sum_{h=1}^{e^{\star}(t_{ijk})} m_{ij}{}^{\star}(h) + m_{ij}} \right]$$

if record t_{ijk} is informative, and $I(t_{ijk}, u_{ij}) = 0$ if t_{ijk} is noninformative. In these equations, m_{ij} is the number of records retrieved in service s_{ij}, $e^{\star}(t_{ijk})$ is the number of the edge in the ideal chain containing t_{ijk}, and $m_{ij}{}^{\star}(h)$ is the number of records in the hth edge of the ideal chain for service s_{ij}.

For $Z(s_{ij})$:

The delay extent is an average of the retrieval delay extent $X(s_{ij})$ and the service delay extent $Y(s_{ij})$, that is,

$$Z(s_{ij}) = \frac{X(s_{ij}) + Y(s_{ij})}{2}.$$

The retrieval delay extent $X(s_{ij})$ is given by the weighted sum of the retrieval disorder extent $X_1(s_{ij})$ and the noninformative record extent $X_2(s_{ij})$:

$$X(s_{ij}) = wX_1(s_{ij}) + (1 - w)X_2(s_{ij}),$$

where the weight $0 \leq w \leq 1$,

$$X_1(s_{ij}) = (1 - R_{ij})/2,$$

where R_{ij} is the rank correlation coefficient between the actual and optimal retrieval ranks, namely

$$R_{ij} = \frac{\sum_{k=1}^{m_{ij}} kr^{\star\star}(t_{ijk}) - \frac{m_{ij}(m_{ij} + 1)^2}{4}}{\sqrt{\frac{m_{ij}(m_{ij}^2 - 1)}{12}[\sum_{i=1}^{m_{ij}} r^{\star\star}(t_{ijk})^2 - \frac{m_{ij}(m_{ij} + 1)^2}{4}]}},$$

and X_2 is the proportion of the retrieved records that are noninformative, that is,

$$X_2(s_{ij}) = \frac{m^\star_{ij}(q')}{m_{ij}}.$$

In these equations, m_{ij} is the total number of retrieved records in the retrieval trail; $m_{ij}(q')$ is the number of noninformative records retrieved. The expression $r^{\star\star}(t_{ijk})$ represents the rank of t_{ijk} in the optimal retrieval chain. If t_{ijk} is in the edge number $e^{\star\star}(t_{ijk})$ of the optimal chain, then its rank is the average rank for all records in this edge, namely

$$r^{\star\star}(t_{ijk}) = \sum_{h=1}^{e^{\star\star}(t_{ijk})-1} m_{ij}{}^{\star\star}(h) + \frac{m_{ij}{}^{\star\star}[e^{\star\star}(t_i)]}{2},$$

where $m_{ij}{}^{\star\star}(h)$ is the number of records in the hth edge of the optimal retrieval trail.

The service delay extent is given by

$$Y(s_{ij}) = [v(s_{ij}) - i]/v,$$

where $v(s_{ij})$ is the time interval in which the sevice s_{ij} originating in interval i was actually provided, and v is the total number of intervals in the time period under consideration.

For $I(s_{ij})$:

$$I(s_{ij}) = I_0(s_{ij})D(s_{ij}),$$

where the discount function $D(s_{ij})$ may have either a linear or exponential form:

$$D(s_{ij}) = 1 - bZ(s_{ij}),\ 0 \le Z(s_{ij}) \le 1/b \le 1;\ 0 \text{ otherwise};$$

or

$$D(s_{ij}) = b^{-Z(sij)},\ 0 \le Z(s_{ij}) \le 1,\ b > 1.$$

2. From a community journal sample, estimate the population proportion π of needs that are brought to the service, as the ratio p of the number of needs brought to the service in the sample to the total needs in the sample.

If different samples are used to determine $I_0(s_{ij})$ and $Z(s_{ij})$ (in Step 1) and π (in Step 2), then the number n'' of unserved needs in the population corresponding to the n' served needs is

$$n'' = n'\,(1 - p)/p,$$

and so a sample of n' served needs would represent a sample of $n = n' + n''$ total needs.

3. A 100% α confidence interval for π is given by

$$p \pm Z_{\alpha/2}\sqrt{\frac{p(1 - p)}{n}} = [p_1, p_u],$$

where $z_{\alpha/2}$ is the z value (from a table of the standard normal distribution) corresponding to a probability of $\alpha/2$ of being exceeded.

Then a 100% α confidence interval for the total number of needs in the population is:

$$[n'/p_u, n'/p_1] = [n_1, n_u].$$

4. If n is known, rather than estimated, as in Step 2, a 100% α confidence interval for the average service informativeness value μ is given by

$$\frac{\sum_{i=1}^{v}\sum_{j=1}^{n'(i)} I(s_{ij})}{n} \pm_{\alpha/2} \sqrt{\frac{\sigma^2}{n}} = [I_1, I_u], \tag{6.1}$$

where $n'(i)$ is the number of needs served in the ith interval and σ^2 represents the variance of the $I(s_{ij})$ values and can be estimated by

$$\sigma^2 = \frac{\sum_{i=1}^{v}\sum_{j=1}^{n'(i)} I^2(s_{ij}) - [\sum_{i=1}^{v}\sum_{j=1}^{n'(i)} I(s_{ij})]^2/n}{n - 1}.$$

5. If n is estimated by a 100% α confidence interval $[n_1, n_u]$, then the interval $[I_1, I_u]$, where

$$I_1 = \frac{\sum_{i=1}^{v}\sum_{j=1}^{n'(i)} I(s_{ij})}{n_u} - z_{\alpha/2}\sqrt{\frac{\sigma^2}{n_u}},$$
$$I_u = \frac{\sum_{i=1}^{v}\sum_{j=1}^{n'(i)} I(s_{ij})}{n_1} + z_{\alpha/2}\sqrt{\frac{\sigma^2}{n_1}}, \tag{6.2}$$

is a $(1 - \alpha)^2 100\%$ confidence interval for the average informativeness μ. So, for example, to obtain a 95% confidence interval for μ, one would set $(1 - \alpha)^2 = .95$, or $\alpha = .0253$, approximately.

6. In Equations (6.1) and (6.2), the standard normal deviate $Z_{\alpha/2}$ statistic should be replaced by the $t_{\alpha/2}(n - 1)$ statistic, that is, the value that is exceeded by a probability of $\alpha/2$ in the Student t distribution with $n - 1$ degrees of freedom.

7. The sample size n needed to estimate the average informativeness μ to within a specified error ($\pm$ e) can be determined if an estimate of σ^2 is available from an earlier sample. If the size of the population of information needs is large, then

$$n = \frac{z_{\alpha/2}^2 \sigma^2}{e^2}.$$

If the population size m is relatively small, then

$$n = \frac{z_{\alpha/2}^2\sigma^2}{e^2 + z_{\alpha/2}^2\sigma^2/m}.$$

6.2 Testing for Differences in Informativeness

In testing for differences in informativeness among different approaches to collection, description, retrieval, and packaging, we will be comparing the average informativeness, in the time period [1,v], over the various approaches. To use parametric techniques from statistical inference to determine differences from sample data, we must develop an appropriate linear model for the variation of the individual informativeness values about the average.

Let I_j represent the informativeness of this service provided for the $_j$th individual user need in the sample. This value can be written as:

$$I_j = \mu + e_j,$$

where μ is the average informativeness of the service and e_j is the variation about this average for the jth user need in the sample. If we are interested in comparing different service approaches, whether distinguished by collection or description or retrieval or packaging, we may use a linear model:

$$I_{hj} = \mu + \eta_h + e_{hj},$$

where η_h represents the effect of the hth service approach and e_{hj} is the deviation of the individual value from the mean for this approach. Different service approaches can then be characterized by different databases or descriptions or retrieval strategies or packaging methods. If random samples are taken of user needs served under each approach, by means of an appropriate statistical analysis, the effect of the different approaches, the η_h, can be compared. This model is called a single-factor design.

The same linear model can be used for other single-factor comparisons. For example, if we are interested in comparing the service in different time periods (perhaps to see if service is improving), we write

$$I_{ij} = \mu + \eta_i + e_{ij},$$

where η_i represents the effect of the ith time period and e_{ij} is the deviation of the individual value from the mean for this time period. Or is we want to compare informativeness of the service for different user groups, η_i represents the effect of the ith group on the mean informativeness.

If we wish to compare service informativeness along two dimensions, for example, using different appraoches *and* in different time periods, we write

$$I_{hij} = \mu + \eta_h + \tau_i + (\eta\tau)_{hi} + e_{hij}, \qquad (6.3)$$

where η_h represents the effect of the hth approach, τ_i represents the effect of the ith time period, $(\eta\tau)_{hi}$ represents the effect of the interaction of the hth approach in the ith time period, and e_{hij} is the deviation of the individual value from the mean for the designated approach and time period. This model is called a two-factor design.

We may also wish to compare the effect of different service approaches and/or different time periods on secondary measures of informativeness. For example, we may be interested in one of the three components of informativeness, that is, initial informativeness I_0 of the records, retrieval delay extent X, and delivery delay extent Y. In experimental situations relating to different approaches to description or retrieval, the concept of delivery delay extent may not be applicable because there is no service delay and we will compare approaches on the basis of initial informativeness scores discounted by retrieval delay only. In these cases, the dependent variable in Equation (4.1) represents the specific secondary measure of interest, and the parameters the overall means and the effects of approaches and time periods on the dependent variable value.

To test for differences in informativeness among different approaches and/or over different time periods or among different groups, random samples of informativeness (or other) scores are taken for users served at the different levels of the factors. If different service approaches are being compared, a random sample is taken of users served under each approach. If changes over time are being examined, a random sample is taken of users served in each time period. If user groups are being compared, a random sample is taken of users in each group. If levels of two factors are being compared, a random sample is taken of users served under each combination of the two factors.

Sometimes, in comparing approaches, we wish to examine the informativeness of each using the same set of user needs. In this case, a repeated measures design is appropriate and the model becomes

$$I_{hj} = \mu + \eta_h + \nu_j + e_{hj},$$

where ν_j is the effect of the jth user.

Other, more complicated experimental designs are available for use, for example, when combinations of approach, time period, and user group are examined or measures are repeated for some effects and not others (e.g., repeated measure samples for approaches, independent samples for time periods). The reader is referred to Winer (1971) for an extended treatment.

Once the samples of informativeness (or other) scores have been collected, the usual technique for statistical analysis to determine if difference exist, assuming the linear models just presented, is the analysis of variance, as described, for example, in Berenson *et al.* (1983) or Winer (1971). Although the intial user–record informativeness ratings are at an ordinal level, the total informativeness score for a serviced used need is a discounted sum of these ordinal values and so may be approximated by a continuum when the numbers of records involved is reasonably large. In this case, the analysis of variance may be appropriate, if the scores satisfy its other assumptions: approximate normality and equality of the variances of the residuals (the e_{hj}, e_{hi}, and e_{hij}) over different factor levels. If the analysis of variance is not appropriate, its rank-based analogs should be used. A good introduction to these rank tests will be found in Meddis (1984). If experience shows that, with a particular application, the rank-based analog and the analysis of variance give the same results, then the latter analysis, which is more generally available on statistical software pachages, may be used. The analysis of variance approach as presented by Berenson is summarized in Appendix 6.1. The rank-based approach as presented by Meddis is summarized in Appendix 6.2. A good overall introduction to statistical testing in a retrieval environment will be found in Hull (1993).

Examples of the applicationof the various models just presented and of the use of both the ANOVA and rank-based approach to data analysis will be found in the remaining sections of this chapter.

6.2.1 Evaluation of Collections or Databases

Evaluation of collections or databases has two aspects, the evaluation of the informativeness of a single record in the collection over some period of time and the evaluation of the collection as a whole. We have addressed the former problem in Chapter 5, Section 5.2, on use trails, where we suggested that user contact time was a variable dependent on the same parameters as informativeness and that it could be used to compare the informativeness of two record over time or to determine changes in the informativeness of a record to a user community over a period of time. As well, we showed how the future informativeness of single records could be predicted under an assumption of exponential record obsolescence.

In this section, we look at the second problem, evaluation of the collection as a whole. This kind of evaluation typically takes one of the following forms:

1. comparison of two or more different collections for the same or similar sets of user needs;

2. comparison of a single collection for different sets of user needs, for example, user needs at different time intervals or in different user groups;
3. comparison of two or more different collections at two or more time periods for the same or similar sets of user needs.

Let us look at some examples of this kind of evaluation.

A professional special library such as a law, medical, or engineering library, has a well-defined user community. It exists to provide the materials (databases, journals, government and legal publications, monographs, reports, etc.) needed by a group of professionals and paraprofessionals in their current work. The library may hold some material in-house and may access other material via external databases or other sources. An evaluation might be undertaken to determine the informativeness of the present collection compared to others in which some in-house materials were discontinued, to be accessed externally, and some external materials were acquired in-house.

Community information centers develop and access databases to serve the needs of a region for information about public and private human services available in that region. To evaluate such a database we need to assess the extent to which it contains records for all such services that are needed by the user community. An evaluation could compare the informativeness of the present database with that of a test database, which was augmented with records in an area not previously covered, to determine if this addition would better meet the needs of the community.

National libraries and large research libraries usually collect material on the basis of an official policy to include all items of a certain type. For example, a national library will seek to include all items published in and about a country. A research library will include all items in designated subject areas. This policy is seen as responding to both present and future user information needs. An evaluation of the collection might look at the informativeness of specific types of material or subject categories relative to present user needs and future user needs as predicted by a panel of experts.

One function of public libraries is to provide popular reading materials to their community. A public library system typically renews the collection in its branches on a periodic basis. A library system might wish to determine how frequently this change should be made by comparing the informativeness of the service in several similar branches, when a different collection renewal period (e.g., three, six, twelve months) was used in each branch.

A corporate information management unit provides access to records of past activities of the company. The retention policy determines the form of material retained (correspondence, internal reports, financial statements, etc.) and the length of time records are retained. The user community consists of company employees and managers and some external sources, for example, customers or tax authorities. An evaluation of the retention policy might look at the informativeness of different classes of material, where classification could be by form or age.

Table 6.2 presents some measures that have been proposed in the past for collection evaluation purposes. Most of these are based on counting the number of uses of the records in the collection, rather than determining their informativeness. A few look at delay times of various sorts. Van House *et al.* (1987) and Lancaster (1988) provide good surveys of most of these measures.

All of these measures are useful ones for evaluating a database or collection. Some of them can be collected in a relatively automated fashion, without the need for additional information from the user. However, except for contact time, they do not measure the informativeness of the collection, only its frequency of use, a variable which, it can be argued, relates more to anticipated than actual informativeness. Also, the unit of analysis is a record, rather than a user need. Informativeness, as we have seen, requires greater input from the users if it is to be assessed. However, it has the advantage of being a more discriminating measure than frequency of use.

The use of the informativeness measure to compare two or more collections or a single collection over time, or both, will now be illustrated by means of several examples, the first of which will be analyzed in detail.

Table 6.2
Measures of Effectiveness of a Collection or Database

Measure	Definition
Annual loans or accesses	Total number of uses over a year
Loans or accesses per capita	Number of uses per member of the community
Ratio of loans or accesses to acquisitions	Number of uses per record acquired
Turnover rate	Number of uses per record in collection or database
Fill rates: author, title, subject	Number of uses per user request of a specified type
Document delivery time	Lengths of time between request for and use of records (averaged or otherwise summarized)
Shelf time	Lengths of time between uses of records (averaged or otherwise summarized)
Contact time	Lengths of time records are used (averaged or otherwise summarized)

A record manager is interested in determining whether the company correspondence should be retained for a period of two years, five years, or eight years. At the present time, the archival correspondence textbase contains records for the past eight years. With a time slice sample of 30 requests for previous correspondence, users are asked to indicate the informativeness and preferred ordering of records from the archival textbase, using a form similar to that presented in Table 6.1. These responses are then analyzed to determine the initial informativeness of each request under three conditions:

Textbase 1: only records from the past two years are supplied;
Textbase 2: only records from the past three years are supplied;
Textbase 3: all records from the past eight years are supplied.

The appropriate design in this case is a single-factor, repeated-measures one, since the informativeness of three different textbases for the same set of requests is analyzed. The analysis is presented in Table 6.3. The result of the analysis is that average informativeness is greater for Textbase 3 than for the other two, a result that would indicate that records should be retained for the longer period.

In some situations, it may not be possible to ask users to supply informativeness and preferred order information, as required in the previous example. For example, a public library may wish to compare the value of changing the popular fiction collection in its branch libraries every three months as opposed to every year; or an online search vendor may wish to determine the informativeness of adding a new database to those available to its customers. However, they may not have the staff resources to implement the kind of data collection implied by the approach we have described, or they may simply not wish to inconvenience their users in this fashion. In these cases, the title fill rate and contact time could be used, respectively, as substitutes for informativeness.

In the public library system example, the purpose of the evaluation is to compare the informativeness of two branch library collections: Library 1, collection updated every three months; Library 2, collection updated once a year. Information about the fill rate for a sample of title requests from each library is collected over a period of a year. Each title request filled has an initial informativeness of one and each title request not filled has an initial informativeness of zero. The service delay discount extent could be calculated as the proportion of the year users had to wait for a title, and used in an appropriate linear or exponential function to discount this initial informativeness.

The dependent variable: $I(s_{ij})$ of the *j*th request for a popular title using collection *i*, $i = 1,2$, is given by

$$I(s_{ij}) = I_0(s_{ij})D(s_{ij}),$$

Table 6.3
Comparison of Three Retention Schedules for a Correspondence Textbase

Hypotheses:

$$H_0: \eta_1 = \eta_2 = \eta_3$$
$$H_1: \eta_1 < \eta_2 < \eta_3$$

where η_1, η_2, and η_3 are, respectively, the contributions of the most recent two, three, and eight years of records to the mean informativeness score.

Data:

	Informative scores		
	Textbase number		
User	*1*	*2*	*3*
1	0.344	0.436	0.724
2	0.214	0.148	0.219
3	0.671	0.867	0.931
4	0.552	0.361	0.324
5	0.834	0.831	0.963
6	0.671	0.799	0.544
7	0.353	0.502	0.735
8	0.442	0.729	0.908
9	0.484	0.730	0.807
10	0.299	0.467	0.342
11	0.171	0.136	0.307
12	0.240	0.220	0.411
13	0.739	0.195	0.140
14	0.723	0.719	0.644
15	0.409	0.268	0.483
16	0.637	0.619	0.634
17	0.100	0.259	0.329
18	0.918	0.821	0.898
19	0.327	0.631	0.883
20	0.504	0.525	0.714
21	0.136	0.090	0.266
22	0.962	0.854	0.944
23	0.960	0.902	0.927
24	0.945	0.979	0.993
25	0.886	0.925	0.898
26	0.334	0.254	0.543
27	0.153	0.432	0.621
28	0.126	0.330	0.466
29	0.516	0.691	0.514
30	0.669	0.553	0.781
Mean	0.511	0.542	0.630
Variance	0.078	0.069	0.061

Since sample sizes are large and since the variances do not differ a great deal for the three samples, the analysis of variance may be used to test for differences in means.

(continues)

Table 6.3 *(Continued)*

ANOVA table

Source of variation	*df*	*Sum of Squares*	*Mean Squares*
Among levels	2	0.229	0.114
Among cases	29	5.284	0.182
Within cells	58	1.009	0.017
Total	89	6.522	

$F = 6.571$
$F[2,29;.05] = 3.33$

Conclusion: Reject H_0.

Test for significant differences in means:

$M_2 - M_1$	0.032
$M_3 - M_2$	0.087 ⋆ significant difference
$M_3 - M_1$	0.119 ⋆⋆ highly significant difference

Critical values for significant differences:

$Q[.05] = 0.082$
$Q[.01] = 0.103$

Conclusion: The collections for two and three years do not differ in informativeness, but the collection for eight years is significantly more informative.

where

$$I_0(s_{ij}) = \begin{cases} 1 \text{ if the request was filled,} \\ 0 \text{ if the request was not filled,} \end{cases}$$

and

$$D(s_{ij}) = 2^{-T/4},$$

where Z is the delay extent and T is the time in weeks between the receipt and the filling of the request. In this example, since the "retrieval trail" consists of a single item, the requested title, there is no retrieval delay, only a service delay, namely $Z = T/52$. The exponential delay discount function assumes that the request loses one-half of its informativeness value if the request is not filled for four weeks. This might be the case, for example, if on average one-half of the holds on books were cancelled if the book was not provided within four weeks.

In the example of the new databases offering for an online vendor, there are two collections to be compared: Collection 1, current databases; Collection 2, current databases and new database. Data is automatically collected on the contact times of users with records in the databases over a time slice sample. This measure is used as the dependent variable in comparing the two collections, since, as we suggested in Chapter 5, Section 5.2, it can be assumed to be proportional to the average initial informativeness of the record, and the two collections are being compared on the basis of averages over uses and records. In the analysis, a repeated measures design is used, in which the average contact per user is compared for the two collections to determine if the addition of Collection 2 significantly increases this value.

6.2.2 Evaluation of Descriptions

Cataloging, classification, indexing, and other forms of description are used to improve access to records in collections or databases and, consequently, the informativeness of the service for its user community. These processes help the user find informative records by allowing her or him to quickly identify sets of records with common features (authors, titles, keywords, subject headings, classification codes, dates) separately and in combination, and to browse the collection in an arrangement in which like records are close together in location.

Information services want to know if one form of description is better than another or if adding a particular kind of description will improve the service. Database producers want to know if their records should be indexed simply by keywords extracted from the text or by assigned terms from a controlled vocabulary, or both. Developers of information retrieval software are interested in the effectiveness of various kinds of weighted indexing. Catalogers want to know what catalog elements are most useful to their users. A librarian charged with providing access to the internal reports of an engineering firm would like to determine the value of letting users search keywords in abstracts as well as titles in an online index to the collection. He would also like to know what arrangement of the reports would be most useful to the users of the collection.

Some specific questions that are frequently asked in connection with an evaluation of description are the following:

1. Which of two or more classification schemes provides the best access to the collection for a particular user community or type of user community, for example, medical, legal, or scientific professionals, or children?

2. Are the components of the catalog record in a particular library appropriate to its user community; should some be added and others removed?

3. What is the best level of indexing exhaustivity (average number of index terms per record) for an online service?

4. What is the best level of indexing specificity (average number of records assigned to each index term) for an online service?

5. Which provide better access to a database: controlled descriptors or text-based keywords?

6. Does the addition of syntactic indicators (role indicators, case indicators, grammatical category) to index terms improve retrieval for an online service?

7. Does the addition of term weights to index terms improve retrieval for an online service? What kind of weighting scheme is optimal?

8. Do the keywords in abstracts improve retrieval from an online service over that provided by the keywords in the titles?

9. Does browsing the shelf via a classification scheme provide a useful alternative to the catalog in locating useful material in a library?

These and similar questions have been investigated by many researchers in information retrieval and in knowledge representation. Our thesis, again, is that the informativeness measure proposed in Chapter 5 is the best basis for comparisons of the quality of different descriptions. When it is not possible to obtain informativeness scores, other measures such as record connect time, which is related to informativeness, may be used.

A major problem in assessing description approaches by means of informativeness or any other measure based on success in retrieval is isolating the effect of the description from that of the search strategy. In effect, we must somehow hold the search strategies constant in making comparisons of descriptions. One solution to this problem is to select, for each form of description and each user need in the evaluation study, the optimal strategy for that form of description. Unfortunately, finding the optimal retrieval strategy for a specified type of description is a problem not always easily solved, though it may be useful in particular cases.

For example, this is the approach taken by Shaw (1993) in his study of the effectiveness of controlled and uncontrolled weighted subject descriptions in a cystic fibrosis collection. He uses cluster-based retrieval for both representations. Clustering is carried out at a number of term exhaustivity and clustering threshold levels by varying the term weight and the document similarity measures. For each query, the cluster giving the best retrieval performance is selected. The retrieval effectiveness measure used in this study is a form of the Van Rijsbergen E measure, which, as we saw in Chapter 5, is related to a special case of the informativeness measure.

Another solution to the problem of isolating the effect of description is to use a repeated measures design, in which the user needs and the resulting search strategies are repeated using each type of description. This solution is viable only if the search strategies *can* be repeated. For example, we could use this approach in comparing two types of document term weighting, but not term weighting and precoordinated subject headings, since the former requires a document ranking type of search strategy and the latter a Boolean set theoretical type of search strategy.

Table 6.4 presents some of the measures that have been proposed in the past for the purpose of evaluating some kind of description.

All of these measures are useful ones for evaluating both the representation and the access approaches. All require some user input, though not input as extensive as that for the informativeness measure. User satisfaction, since it does not assign a value to individual records, only the service as a whole, may be related to informativeness but is not sufficiently analytic to be used as an estimate of informativeness. The user–system vocabulary similarity measure may correlate positively with informativeness of the service, since one might assume that if users and system "speak" the same vocabulary an improved search will result. Again, though, it cannot be used to determine informativeness of individual records.

For fill rates and location times, the unit of analysis is a record, rather than a user need. They may thus be considered a special case of the informativeness measure in which the need is for a single record, or record on some subject. The informativeness, then, will be one if the item is located, and zero

Table 6.4
Measures of Effectiveness of Various Types of Description

Measure	Definition
Fill rates: author title subject	Proportion of collection items that users identify by author(s), title, subject(s), etc., and that are located
Location time: author title subject	Length of time required to locate item identified by author(s), title, subject(s), etc. (averaged or otherwise summarized)
User satisfaction	Postsearch user ratings of classification schemes, indexes, catalogs, etc. (averaged or otherwise summarized)
Recall (R)	Proportion of relevant items that are retrieved for a query
Precision (P)	Proportion of retrieved items that are relevant for a query
User–system vocabulary similarity	Proportion of user vocabulary the system recognizes or Proportion of system vocabulary the user uses

otherwise. Location time, suitably normalized, can be considered another version of the retrieval delay discount. We have already, in Chapter 5, Section 5.1.1, shown that recall and precision are special cases of informativeness. As we shall see in the next section, they are also used to assess the effectiveness of search strategies.

The use of the informativeness measure to compare two or more approaches to description will now be illustrated by means of several examples, the first of which will be analyzed in detail.

A university medical library, which currently uses the Library of Congress Classification scheme (LCC), Class R, to classify its collection wishes to determine if the more detailed National Library of Medicine scheme (NLM) would better serve its users, both students and researchers. The purpose of a library shelf classification is to bring together similar items. The medical library in a nearby university uses the NLM scheme and agrees to cooperate in an experimental comparison of the two systems.

Samples of 21 users are recruited at each institution to participate in a comparison of the informativeness of the two classification schemes for browsing purposes, to locate material relevant to their needs. Each participant is asked, over the period of a term, to bring to a designated librarian in each institution a subject-based (rather than known-item) information need that might be satisfied by the library's collection. Following an interview about the need with a librarian, the user is directed to a particular class number and asked to browse for relevant material. The participants record the call number of each volume they browse during the search process (the retrieval trail) and determine which of these items is informative (in the ideal chain). Subsequent to this browsing, additional items in the ideal chain are determined using the subject headings and title keywords in the online catalogs to the libraries. The participants rank all informative items located, either through browsing or subsequent searching, in order to develop the ideal chain. However, only those located through browsing are considered to be in the retrieval trail for purposes of comparing the two classification schemes. The dependent variable is the initial informativeness of each retrieval trail discounted by an exponential retrieval delay discount function.

The details of the analysis are shown in Table 6.5. Because there is some doubt, from the sample data, that variances are equal across the three aproaches, a rank-based test is used. The result shows that there is no difference between the LCC and NLM classifications in median informativeness for this type of user environment (university medical library).

As a second example of the comparison of different description methods, suppose the producer of a database of statistical information such as that produced by the census or workforce sample surveys wished to investigate the value of adding a keyword index to the table of contents that was traditionally used to locate specific pieces of statistical information. An index is developed for one module of the database and made available to a random

Table 6.5
Comparison of Two Classification Schemes

Hypotheses:

$H_0: \eta_1 = \eta_2,$
$H_1: \eta_1 > \eta_2,$

where η_1 is the contribution of the NLM classification to average informativeness and μ_2 is the contribution of the LCC classification.

	NLM		LCC	
	Scores	*Ranks*	*Scores*	*Ranks*
	0.527	12	0.255	8
	0.941	36.5	0.977	40
	0.515	11	0.237	7
	0.838	26	0.015	1
	0.843	28.5	0.921	34
	0.937	35	0.982	42
	0.760	22	0.891	31
	0.911	32	0.789	24
	0.694	20	0.026	2
	0.843	28.5	0.978	41
	0.717	21	0.475	10
	0.692	19	0.948	38
	0.638	17	0.030	3
	0.839	27	0.204	6
	0.775	23	0.599	14
	0.619	15	0.035	4
	0.578	13	0.157	5
	0.644	18	0.941	36.5
	0.637	16	0.452	9
	0.827	25	0.920	33
	0.883	30	0.967	39
Mean	0.745		0.562	
Variance	0.017		0.145	
Rank sum		475.5		427.5
Number of scores		2121		

Because of the large difference between the two sample variances a rank test will be used.

Lambda values for H_1:

$\lambda_1 = 1, \lambda_2 = -1.$

Key Statistics:

$L = 475.5 - 427.5 = 48$

Correction for ties:

2 ties: $n^\star = 2$; $T = .999$
$E(L) = 0$; $V(L) = 6321.000$; $SD(L) = 79.505$
$Z_{test} = 0.591$; $Z[.025] = 1.960$

Conclusion: Accept H_0.

sample of users of that module. An equal-sized sample of users is not provided with the keyword index. All users are asked to signal online the point at which they find the statistical data they are seeking. If the data is not found, no signal is transmitted. In this case, the comparison of the two treatments (table of contents only and table of contents with index) is carried out by using an initial informativeness function of the form: $I_0(u) = 1$ if the data is located and $I_0(u) = 0$ otherwise. $I_0(u)$ is discounted by an appropriate delay discount function in which the delay extent represents the time to find the desired information.

6.2.3 Evaluation of Search Strategies

The evaluation of search strategies has been a major preoccupation of the information retrieval field since the early days of Perry and Kent's Searching Selector (see Perry and Kent, 1958) and Salton's SMART system (see Salton, 1971) in the late fifties and early sixties. To some extent the interest in strategies has been created by the computerization of information stores, since a greater variety of approaches is possible with electronic records than with printed records. However, even with print collections and card indexes or catalogs, it may make sense to talk about a search strategy (e.g., what to look at first, the keyword index or the citation index?).

The author (Tague-Sutcliffe, 1992c) has provided an earlier overview of the process of comparing different search strategies. A search strategy is based on a user need or, particularly if done by an intermediary, that is, an employee of the information service, on a query or verbalization of the need. A search statement is a single string, expressed in the language of the retrieval system, which triggers a search of the database (i.e., causes a search algorithm to scan the database and identify a sequence of records for the retrieval trail). A search process is a sequence of search statements, all relating to the same user need.

Search strategies differ along a number of dimensions:

- Search logic or technique used. Belkin and Croft (1987) distinguish techniques based on individual documents (Boolean, weighted vector, extended Boolean, natural language, relevance feedback) with those based on networks of documents (clustering, browsing, spreading activation).
- Delegated versus end-user searches. Searches may be carried out by the original user, by an information service intermediary, or by both together.
- Access mode for searchers. Searches may be implemented via commands, menus, dialogue boxes, hypertext links, or combinations of these.
- Length of search process. Searches vary in the number of statements or steps in the search process.

• Type of search process. Bates (1979) has defined a variety of search tactics, each of which may consist of one or more search statements.

Users, intermediaries, managers, and developers of retrieval software are all interested in the question of evaluating search strategies; as a result, there is a large literature on this subject. Particularly useful for learning about the many approaches to search strategies are the *Proceedings of the International ACM SIGIR Conference on Research and Development in Information Retrieval*. Some typical questions that arise concerning retrieval effectiveness are the following:

1. Which search logic, Boolean retrieval or vector-based ranking, is best?
2. In ranking-type logic, which query–record matching function, cosine, Jaccard, maximum entropy, is best?
3. In relevance feedback searching, what function should be used to weight the query terms?
4. Which access method (commands, menus, hypertext links, etc.) is best for particular types of needs (e.g., browsing vs. specific item request) or for particular types of users (novices, occasional users, experienced users)?
5. Does query negotiation between the user and a trained search intermediary improve a search?
6. Under what conditions of query and user types are delegated searches better than end-user searches?
7. In online searching, is it best to search the title first, the abstracts first, or to go directly to the full-text documents?

The measures that have been used in the past to evaluate search strategies are listed in Table 6.6.

The first two measures, search length and number of hits, are objective measures of system performance, but involve no judgment on the part of the user. We have already pointed out in Chapter 1 the close relationship between the concepts of relevance and informativeness, both of which are subjective measures. The relevance-based measures of recall and precision have been used in retrieval evaluation since the pioneering Cleverdon (1960) tests. The standardized forms of precision are found in the many tests based on the SMART system (Salton, 1971) and, most recently, in the large-scale TREK tests (Harman, 1993). As we have seen (Chapter 5, Section 5.1.1) precision and recall are special cases of informativeness. Informativeness is similar to the derived measures (E measure and MZ metric) in that it is a function of both recall and precision, though of a multiplicative rather than additive form. Fallout, like precision, seems more a measure of efficiency rather than effectiveness, since nonretrieval of nonrelevant items will reduce delay but says nothing about informativeness. Expected search length is related to the delay extent, since it is a function of the number of nonrelevant

Table 6.6
Measures of Effectiveness of Various Types of Search Strategies

Measure	Definition
Number of hits	Number of records retrieved in search
Search length	User–system connect time or number of commands issued
Recall (R)	Proportion of relevant items that are retrieved
Precision (P)	Proportion of retrieved items that are relevant
k-Record Precision	Precision when k relevant records have been retrieved, determined for k = 1,2, . . .
x% Recall Precision	Precision at the x% recall level, determined for $0 \leq x \leq 100$
Fallout	Proportion of nonrelevant items that are retrieved
E measure	$1 - \dfrac{1}{\alpha P^{-1} + (1 - \alpha)R^{-1}}$ $0 \leq \alpha \leq 1$
MZ metric	$1 - \dfrac{1}{P^{-1} + R^{-1} - 1}$
Expected search length	Expected number of nonrelevant documents retrieved before a given number of relevant documents
User satisfaction	Postsearch user ratings of search strategy
Accuracy	Number or proportion of questions answered correctly

documents. User satisfaction, though usually measured on an ordinal scale and hence related to informativeness, has less explanatory power, since it does not relate the overall informativeness of a search to other characteristics of the search such as the informativeness of individual records or delays in providing the result. The number or proportion of correctly answered questions can be considered to be a special case of the initial informativeness measure: the ideal chain has a single record with the correct answer, and so the undiscounted informativeness is one if this answer is provided and zero if it is not.

As an example of an investigation of the informativeness of different approaches to searching, consider the following problem. Hypertext-style interfaces, which incorporate structural and semantic links from one part of a database to another, have been proposed as a means of providing better browsing capabilities to users of online systems. However, research has shown that many users prefer to use traditional Boolean keyword searches when these are made available as an added feature of a hypertext system. One hypothesis is that hypertext-style interfaces are best for users who do not have a clear idea of what they are searching and Boolean searching is best for those looking for a specific piece of information.

Suppose, then, that two test user interfaces are developed for a database for tourist and information centers in a particular city. The database contains such information as places of historic interest, museums, galleries, parks, recreational facilities, shopping facilities, hotels and other forms of accommodation, restaurants, special events, and so on. The hypertext-style interface is installed at one tourist and information center and the keyword searching interface at another. For a trial period of one month, staff at each center recruit visitors to participate in an evaluation of the interface by providing them with a reward (e.g., tickets to a special event, a detailed guidebook for the city).

Participants in the test are asked to describe the purpose of their visit to the center to a staff member in sufficient detail that it will be possible to categorize their search as a browsing search or a specific query search. As the users search the database, they are asked to indicate, for each screen displayed, whether or not it was informative for them. A log is kept of all the screens displayed and the user's informativeness ratings. After the search, the user is asked whether or not she or he is satisfied. If not, the staff member will provide additional screens of information from the database and these additional records are then evaluated by the user.

The ideal chain then contains all records (screens) that the user has selected as informative. The user is given a printout of these screens and asked to rank them as to informativeness and also to indicate a preferred retrieval ordering. These rankings are then used to create the edges of the ideal chain and the optimal retrieval chain. In this example, we are not particularly concerned with service delays, and so the dependent variable in the experiment will be the initial informativeness of the records that the user retrieved without help from the staff member, discounted by the retrieval delay.

There are two factors in this experiment: type of interface (hypertext or keyword search) and type of query (browsing or specific information). The research hypothesis is that the hypertext interface is best for browsing searches and the keyword interface for keyword searches. In terms of informativeness and the two-factor design, the alternative hypothesis is that the interaction of hypertext interface and browsing search and the interaction of keyword interface and specific information search will provide higher informativeness scores than the interaction of hypertext interface and specific information search and the interaction of keyword interface and browsing search.

Because of the nature of data collection, it is unlikely that equal numbers of users will be found in each cell of the two-factor design. Procedures for analyzing a two-factor design with unequal cell frequencies will be found in both Berenson *et al.*, (1983) and Meddis (1984). Another approach is to randomly discard user data sets so that equal cell frequencies are obtained. We will use this latter approach, with a resulting five searches in each cell.

Because of the small sample size, the rank-based approach for a two-factor design will be followed. The results are given in Table 6.7.

The results of the rank tests are that: (1) there is no difference in the two interfaces in terms of median informativeness; (2) with the hypertext interface the median informativeness is better for browsing searches than for specific information searches; and (3) with the keyword interface there is no difference in median informativeness for browsing and specific information searches.

Repeated measure designs in which the same set of user needs are used to compare a number of search strategies are often difficult to develop since learning effects occur when the searcher searches for the same information using a sequence of different strategies. When the actual searching process is automatically controlled by the selected strategy and the user simply determines the informativeness and optimal retrieval rankings, then it may

3176$$0347
#3176 Tague 347-366 (Ch6d) - ag - 10-13-94
oc gal updated 10-15-94 dm
ac galleys updated sab 11-21-94
oc galleys updated sab 12-1-94, 12-2-94
ac pgs updated 12-12-94 kz

Table 6.7
Comparison of Two Interfaces with Two Types of Searches

Hypotheses:

H_{01}: $\eta_1 = \eta_2$ H_{11}: $\eta_1 > \eta_2$
H_{02}: $(\eta\gamma)_{11} = (\eta\gamma)_{12}$ H_{12}: $(\eta\gamma)_{11} > (\eta\gamma)_{12}$
H_{03}: $(\eta\gamma)_{21} = (\eta\gamma)_{22}$ H_{13}: $(\eta\gamma)_{21} < (\eta\gamma)_{22}$,

where η_1 and η_2 represent, respectively, the effects of the hypertext and keyword interfaces and the $(\eta\gamma)_{ij}$, $i = 1,2; j = 1,2$, represent, respectively, the interactions of the hypertext interface with the browsing and specific information search and the keyword interface with the browsing and specific information search.

Type of interface	*Type of search*			
	Browsing		*Specific info*	
	Score	*Rand*	*Score*	*Rank*
Hypertext	0.873	18	0.259	2
	0.918	20	0.366	5
	0.473	7	0.450	6
	0.550	8	0.100	1
	0.847	17	0.633	10
Mean	0.732		0.362	
Variance	0.034		0.032	

(continues)

Table 6.7 (*Continued*)

Type of interface	*Type of search*			
	Browsing		*Specific info*	
	Score	*Rand*	*Score*	*Rank*
Rank sum		70		24
Number of scores	55			
Keyword	0.295	3	0.764	14
	0.730	12	0.712	11
	0.593	9	0.839	16
	0.776	15	0.916	19
	0.302	4	0.740	13
Mean	0.539		0.794	
Variance	0.042		0.005	
Rank sum		43		73
Number of scores	55			

Lambda coefficients:

H_{11}: $\lambda_{11} = \lambda_{12} = -1$, $\lambda_{21} = \lambda_{22} = 1$
H_{12}: $\lambda_{11} = 1$, $\lambda_{12} = -1$
H_{13}: $\lambda_{21} = -1$, $\lambda_{22} = 1$

Key Statistics:

$L_1 = (-1)(70 + 24) + (1)(43 + 73) = 22$
$E(L_1) = 0$; $V(L_1) = 700$
$Z_{test} = 0.832$; $Z[.05] = 1.96$

Conclusion: Accept H_{01}.

$L_2 = (1)(70) + (-1)(24) = 46$
$E(L_2) = 0$; $V(L_2) = 350$
$Z_{test} = 2.459$; $Z[.05] = 1.96$

Conclusion: Reject H_{02}.

$L_3 = (-1)(43) + (1)(73) = 30$
$E(L_3) = 0$; $V(L_3) = 350$
$Z_{test} = 1.604$; $Z[.05] = 1.96$

Conclusion: Accept H_{03}

6.2.4 Evaluation of Packaging

Packaging refers to the form of the output that is presented to the user. The output may be full-text records or it may be record surrogates, for example, titles or abstracts. The output may be a record that is extracted from one or more others, in order to more precisely answer the user's query. It may be a record that summarizes, reviews, or applies statistical or financial analyses to a set of other records. Such packaging necessitates additional effort on the part of the staff of the information service. However, it also adds value to the service by saving the time of the user and so we need to have a measure of this added value.

Examples of questions that relate to the form of packaging are:

1. How informative is an abstract or summary of a record or set of records compared to the original?
2. How much more informative is an abstract than a title?
3. How much time does a review paper save the user?
4. How much information does a statistical analysis add to a numeric dataset? How much information does it provide without the original dataset?

There have been limited investigations of questions like these in the past. Marcus *et al.* (1978) examined the "indicativity" of documents based on different surrogates. Indicativity measures how well a given output (e.g., catalog field) conveys the content of the original document. It is measured by comparing the user's evaluation of the relevance of a document on the basis of the output field alone, compared with his or her evaluation on the basis of the full text. The investigators found that indicativity increased with the length of the field. Janes (1991) looked at how users' relevance judgments changed as they were presented with retrieved document representations incrementally (e.g., title, abstract, indexing). Relevance was measured using Eisenberg's magnitude estimation technique. He found that relevance judgments do change as text is added: abstracts provide the largest change, then titles, then bibliographic information, and, finally, indexing.

There appear to be three aspects to the evaluation of packaging:

- Indicativity: how well does a package (surrogate) represent the record it is replacing?
- Efficiency: how much user time is saved by providing the package rather than the original record or set of records?
- Added informativeness: how much additional information does the package provide over that in the original record or set of records?

A straightforward way of determining the informativeness of a type of surrogate would be to consider the surrogates as determinants of the search strategy. This approach involves a two-stage procedure, as follows:

1. As a result of an initial search of the surrogates database (e.g., titles, abstracts), the user is presented with a set of surrogate records that indicate potentially informative full-text records.

2. From the surrogates, the user determines those records she or he wishes to examine and the preferred order of examination. This sequence becomes the retrieval trail **t** for the second search.

3. The user then examines all the full-text records corresponding to the retrieved set for the initial search.

4. From these full-text records, the user determines the records that are actually informative and their informativeness ranking, that is, the ideal chain **C*(u)**.

5. The user determines the optimal retrieval chain **C**(u)** of the informative full-text records that were in the retrieval trail for the second search, the search of the full-text database.

6. The overall informativeness value is then determined as follows:

- the initial informativeness I_0[**t,C*(u)**] is determined from the ideal chain by summing the informativeness values for the records in the full-text retrieval trail as determined in Step 2;
- an appropriate delay discount D[**t,C**(u)**] is selected and evaluated using the retrieval trail **t** determined in Step 2 and the optimal retrieval order **C**(u)** determined in Step 5.
- The informativeness of the surrogate is calculated as the product of the initial informativeness I_0[**t,C*(u)**] and the delay discount D[**t,C**(u)**].

The informativeness of the surrogates represents the proportion of the retrieved items' informativeness, which is "indicated" by the surrogate. An example of this procedure involving a set of twelve titles, a retrieval trail of eleven titles, an ideal chain of nine full-text items, and an optimal retrieval trail of eight items is shown in Table 6.8. The resulting value shows that titles indicate approximately 70% of the informativeness of the full-text items.

One might use such informativeness scores to compare the indicativity or informativeness relative to the full text of different types of surrogates in an online information retrieval system, such as: (1) bibliographic record (author, title, journal, etc.); (2) bibliographic record and subject descriptors; (3) bibliographic record and an abstract.

For this purpose, a repeated measures design could be used. Users in the test carry out the initial searches by first scanning the bibliographic record, then the subject descriptors, then the abstracts for each record in the search. Three retrieval trails are determined for the full-text search, based on records selected as potentially informative from, respectively, the bibliographic record alone, the bibliographic record and subject descriptors, and the bibliographic record and abstract.

Efficiency describes the extent to which the information service saves the user's time by not providing more material than is needed to satisfy his or her need. In the model we developed in Chapter 4, we pointed out that in general there might be more than one ideal chain, that is, that there might be more than one way of satisfying the user's need from the database. Given two ideal chains, we define the efficiency of one chain relative to another as the ratio of the length of the second chain compared to the first chain, expressed as a percentage. Length, in this context, is defined as the number

Table 6.8
Determination of the Amount of Information a Set of Titles Provides about the Full-Text Items

Retrieval order of item			
From title i	From full text $r^{**}(t_i)$	Ideal chain edge $e^*(t_i)$ $I(t_i)$	Item informativeness
1	2	1	0.145
2	1	1	0.145
3	10 *		
4	5	2	0.101
5	10*		
6	3	2	0.101
7	4	2	0.101
8	8	2	0.101
9	10 *		
10	6	2	0.101
11	7	2	0.101
**		2	0.101

* Indicates a noninformative item.
** Indicates an informative item not in the retrieval trail.

$$I_0[\mathbf{t},\mathbf{C^*(u)}] = 0.899 \text{ [from Chapter 5, Equation (5.2)]}$$

Let the delay discount function be

$$D_0[t,C^*(u)] = 2^{-(.5X_1+.5X_2)}$$

$$X_1 = 0.413 \text{ [from Chapter 5, Equation (5.4)]}$$
$$X_2 = .273 \text{ [from Chapter 5, Equation (5.4)]}$$

So $I[\mathbf{t},u] = .899(2^{-.343}) = 0.708$.

of records in the chain. Extending this concept to apply to two retrieval trails of equal informativeness, the efficiency of one relative to the other will again be the percentage ratio of the lengths. Thus, if a review paper t′ is as informative for a user as the record sequence $\mathbf{t} = t_1t_2, \ldots t_k$ of reviewed papers, the efficiency of t′ relative to **t** is $100/k$ percent. One might determine an equivalent sequence by asking such a question as: What items that you might have needed to read does this summary item replace?

The definition of length as the number of records in the chain assumes all records are of approximately the same length. If this is not a reasonable assumption, the length of a sequence may be defined as the sum of the lengths of the records in it, where length might be the number of pages or screens of text in the record.

Some kinds of packaging provide additional information to the user, as well as saving his or her time. For example, a review paper synthesizes concepts in a set of papers on some topic. A statistical summary of a survey dataset describes the population surveyed in terms of general characteristics. We may wish to measure the amount of additional information this package provides to the user.

One approach would be to simply add the review or summary record in an appropriate position in the ideal chain. However, in this case, we may have several equivalent ideal chains, containing the summary record and some or all of the summarized records. For example, if a review paper t' summarized 10 other papers $t_1, t_2, \ldots t_{10}$, a user might assess the following ideal chains as equally informative

$$C_1 = \langle\{t'\}, \{t_1, t_2\}\rangle$$
$$C_2 = \langle\{t'\}, \{t_1, t_2, \ldots t_{10}\}\rangle.$$

In other words, the review paper replaces the information that would be provided by eight of the reviewed papers, but does not totally replace the information provided by two of the papers. In this case, C_1 is clearly the more efficient of the two ideal chains.

Suppose that we are interested in determining the informativeness of the retrieval trail $\mathbf{t} = \langle t_1, t_2, \ldots t_{10}\rangle$. Which ideal chain should we use as the standard, C_1 or C_2? Clearly, the informativeness will be greater if it is compared to C_2, since it then contains fewer noninformative records. However, "ideally" the service should have provided the review paper in order to save the user's time.

There is no one answer to this question; it depends on the priorities of the service. If saving the user's time has a high priority, then C_1 should be used as the standard. If minimizing use of the service's resources, while at the same time satisfying the user in some form, then C_2 may be used as the standard when it results in a higher informativeness value.

6.3 Summary

In this chapter we have suggested some applications of the informativeness measure developed in Chapters 4 and 5 to evaluation of the collection, description, retrieval, and packaging activities that go on in information services and to an overall evaluation of how well the service is serving its community. We have presented some ways of assessing the reliability or standard error of average informativeness estimates and some experimental designs and data analysis methods for comparing different approaches to the various information service activities.

This chapter is not intended as a complete exposition of the possible research designs that could be used in assessing and comparing informativeness values in different situations. We have tried to make our examples suggestive of different approaches to the collection of informativeness data and its analysis through appropriate designs and statistical techniques. We leave it to the ingenuity of the reader to develop designs and techniques appropriate to her or his evaluation concerns.

6.4 Review Problems

6.7.1 Give examples of questions that would have high and low values on the three dimensions of user need: specificity of need, size of answer sequence, and substitutability of answer sequence from one user to another.

6.7.2 Identify an information service that you use on a regular basis. Suggest how you would sample users and nonusers from its community in order to determine the average informativeness of this service over the needs in its user community.

6.7.3 Suppose that a sample of 100 users of an online service had an average informativeness of .73 over all the searches that they ran during a one-month period, with a standard deviation of .09. Suppose, also, that in the same period, among 200 subscribers to the service who were contacted, 120 had needs that could have been satisfied at least in part by the service, but only 80 of these actually performed an online search. Determine a 95% confidence interval for the average informativeness of the service during the month.

6.7.4 A telephone-based community information service is considering augmenting its database with an additional database of community events. However, it is concerned that its present users will experience delays in access if a large number of calls about events are received. The new database is mounted on a trial basis for a one-month period and the following information is recorded during the month preceding the trial and during the trial period:

(1) Was the service able to satisfy the user?
(2) What was the length of the delay, if any, that the user experienced in trying to reach the service on the telephone?

Responses to users were rated as at informativeness value 1 if they satisfied the user, .5 if they partially satisfied the user, and 0 if they did not satisfy the user. Since the telephone service is open for ten hours each day and functions on the basis of providing same-day service, it adopted a service delay discount function of

$$D(T) = 1 \text{ if } T \leq 10; 0 \text{ otherwise},$$

where T is the number of hours delay. The results of the one-month trial are as follows:

Month	*Delay discount*	*Number of users with initial informativeness*		
		0	*.5*	*1*
Pretrial	1	258	369	725
	0	79	110	284
Trial	1	163	459	815
	0	93	286	357

Do the results indicate that the new database has improved or reduced informativeness of the service?

6.7.5 In a retrieval test, three different query term weighting schemes are used in search strategies. The first scheme W_1 is the existing scheme, the second and third schemes W_2 and W_3 are potential replacements for it. A set of 12 queries is searched, 6 requiring large answer sets and 6 requiring small answer sets, using each weighting scheme. The initial informativeness I_0 and the delay discount D are then determined for each query based on the user's ideal chain and optimal retrieval chain. The results are as follows:

Query size and number	W1		W2		W3	
	I_0	D	I_0	D	I_0	D
Small						
1	0.26	0.61	0.68	0.17	0.97	0.23
2	0.59	0.75	0.49	0.46	0.93	0.49
3	0.15	0.06	0.77	0.26	0.93	0.06
4	0.77	0.04	0.88	0.70	0.34	0.11
5	0.97	0.19	0.82	0.30	0.88	0.48
6	0.59	0.14	0.88	0.89	0.79	0.87
Large						
1	0.28	0.59	0.30	0.15	0.31	0.21
2	0.64	0.00	0.66	0.44	0.67	0.47
3	0.20	0.04	0.22	0.24	0.22	0.98
4	0.98	0.01	1.00	0.03	1.00	0.05
5	1.00	0.17	1.00	0.65	1.04	0.46
6	0.64	0.12	0.64	0.87	0.65	0.45

Determine if, on the basis of discounted informativeness in the retrieval test, either of the two experimental weighting schemes should replace the existing one on a permanent basis, for either large-size or small-size queries.

Appendix A6.1

Comparing Informativeness Using the Analysis of Variance

A6.1.1 ANOVA Test for a Difference in Informativeness, Single-Factor Design

The following steps present, in outline, the analysis of variance procedure for testing for a difference in mean informativeness among approaches such as different databases, indexing methods, search strategies, and packaging techniques, or over different time periods, or among different user groups. The approaches or periods or groups are the levels of a single independent variable and the informativeness scores are the values of the dependent variable.

1. Determine the following values:

a: number of levels of the independent variable (approaches or periods);

n_h: number of cases (observations) in the sample from the hth level of the independent variable;

$N = \Sigma_h n_h$: total number of cases in the sample;

I_{hj}: independent variable value (score) for the jth case under the hth level, $h = 1,k; j = 1,n_h$:

$I_h = \sum_{j=1}^{nh} I_{hj}$: the sum of the scores for the n_h cases at the hth level;

$M_h = I_h/n_h$: the average score for sample cases at the hth level;

$I.. = \sum_{h=1}^{a}\sum_{j=1}^{nh} I_{hj}$: the sum of the scores from all n cases;

$S_h^2 = \dfrac{\sum_{j=1}^{nh} I_{hj}^2 - I_{h\cdot}^2/n_h}{n_h - 1}$: the variance of the scores for the sample cases at the hth level.

2. If the variances S^2_h are not approximately equal over the a levels, use the rank-based approach described in Appendix 6.2.1. An F_{max} or other similar test may be used to test for equality of variances (see Berenson *et al.*, 1983, pp. 66ff. for details).

3. Specify the null hypothesis, that the population mean scores for all levels of the independent variable are equal, that is, that

$$H_0: \eta_1 = \eta_2 = \ldots \eta_a = 0.$$

4. Calculate the ANOVA table as follows:

Source of Variation	*Degrees of Freedom*	*Sum of Squares*	*Mean Square*
Between levels	$a - 1$	$SSA = \sum_{h=1}^{a} \frac{I_{h\cdot}^2}{n_h} - \frac{I_{..}}{N}$	$MSA = \frac{SSA}{a-1}$
Within levels	$N - a$	$SSW = \sum_{h=1}^{a}\sum_{j=1}^{n_h} I_{hj}^2 - \sum_{h=1}^{a} \frac{I_{h\cdot}^2}{n_h}$	$MSW = \frac{SSW}{N-a}$
Total	$N - 1$	$SST = \sum_{h=1}^{a}\sum_{j=1}^{n_h} I_{hj}^2 - \frac{I_{..}^2}{N}$	

5. If F = /MSA/MSW > $F(a - 1, N - a;\alpha)$, reject H_0; at least one pair of levels of the independent variable differ in their mean scores. $F(a - 1, N - a;\alpha)$ is the value in the F table for a significance level of α and $k - 1$ and $N - k$ degrees of freedom in the numerator and denominator, respectively.

6. If the test in Step 5 is significant, then use a Tukey *t* test to determine which pairs of means differ. Specifically, determine the critical range Q as

$$Q = Q[a, N - a;\alpha]\sqrt{\frac{MSW\sum_{h=1}^{a}\frac{1}{n_h}}{a}},$$

where the value $Q[a, N - a;\alpha]$ is the upper-tail α critical value obtained from the Studentized range distribution (see Berenson *et al.*, 1983, pp. 551ff. for Tables) and MSW is the mean square within levels from the ANOVA table.

If the difference between any pair of means $M_h - M_i$ is greater than the critical range Q, then the two means differ significantly at the α significance level.

A6.1.2 ANOVA Test for a Difference in Informativeness, Single-Factor, Repeated Measures (within Subjects) Design

The following steps present, in outline, the analysis of variance procedure for testing for a difference among approaches such as different databases, indexing methods, search strategies, and packaging techniques when the same set of user needs is used to assess the informativeness scores under each approach.

1. Determine the following values:

a: number of levels (approaches) of the independent variable (single factor);
b: number of cases (subjects);
I_{hj}: dependent variable value (score) for the *j*th case under the *h*th approach, $h = 1,a; j = 1,b;$

$I_{h.} = \sum_{j=1}^{b} I_{hj}$: the sum of the scores for the b cases at the hth level;

$I_{.j} = \sum_{h=1}^{a} I_{hj}$: the sum of the a scores for the bth sample case;

$M_h = I_{h.}/b$: the average score for sample cases at the hth level;

$I_{..} = \sum_{h=1}^{a}\sum_{j=1}^{b} I_{hj}$: the sum of the scores from all cases and levels;

$S_h^2 = \dfrac{\sum_{j=1}^{b} I_{hj}^2 - I_{h.}^2/b}{b-1}$: the variance of the scores for the sample cases at the hth level.

2. If the variances S^2_h are not approximately equal over the a levels, use the rank-based approach described in Appendix 6.2.3.

3. Specify the null hypotheses, that the population mean scores for levels of the independent variable are the same, that is, in terms of the linear model:

$$H_0: \eta_1 = \eta_2 = \ldots \eta_a = 0.$$

4. Calculate the ANOVA table as follows:

Source of Variation	*Degrees of Freedom*	*Sum of Squares*	*Mean Square*
Among levels	$a-1$	$SSA = \sum_{h=1}^{a} \frac{I_{h.}^2}{b} - \frac{I_{..}^2}{ab}$	$MSA = \frac{SSA}{a-1}$
Among cases	$b-1$	$SSB = \sum_{j=1}^{b} \frac{I_{.j}^2}{a} - \frac{I_{..}^2}{ab}$	$MSB = \frac{SSB}{b-1}$
Within cells	$(a-1) \times (b-1)$	$SSW = \sum_{h=1}^{a}\sum_{j=1}^{b} I_{hj}^2 - \sum_{h=1}^{a} \frac{I_{h.}^2}{b} - \sum_{j=1}^{b} \frac{I_{.j}^2}{a} + \frac{I_{..}^2}{ab}$	$MSW = \frac{SSW}{(a-1)(b-1)}$
Total	$ab-1$	$SST = \sum_{h=1}^{a}\sum_{j=1}^{b} I_{hj}^2 - \frac{I_{..}^2}{ab}$	

5. If $F = MSA/MSW > F[a-1,(a-1)(b-1);\alpha]$, reject H_0; at least one pair of levels differ in their mean scores.

6. If the F test in Step 5 is significant, then a Tukey t test may be used to determine which pairs of means differ.

Specifically, determine the critical range Q as

$$Q = Q[a,(a-1)(b-1);1-\alpha]\sqrt{\frac{MSW}{b}},$$

where the value $Q(a,n-a;1-\alpha)$ is the upper-tail α critical value obtained from the Studentized range distribution and MSW is the mean square within cells from the ANOVA table. Then any two means M_g and M_h differ significantly if $M_g - M_h > Q$.

A6.1.3 ANOVA Test for a Difference in Informativeness, Two-Factor Design with Equal Observations per Cell

The following steps present, in outline, the analysis of variance procedure for testing for a difference in mean informativeness scores among approaches such as different databases, indexing methods, search strategies, and packaging techniques, when the effect of another factor, such as different time periods or different user groups, and its interaction with the approach, are also being assessed. The approaches are the levels of the first independent variable (first factor), the time periods or groups are the levels of the second independent variable (second factor), and the informativeness scores are the values of the dependent variable. In the two-factor design presented here, there should be equal numbers of observations for each combination of approach and time period. For unequal sample designs, see Berenson, *et al.*, (1983).

1. Determine the following values:

a: number of levels of the first factor (approaches);
b: number of levels of the second factor (time periods or user groups);
n: number of cases (informativeness scores) in the sample for the each of the *ab* combinations (cells) of a level of the first factor and a level of the second factor;
abn: total number of cases in the sample;
I_{hij}: dependent variable value (score) for the *j*th case under the *h*th level of the first factor and the *i*th level of the second factor, $h = 1,a; i = 1,b; j = 1,n;$

$I_{hi.} = \sum_{j=1}^{n} I_{hij}$: the sum of the scores for the *n* cases in the *hi*th cell;

$I_{h..} = \sum_{i=1}^{b}\sum_{j=1}^{n} I_{hij}$: the sum of the scores for the *bn* cases at the *h*th level of the first factor;

$I_{.i.} = \sum_{h=1}^{a}\sum_{j=1}^{n} I_{hij}$: the sum of the scores for the *an* cases at the *i*th level of the second factor;

$M_{hi} = I_{hi.}/n$: the average score for sample cases in the *hi*th cell;
$M_{h.} = I_{h..}/bn$: the average score for sample cases at the *h*th level of the first factor;
$M_{.i.} = I_{.i.}/an$: the average score for sample cases at the *i*th level of the second factor;

$I_{...} = \sum_{h=1}^{a}\sum_{i=1}^{b}\sum_{j=1}^{n} I_{hij}$: the sum of the scores from all *n* cases;

$S_{hi}^2 = \dfrac{\sum_{j=1}^{n} I_{hij}^2 - I_{hi.}^2/n}{n-1}$: the variance of the scores for the sample cases in the *hi*th cell.

2. If the variances $S^2_{hi.}$ are not approximately equal over the *ab* cells, use the rank-based approach described in Appendix 6.2.2.

3. Specify the null hypotheses, that the population mean scores for all levels of both factors and all combinations of the two factors (interactions) are the same, that is, in terms of the linear model:

$$H_{01}: \eta_1 = \eta_2 = \ldots \eta_a = 0$$
$$H_{02}: \tau_1 = \tau_2 = \ldots \tau_a = 0$$
$$H_{03}: (\eta\tau)_{11} = (\eta\tau)_{12} = \ldots (\eta\tau)_{ab} = 0.$$

4. Calculate the ANOVA table as follows:

Source of Variation	*Degrees of Freedom*	*Sum of Squares*	*Mean Square*
First factor	$a - 1$	$SSA = \sum_{h=1}^{a} \frac{I_{h..}^2}{bn} - \frac{I_{...}^2}{abn}$	$MSA = \frac{SSA}{a-1}$
Second factor	$b - 1$	$SSB = \sum_{i=1}^{b} \frac{I_{.i.}^2}{an} - \frac{I_{...}^2}{abn}$	$MSB = \frac{SSB}{b-1}$
Interaction	$(a - 1) \times (b - t1)$	$SSAB = \frac{\sum_{h=1}^{a}\sum_{i=1}^{b} I_{hi.}^2}{n} - \frac{\sum_{h=1}^{a} I_{h..}^2}{bn} - \frac{\sum_{i=1}^{b} I_{.i.}^2}{an} + \frac{I_{...}^2}{abn}$	$MSAB = \frac{SSAB}{(a-1)(b-1)}$
Within cells	$ab(n - 1)$	$SSW = \sum_{h=1}^{a}\sum_{i=1}^{b}\sum_{j=1}^{n} I_{hij}^2 - \frac{\sum_{h=1}^{a}\sum_{i=1}^{b} I_{h}^2}{n}$	$MSW = \frac{SSW}{ab(n-1)}$
Total	$n - 1$	$SST = \sum_{h=1}^{a}\sum_{i=1}^{b}\sum_{j=1}^{n} I_{hij}^2 - \frac{I_{...}^2}{abn}$	

5. If $F = MSA/MSW > F[a - 1, ab(n - 1); \alpha]$, reject H_{01}; at least one pair of levels of the first factor differ in their mean scores.
If $F = MSB/MSW > F[b - 1, ab(n - 1); \alpha]$, reject H_{02}; at least one pair of levels of the second factor differ in their mean scores.
If $F = MSB/MSW > F[(a - 1)(b - 1), ab(n - 1); \alpha]$, reject H_{03}; there is an interaction between at least one pair of levels of the two factors.

6. If the interaction effect (H_{03}) is not significant and either or both of the factors show significant differences in means for the different levels in Step 5, then a Tukey *t* test may be used to determine which pairs of means differ. Specifically, for factor A, determine the critical range Q as

$$Q = Q[a,ab(n - 1);1 - \alpha]\sqrt{\frac{MSW}{bn}},$$

where the value $Q(a,n - a;1 - \alpha)$ is the upper-tail α critical value obtained from the Studentized range distribution and MSW is the mean square within cells from the ANOVA table.
Similarly, for factor B, determine the critical range Q as

$$Q = Q(b,ab(n - 1);1 - \alpha)\sqrt{\frac{MSW}{an}}.$$

If the difference between any pair of means $M_{h.} - M_{i.}$ or $M_{.h} - M_{.i}$ is greater than the corresponding critical range Q, then the two means differ significantly at the α significance level.

If there is a significant interaction effect, then differences in means for the levels of one factor should be tested at fixed levels of the other factor. For example, the difference $M_{hi} - M_{gi}$ is significant if it is greater than the critical range

$$Q = Q[(a - 1)(b - 1),ab(n - 1);1 - \alpha]\sqrt{\frac{MSW}{abn}}.$$

Appendix A6.2

Comparing Informativeness Using the Meddis Rank-Based Approach

A6.2.1 Rank Test for a Difference in Informativeness, Single-Factor Design

The following steps present, in outline, the rank-based procedure for testing for a difference in median informativeness among approaches such as different databases, indexing methods, search strategies, and packaging techniques, or over different time periods, or among different user groups. The approaches or periods are the levels of the independent variable and the informativeness scores are the values of the dependent variable.

1. Determine the following values:
a: number of levels of the independent variable;
n_h: number of cases in the sample for the *h*th level;
$N = \Sigma_h n_h$: total number of cases in the sample.

2. Specify the null hypothesis that the population median scores are the same for all levels of the independent variable.

H_0: $\eta_1 = \eta_2 = \ldots \eta_a = 0$.

3. Specify alternative hypotheses. If possible, the alternatives should be specific (e.g., for three different approaches, $\eta_1 > \eta_2 > \eta_3$) and should be based on expectations arising from the original research problem. Nonspecific tests require a greater difference to be significant.

4. Identify the expected ordering of the means at the a different levels under the alternative hypothesis. Assign coefficients λ_i, $i = 1,a$, to represent this pattern. (For example, for the three approach examples given in Step 3, the coefficients might be $\lambda_1 = 1$, $\lambda_2 = 0$, $\lambda_3 = -1$.) It is desirable to have the coefficients sum to zero.

5. Sort the scores from all samples into one sequence and assign ranks so that low scores get low ranks, high scores high ranks, and tied scores receive their average rank. Note the length of the ties. Let:

R_{hj} = rank of the jth score in the sample for the hth level;
$R_h = \Sigma_j R_{hj}$ = sum of ranks in the sample for the hth level;
t_q = number of scores in the qth set of tied scores;
$n^\star$ = number of sets of tied scores.

6. Compute and evaluate the key statistics.

The key statistic reflects the disagreement between the data and the null hypothesis of no difference among levels of the independent variable. The key statistics are as follows for specific and nonspecific tests.

For specific tests the key statistic is:

$$L = \sum_{h=1}^{a} \lambda_h R_h.$$

The expected value and variance of this key statistic are:

$$E(L) = \frac{(n+1)}{2} \sum_{h=1}^{a} n_h \lambda_h$$

$$V(L) = \frac{(n+1)}{12}\left[n \sum_{h=1}^{a} n_h \lambda_h^2 - \left(\sum_{h=1}^{a} n_h \lambda_h\right)^2\right]T,$$

where the correction for ties T is given by

$$T = 1 - \frac{\sum_{q=1}^{n^\star} (t_q^3 - t_q)}{n^3 - n}.$$

For large samples, the key statistic L has a normal distribution if the null hypothesis is true. Thus, we reject H_0 if

$$\left|\frac{L-E(L)}{\sqrt{V(L)}}\right| \geq Z[\frac{\alpha}{2}],$$

where $Z[\alpha/2]$ is the standard normal curve value for which the probability of exceeding is $\alpha/2$. For small samples, the significance of its value under the null hypothesis may be found using the tables in Meddis.

For nonspecific tests the key statistic is:

$$H = [\frac{12}{N(N+1)}\sum_{h=1}^{a}\frac{R_h^2}{n_h} - 3(N+1)]/T.$$

This statistic has a chi square distribution with a-1 degrees of freedom for large samples if the null hypothesis is true. Thus, we reject H_0 if $H \geq \chi^2[a-1;\alpha]$, the value in the chi square distribution table for a-1 degrees of freedom for which the probability of exceeding is α. Small-sample significance values are given in Meddis.

7. If p additional specific alternative hypotheses are being tested, for example, that pairs of means vary in a certain direction, then the significance level for each testing should be set to α/p.

If the nonspecific test statistic H is significant, it can be concluded that the observed pattern of sample rank means represents a significant specific hypothesis, for example, that $\eta_1 > \eta_2, \ldots > \eta_a$.

A6.2.2 Rank Test for a Difference in Informativeness, Single-Factor, Repeated Measures (within Subjects) Design

The following steps present, in outline, the rank-based procedure for testing for a difference in median informativeness among approaches such as different databases, indexing methods, search strategies, and packaging techniques, when the same set of user needs are analyzed with each approach. The approach is the independent variable or factors and the informativeness scores are the values of the dependent variable.

1. Determine the following values:
*a:*number of different approaches, or levels of the first factor;
*b:*number of cases (subjects);
*ab:*total number of observed scores.

2. Specifiy the null hypothesis that the population median scores are the same for all approaches.

$$H_0: \eta_1 = \eta_2 = \ldots \eta_a = 0$$

3. Specify alternative hypotheses. If possible, the alternatives should be specific (e.g., for three different approaches, $\eta_1 > \eta_2 > \eta_3$) and should be based on expectations arising from the original research problem. Non-specific tests requires a greater difference to be significant.

4. Identify the expected ordering of the medians at the a different levels under the alternative hypothesis. Assign coefficients λ_i, $i = 1,a$, to represent this pattern. (For example, for the three approach examples given in Step 3, the coefficients might be $\lambda_1 = 1$, $\lambda_2 = 0$, $\lambda_3 = -1$.) It is desirable to have the coefficients sum to zero.

5. Sort the a scores for each user in one sequence and assign ranks so that low scores get low ranks, high scores high ranks, and tied scores receive their average rank. Note the length of the ties. Let:

R_{hj} = rank of the jth user's score under the hth approach;
$R_h = \Sigma_j R_{hj}$ = sum of ranks in the sample for the hth level;
t_{jq} = number of scores in the qth set of tied scores for the jth user;
$n^*(j)$ = number of sets of tied scores for the jth user.

6. Compute and evaluate the key statistics.

The key statistic reflects the disagreement between the data and the null hypothesis of no difference among treatments.

For specific tests the key statistic is:

$$L = \sum_{h=1}^{a} \lambda_h R_h.$$

The expected value and variance of this key statistic are:

$$E(L) = \frac{b(a + 1)}{2} \sum_{h=1}^{a} \lambda_h$$

$$V(L) = \frac{b(a + 1)}{12} [a \sum_{h=1}^{a} \lambda_h^2 -) \sum_{h=1}^{k} \lambda_h)^2] T,$$

where the correction T for ties is given by

$$T = \frac{\sum_{j=1}^{b} T_j}{b}, \text{ where } T_j = 1 - \frac{\sum_{q=1}^{n^*(j)} (t_{jq}^3 - t_{jq})}{a^3 - a}.$$

For large samples, the key statistic L has a normal distribution if the null hypothesis is true. Thus, we reject H_0 if

$$\left| \frac{L - E(L)}{\sqrt{V(L)}} \right| \geq Z[\tfrac{\alpha}{2}],$$

where $Z[\alpha/2]$ is the standard normal curve value for which the probability of exceeding is $\alpha/2$. For small samples, the significance of its value under the null hypothesis may be found using the tables in Meddis.

For nonspecific tests the key statistic is:

$$H = \{\frac{12}{ab(a + 1)}\sum_{h=1}^{a} [R_h^2 - 3b(a + 1)]\}/T.$$

This statistic has a chi square distribution with a-1 degrees of freedom for large samples if the null hypothesis is true. Thus, we reject H_0 if $H \geq \chi^2[a-1;\alpha]$, the value in the chi square distribution table for a-1 degrees of freedom for which the probability of exceeding is α. Small-sample significance values are given in Meddis.

7. If p additional specific alternative hypotheses are being tested, for example, that pairs of means vary in a certain direction, then the significance level for each testing should be set to α/p.

If the nonspecific test statistic H is significant, it can be concluded that the observed pattern of sample rank means represents a significant specific alternative for example, that $\eta_1 > \eta_2, \ldots > \eta_a$.

A6.2.3 Rank Test for a Difference in Informativeness, Two-Factor Design with Equal Observations per Cell

The following steps present, in outline, the rank-based procedure for testing for a difference in median informativeness among approaches such as different databases, indexing methods, search strategies, and packaging techniques, when the effect of another factor, such as different time periods or different user groups, and its interaction with the approach, are also being assessed. The approaches are the levels of the first independent variable (first factor), the time periods are the levels of the second independent variable (second factor), and the informativeness scores are the values of the dependent variable. In the two-factor design presented here, it is assumed there are equal numbers of observations for each combination of approach and time period. For unequal samples, see Meddis.

1. Determine the following values:

a: number of levels of the first factor (approaches);

b: number of levels of the second factor (time periods or user groups);

n: number of cases (informativeness scores) in the sample for each of the *ab* combinations (cells) of a level of the first factor and a level of the second factor;

abn: total number of cases in the sample.

2. Specify the null hypotheses, that the population median scores for

all levels of both factors and all combinations of these two factors (interactions) are the same, that is, in terms of the linear model:

$$H_{01}: \eta_1 = \eta_2 = \ldots \eta_a = 0$$
$$H_{02}: \tau_1 = \tau_2 = \ldots \tau_b = 0$$
$$H_{03}: (\eta\tau)_{11} = (\eta\tau)_{12} = \ldots (\eta\tau)_{ab} = 0.$$

3. Specify alternative hypotheses for each null hypothesis. If possible, the alternatives should be specific (e.g., for three different approaches, $\eta_1 > \eta_2 > \eta_3$). The specific tests should be based on expectations arising from the original research hypotheses of the investigation. Nonspecific tests require a greater difference to be significant.

4. Identify the expected ordering of the sample medians for each combination of the two factors under each specific alternative hypothesis. Assign coefficients λ_{hi}, $h = 1,a$, $i = 1,b$, to represent this pattern. For example, for three approaches, two time periods, and six interactions, the specific alternative hypotheses and the coefficients might be as follows:

$$H_{11}: \eta > \eta_2 > \eta_3$$
$$\lambda_{11} = \lambda_{12} = 1,\ \lambda_{21} = \lambda_{22} = 0,\ \lambda_{31} = \lambda_{32} = -1$$
$$H_{12}: \tau_1 > \tau_2$$
$$\lambda_{11} = \lambda_{21} = \lambda_{31} = 1,\ \lambda_{12} = \lambda_{22} = \lambda_{32} = -1$$
$$H_{13}: (\eta\tau)_{11} - (\eta\tau)_{12} > (\eta\tau)_{21} - (\eta\tau)_{22} > (\eta\tau)_{31} - (\eta\tau)_{32}$$
$$\lambda_{11} = 1,\ \lambda_{12} = -1,\ \lambda_{21} = 0,\ \lambda_{22} = 0,\ \lambda_{31} = -1,\ \lambda_{32} = 1.$$

5. Sort the *abn* scores in one sequence and assign ranks so that low scores get low ranks, high scores high ranks, and tied scores receive their average rank. Note the length of the ties. Let:

R_{hij} = rank of the *j*th user's score under the *h*th approach in the *i*th time period;
$R_{hi} = \Sigma_j R_{hij}$ = sum of ranks in the sample for the *h*th approach and the *i*th time period;
t_q = number of scores in the *q*th set of tied scores;
$n^\star$ = number of sets of tied scores.

6. Compute and evaluate the key statistic for each alternative hypothesis. The key statistic, which reflects the disagreeement between the data and the null hyposthesis, is:

$$L = \sum_{h=1}^{a}\sum_{i=1}^{b} \lambda_{hi} R_{hi}.$$

The expected value and variance of the key statistic is:

$$E(L) = \frac{n(abn + 1)}{2}\sum_{h=1}^{a}\sum_{i=1}^{b}\lambda_{hi}$$

$$V(L) = \frac{(abn + 1)\,T}{12}[abn^2\sum_{h=1}^{a}\sum_{i=1}^{b}\lambda_{hi}^2 - (n\sum_{h=1}^{a}\sum_{i=1}^{b}\lambda_{hi})^2],$$

where the correction for ties T is given by

$$T = 1 - \frac{\sum_{q=1}^{n^*}(t_q^3 - t_q)}{(abn)^3 - abn}.$$

For large samples, the key statistic L has a normal distribution if the null hypothesis is true. Thus, we reject H_0 if

$$\frac{L - E(L)}{\sqrt{V(L)}} \mid \geq Z\left[\frac{\alpha}{2}\right],$$

where $Z[\alpha/2]$ is the standard normal curve value for which the probability of exceeding is $\alpha/2$. For small samples, the significance of its value under the null hypothesis may be found using the tables in Meddis.

For nonspecific tests there are also individual key statistics for each alternative hypothesis, namely:

H_{01}: $\eta_1 <> \eta_2 <> \ldots \eta_a$
H_{01}: $\tau_1 <> \tau_2 <> \ldots \tau_b$
H_{03}: $(\eta\tau)_{11} <> (\eta\tau)_{12} <> \ldots (\eta\tau)_{ab}$.

The alternative hypotheses simply say the main effects and the interactions are significantly different, without indicating the direction of the differences. The key statistics are:

$$H_1 = \left[\frac{12\sum_{h=1}^{a} R_{h\cdot}^2}{ab^2n^2(abn + 1)} - 3(abn + 1)]\right]/T$$

$$H_2 = \left[\frac{12\sum_{i=1}^{b} R_{\cdot i}^2}{a^2bn^2(abn + 1)} - 3(abn + 1)\right]/T$$

$$H_3' = \left[\frac{12}{abn^2(abn + 1)}\sum_{h=1}^{a}\sum_{i=1}^{b} R_{hi}^2 - 3(abn + 1)]\right]/T$$

and $H_3 = H_3' - H_1 - H_2$.

These statistics have chi square distributions with, respectively, $(a - 1)$, $(b - 1)$, and $(a - 1)(b - 1)$ degrees of freedom (df) for large samples if the null hypotheses are true. Thus, we reject H_{0i} if $H_i \geq \chi^2[df_i;\alpha]$, the value in the chi square distribution table for the indicated degrees of freedom for which the probability of exceeding is α. Small-sample significance values are given in Meddis.

7. If p additional specific alternative hypotheses are being tested, for example, that pairs of means vary in a certain direction, then the significance level for each test should be set to α/p.

If the nonspecific test statistic H is significant in any hypothesis, it can be concluded that the observed patern of sample rank means represents a significant specific alternative for example, that $\eta_1 > \eta_2, \ldots > \eta_a$.

7

Conclusion

A mathematician who had some interest in library science said:

- Books are for use
- Every reader his book
- Every book its reader
- Save the time of the reader
- The library is a growing organism (Ranganathan, 1931).

The approach we have taken in this book to the measurement of information embodies these famous principles, translated to a modern information service environment:

- Information services exist for the user community.
- The amount of information provided by a record depends on the user.
- Records accessible through an information service must be informative for at least one user.
- Delays diminish the amount of information.
- The informativeness of a record for the user community is always changing.

Many views of information have been held in the past. In the initial sections of the book we present the view that the information provided by a record to a user is: (1) subjective, depending on the user's conceptual structure and the user's situation; and (2) dynamic, depending on what records the user has already seen; (3) capable of being assessed by the user at the ordinal level as it relates to the user's present need or interest. We also present the view that the *amount* of information provided by a set of records to a user with a particular need or interest, that is, the informativeness of the set, is:

- a measure that forms an underlying continuum;
- logarithmically related to the amount of information already obtained relating to the user's present need or interest;

- discounted by delays resulting from viewing of noninformative records, and slow response by the information service;
- standardizable by defining as one unit of informativeness the amount of information needed to satisfy a single user need or interest.

Thus, we see the informativeness of a set of records as being unique to a user and expressible by the user at the level of preferences among records. Informativeness of records for a user may be an underlying continuum, and, indeed, some users may be able to assign values from this continuum. However, our opinion is that for the majority of users such an assignment would not be reliable.

Based on the ability of the user to make preference judgments of a particular kind and the other characteristics just listed, we develop informativeness measures to answer four kinds of questions:

- How much information a record provides to a user;
- How much information a sequence of records provides to a user;
- How much information a sequence of uses of a record provides to a user community;
- How much information a service provides to a user community over a specified time period.

The development is an integrated one in that the last three measures are aggregations of the first. To derive it, we introduce the concepts of:

1. an ideal chain, that is, a sequence of record sets that are sufficient and necessary to the satisfaction of the user need or interest and that are ordered with respect to that need or interest;
2. an optimal retrieval chain, that is, the user's preferred order for viewing the retrieved records;
3. a delay discount function, which reduces the informativeness of a service to the extent that retrieval is delayed by improper record order and noninformative records and that service is provided at a time later than when it is needed.

Following the initial development, we show how these informativeness measures may be used in many different assessment situations. We construct a measure of the informativeness of a retrieval trail, the sequence of records provided by an information service to a user in response to a query. As well, we suggest that the cumulated informativeness values for an individual record may be used to measure the value of the record to the user community over a period of time and may be estimated by the more easily obtainable measure of record contact time. Finally, we propose that a cumulated informativeness value averaged over both served and unserved user needs in the community be used to assess how well the service is meeting its primary objective of providing information to this community.

The informativeness measure developed in this book provides an integrated approach to the measurement of the effectiveness of an information service in serving its user community. It may also be used, in conjunction with appropriate experimental designs and techniques of statistical analysis, in comparing different approaches to collection building, database development, indexing, knowledge representation, querying, browsing, output packaging, the analysis and synthesis of sets of records, and other functions carried out as a part of the work of an information service.

Should we care about measuring information? Is the model presented here too analytic, too reductionist? Can we approach the problem of how well an information service is meeting its objective to serve a particular community on any level than the qualitative? Certainly, qualitative methods are important. Managers and system developers from a service need to talk to users and nonusers in the community to gain a qualitative understanding of their needs and their understanding of the records provided by the service. They need to seek the qualitative opinions of experts and community leaders and of their own front-line staff, who deal with users on a daily basis. They need to carry out individual failure analyses, determinations of the reasons why a user was not provided with an optimal service.

All of this qualitative analysis is important. However, in deciding what to do to improve a service, at some point we must offer more than subjective judgments: "It all depends on the circumstances" or "Only the user knows." Our resources are not unlimited. Sometimes we have to make a decision about what is best overall or on average, rather than just for an individual case. It is at this point that we need a *measure* of information, something that can be cumulated, summarized, and averaged. We have to be able to say: "This way is better than that way" or "We did a better job of providing service this year than last year" or "This part of our service performed better than that part" or "We served this group of people better than that group."

To make such extensive and unambiguous judgments and to convince others that we are right, we need to base them on a measure, and since information is what our service is set up to provide, this measure must be one of information. If the measure is a valid one it will give results that will support at least some of the qualitative judgments, though perhaps not all, since it represents a cumulation or averaging and there may well be individual outliers. However, by dealing with numbers, outliers can be identified and, if there are enough of them, special services can be developed to meet these needs. This identification process is made possible by the measure, which allows us to compare how well different groups are being served.

The model that we have developed and elaborated in this book is not the only way of measuring information. We have reviewed many of the other measures of information that earlier writers have proposed and explained why we find them wanting. We have presented the assumptions upon which our measure is based and provided a justification for these assumptions. Our starting point was that we wanted an information measure that makes sense in an information service environment, which is based on a user-centered view of information, and which can be used to provide clear direction for improving the service.

The philosopher Wittgenstein (1958) shared, in an earlier era, the view of language we have taken as the theoretical basis for our development of the information measure, namely that of Lakoff. Wittgenstein said, "The arrow points only in the application a being makes of it." This statement has a double meaning within the context of this book. First, it lays the foundation for our view of information. A printed page or a computer screen or an audio or video recording provides information only to the degree that it is understood and interpreted by a human being. Secondly, a measure of information has meaning only to the extent that the user of the measure understands the basis upon which the measure is constructed.

I hope that the measure of information I have presented here is understood in this way. I have attempted in this book to develop a theory of information measurement that can be understood by those who develop, administer, study, and use information services. Whether or not I have succeeded for an individual reader, only that reader can judge.

I also hope that at the macro level, information services will assess the utility of this information measurement approach to their particular environment. The theory and application models presented in this book are just a first step, the laying of the foundation. The next step is the testing and validation of the approach in many different information service environments. If this testing does occur, then I will embark upon a sequel to the present volume, which will be a casebook of its applications. I invite any who undertake this task to keep me informed of the outcome.

References

Bar-Hillel, Y., and Carnap, R. (1953). Semantic information. *Br. J. Philos. Sci.* **4**(13), 147–157.

Bates, M. (1979). Information search tactics. *J. Am. Soc. Inf. Sci.* **30,** 205–214.

Bates, B. J. (1988). Information as an economic good: Sources of individual and social value. *In* "The Political Economy of Information" (V. Mosco and J. Wasko, eds.), pp. 76–94. Univ. of Wisconsin Press, Madison.

Beheshti, J. (1989). A longitudinal study of the use of library books by undergraduate students. *Inf. Process. Manage.* **25**(6), 737–744.

Belkin, N. (1978). Information concepts for information science. *J. Doc.* **34**(1), 55–95.

Belkin, N. J. (1980). Anomalous states of knowledge as a basis for information retrieval. *Canadian Journal of Information Science* **5,** 133–144.

Belkin, N., and Croft, B. (1987). Retrieval techniques. *Annu. Rev. Inf. Sci. Technol.* **22,** 109–146.

Belkin, N., and Robertson, S. (1976). Information science and the phenomenon of information. *J. Am. Soc. Inf. Sci.* **27,** 197–210.

Berenson, M., Levine, D., and Goldstein, M. (1983). "Intermediate Statistical Methods and Applications; A Computer Package Approach." Prentice-Hall, Englewood Cliffs, NJ.

Bollmann, P., and Cherniavsky, V. S. (1981). Measurement—theoretical investigations of the MZ-metric. *In* "Information Retrieval Research" (R. N. Oddy, S. E. Robertson, C. J. Van Rijsbergen, P. W. Williams, eds.). pp. 256–267, Butterworth, London.

Bookstein, A., and Klein, S. T. (1990). Compression, information theory, and grammars: A unified approach. *ACM Trans. Inf. Syst.* **8**(1), 27–49.

Bradford, S. C. (1948). "Documentation." Crosby Lockwood, London.

Brookes, B. C. (1970). The growth, utility, and obsolescence of scientific periodical literature. *J. Doc.* **26**(4), 283–294.

Brookes, B. C. (1974). Robert Fairthorne and the scope of information science. *J. Doc.* **30**(2), 139–152.

Brookes, B. C. (1980a). The foundations of information science. I. *J. Inf. Sci.* **2,** 125–133.

Brookes, B. C. (1980b). The foundations of information science. III. *J. Inf. Sci.* **2,** 269–275.

Brookes, B. C. (1983). Popper's three worlds and their relevance to information science. *Proceedings of the Canadian Association for Information Science* **11,** 214–225.

Buckland, M. (1991). Information as thing. *J. Am. Soc. Inf. Sci.* **42**(5), 351–360.

Burrell, Q. L. (1985). A note on ageing in a library circulation model. *J. Doc.* **41,** 100–115.

Chaitin, G. J. (1974). Information–theoretic computational complexity. *IEEE Trans. Inf. Theory* **IT-20**(1), 10–15.

Cleverdon, C. W. (1960). Information and its retrieval. *ASLIB Proc.* **22,** 538–49.

Cole, C. (1993). Shannon revisited: information in terms of uncertainty. *J. Am. Soc. Inf. Sci.* **44,** 204–211.

De Luca, A., and Termini, S. (1972). A definition of nonprobabilistic entropy in the setting of fuzzy sets theory. *Inf. Control* **20,** 301–312.

Derr, R. L. (1985). The concept of information in ordinary discourse. *Inf. Process. Manage.* **21**(6), 489–499.

Dervin, B. (1980). Communication gaps and inequities: moving toward a reconceptualization. *In* (B. Dervin and M. Voigt, eds.), "Progress in Communication Sciences" Vol. 2, pp. 73–112. Norwood, New Jersey: Ablex.

Dolby, J. L. (1977). On the notion of ambiguity and information loss. *Inf. Process. Manage.* **13,** 69–77.

Dretske, F. I. "Knowledge and the Flow of Information," Part I. MIT Press, Cambridge, MA.

Eisenberg, M. B. (1988). Measuring relevance judgments. *Inf. Process. Manage.* **24**(4), 373–389.

Eisenberg, M. B., and Barry, C. (1988). Order effects: A study of the possible influence of presentation order on user judgments of document relevance. *J. Am. Soc. Inf. Sci.* **39,** 293–300.

Fairthorne, R. A. (1975). Information: One label, several bottles. *In* "Perspectives in Information Science" (W. Cameron and A. Debons, eds.), pp. 65–73. Noordhoff Int. Publ., Gröningen, Leyden, The Netherlands.

Fisher, R. A. (1938). "Statistical Methods for Research Workers." Hafner, New York.

Fox, C. J. (1983). "Information and Misinformation: An Investigation of the Notions of Information, Misinformation, Informing, and Misinforming." Greenwood Press, Westport, Conn.

Froehlich, T. (1991). Towards a better conceptual framework for understanding relevance for information science research. *Proc. Am. Soc. Inf. Sci.* **28,** 118–125.

Frohmann, B. (1992). The power of images: A discourse analysis of the cognitive viewpoint. *J. Doc.* **48**(4), 365–386.

Good, I. J. (1983). Explicativity: A mathematical theory of explanation with statistical applications. *In* "Good Thinking: The Foundations of Probability and its Applications," Chapter 23. Univ. of Minnesota Press, Minneapolis.

Green, R. (1991). The profession's models of information: a cognitive linguistic analysis. *J. Doc.* **47**(2), 130–148.

Guiasu, S. (1977). "Information Theory with Applications." McGraw-Hill, New York.

Guazzo, M. (1977). Retrieval performance and information theory. *Inf. Process. Manage.* **13,** 155–165.

Harman, D. (1993). Overview of the first Text Retrieval Conference. *SIGIR '93; Proc. Annu. Int. ACM SIGIR Conf. Res. Dev. Inf. Retr.*, Pittsburgh, *1993,* pp. 36–48.

Hayes, R. M. (1993). Measurement of information. *Inf. Process. Manage.* **29**(1), 1–12.

Heaps, H. S. (1987). "Information Retrieval: Computational and Theoretical Aspects." Academic Press, Orlando, FL.

Hoffman, E. (1980). Defining information: An analysis of the information content of documents. *Inf. Process. Manage.* **16**(6), 291–304.

Hoffman, E. (1982). Defining information. II. A quantitative evaluation of the information content of documents. *Inf. Process. Manage.* **18**(3), 133–139.

Hull, D. (1993). Using statistical testing in the evaluation of retrieval experiments. *SIGIR '93; Proc. Annu. Int. ACM SIGIR Conf. Res. Dev. Inf. Retr.*, Pittsburgh, *1993,* pp. 329–338.

Janes, J. W. (1991). Relevance judgments and the incremental presentation of document representations. *Inf. Process. Manage.* **26**(6), 629–646.

Johnson, N. L., and Kotz, S. (1970). "Distributions in Statistics: Continuous Univariate Distributions," Vol. 1. Wiley, New York.

Johnson-Laird, P. N. (1983). "Mental Models." Harvard Univ. Press, Cambridge, MA.

Jumarie, G. (1990). "Relative Information: Theories and Applications." Springer-Verlag, Berlin.

Kampé de Fériet, J., and Forte, B. (1967). Information et probabilité. I. II. III. *C. Hebd. Seances R. Acad. Sci. Ser. A* **265,** 110–114, 142–146, 350–353.

Knightly, J. J. (1979). Overcoming the criterion problem in the evaluation of library performance. *Special Libraries* **70,** 173–178.

Kolmogorov, A. N. (1968). Logical basis for information theory and probability theory. *IEEE Trans. Inf. Theory* **IT-14,** 662–664.

Kullback, S. (1959). "Information Theory and Statistics." Wiley, New York.

Lakoff, G. (1987). "Women, Fire and Dangerous Things: What Categories Reveal about the Mind." Univ. of Chicago Press, Chicago.

Lancaster, F. W. (1988). "If you want to evaluate your library. . . ." University of Illinois, Urbana.

Losee, R. M. (1990). "The Science of Information." Academic Press, San Diego.

Machlup, F. (1983). Semantic quirks in studies of information. *In* "The Study of Information: Interdisciplinary Messages" (F. Machlup and U. Mansfield, eds.), pp. 641–672. Wiley (Interscience), New York.

MacKay, D. M. (1969). "Information, Mechanism and Meaning." MIT Press, Cambridge, MA.

Marcus, R. S., Kugel, P., and Benenfeld, A. R. (1978). Catalogue information and text as indicators of relevance. *J. Am. Soc. Inf. Sci.* **29,** 15–30.

Marschak, J. (1971). Economics of information systems. *J. Am. Stat. Assoc.* **66**(333), 192–219.

May, K. O. (1968). Growth and quality of the mathematical loiterature. *Isis* **69**(199), 363–371.

Meddis, R. (1984). "Statistics Using Ranks: A Unified Approach." Blackwell, Oxford.

Nauta, D. (1972). "The Meaning of Information." Mouton, The Hague.

Perry, J. W., and Kent, A. (1958). "Tools for Machine Literature Searching." Wiley (Interscience), New York.

Phillips, D. C. (1987). "Philosophy, Science and Social Inquiry." Pergamon, Oxford.

Picard, C. (1980). "Graphs and Questionnaires." North-Holland, Publ., Amsterdam.

Pierce, J. R. (1965). "Symbols, Signals and Noise: the Nature and Process of Communication." Freeman, San Francisco.

Popper, K. R. (1972). "Objective Knowledge: An Evolutionary Approach." Clarendon Press, London.

Powell, R. R. (1992). Impact assessment of university libraries: A consideration of issues and research methodologies. *Libr. Inf. Sci. Res.* **14,** 235–257.

Pratt, A. D. (1982). "The Information of the Image." Ablex, Norwood, NJ.

Ranganathan, S. R. (1931). "The Five Laws of Library Science." Asia Publishing House, Bombay.

Resnikoff, H. L. (1989). "The Illusion of Reality." Springer-Verlag, Berlin.

Roberts, F. S. (1979). "Measurement Theory." Addison-Wesley, Reading, MA.

Salton, G. (1971). "The SMART Retrieval System—Experiments in Automatic Document Processing." Prentice-Hall, Englewood Cliffs, NJ.

Salton, G. (1975). "Dynamic Information and Library Processing." Prentice-Hall, Englewood Cliffs, NJ.

Schamber, L., Eisenberg, M. B., and Nilan, M. S. (1990). A re-examination of relevance: Toward a dynamic, situational definition. *Inf. Process. Manage.* **26,** 755–776.

Schreider, Y. (1965). On the semantic characteristics of information. *Inf. Storage Retr.* **2**(4), 221–233.

Schreider, Y. A. (1975). "Equality, Resemblance, and Order." Mir, Moscow.

Schutz, A. (1970). "Reflections on the Problem of Relevance." Yale Univ. Press, New Haven, CT.

Shannon, C., and Weaver, W. (1949). "The Mathematical Theory of Communication." Univ. of Illinois Press, Urbana.

Shaw, W. (1986). On the foundation of evaluation. *J. Am. Soc. for Inf. Sci.* **37**(5), 346–348.

Shaw, W. M. (1993). Controlled and uncontrolled subject descriptions in the CF database: A comparison of optimal cluster-based retrieval results. *Inf. Proc. Manage.* **29**(6), 751–64.

Tague, J., and Schultz, R. (1989). Evaluation of the user interface in an information retrieval system: A model. *Inf. Process. Manage.* **25**(4), 377–389.

Tague, J., Salminen, A., and McClellan, C. (1991). A complete model for information retrieval systems. *SIGIR '91: Proc. Int. Conf. Res. Dev. Inf. Retr.*, Vol. 14, pp. 14–20.

Tague-Sutcliffe, J. (1992a). Measuring the informativeness of a retrieval process. *SIGIR '92; Proc. Int. Conf. Res. Dev. Inf. Retr.*, Vol. 15, pp. 23–36.

Tague-Sutcliffe, J. (1992b). How good is a model? Explicativity as a goodness-offit measure. *In* "Informetrics '91; Selected Papers from the Third International Conference on Informetrics, 1991, Bangalore," pp. 484–505. Sarada Ranganathan Endowment for Library Science, Bangalore, India.

Tague-Sutcliffe, J. M. (1992c). The pragmatics of information retrieval testing, revisited. *Inf. Proc. Manage.* **28**(4), 467–490.

Tague-Sutcliffe, J. M. (1994). Modelling and forecasting contact time as a measure of item informativeness. *Scientometrics* **30**(1), 259–267.

Tompa, F. (1989). A data model for flexible hypertext database systems. *ACM Trans. Inf. Syst.* **7**(1), 85–100.

Trueswell, R. W. (1975). Growing libraries; who needs them? A statistical basis for the no-growth collection. In "Farewell to Alexandria" (D. Gore, ed.) pp. 72–104. Greenwood Press, Westport, Conn.

Van House, N., Lynch, M. J., McClure, C. R., Zweizig, D. L., Rodger, E. J. (1987). "Output Measures for Public Libraries." American Library Association, Chicago.

Van Rijsbergen, C. J. (1979). "Information Retrieval." 2nd ed. Butterworths, London.

Watters, C., and Shepherd, M. (1990). A transient hypergraph-base model for data access. *ACM Trans. Inf. Syst.* **8**(2), 77–102.

Wells, R. (1961). A measure of subjective information. *Struct. Lang. Math. Aspects, Proc. Symp. Appl. Math., 12th, 1961,* pp. 237–244.

Wilbur, J. (1992). An information measure of retrieval performance. *Inf. Syst.* **17**(4), 283–298.

Winer, B. J. (1971). "Statistical Principles in Experimental Design," 2nd ed. McGraw-Hill, New York.

Wittgenstein, L. (1958). "Philosophical Investigations." Sect. 580. Macmillan, New York.

Yovits, M. C., and Kleyle, R. M. (1993). The average decision maker and its properties utilizing the generalized information system model. *J. Am. Soc. Inf. Sci.* **44**(6), 352–363.

Yovits, M. C., Foulk, C. F., and Rose, L. L. (1981). Information and analysis: Theory, simulation and experiment. *J. Am. Soc. Inf. Sci.* **32,** 187–210.

Index

A

Absolute scale, 35
Abstracting, 22, 162, 171–173
Abstraction, 4
Access method, 167
Accuracy, 168
Acquisition, 157
Additive measurement, 26, 34, 41–43
Aggregation, *see* Informativeness, aggregation; Ordinal measurement, aggregation
Algorithmic measure, 57, 81
Ambiguity, 62, 64
Analysis of variance, 154–155, 159–160, 179–183
Ancillary value, 27
Anomaly, 14, 23, 143–144
Anova, *see* Analysis of variance
Archimedean property, 41
Asymmetry, 36, 89, 108
Atomic event, 20
Atomic statement, 69
Authority, 9
Averaging, *see* Informativeness, averaging
Axiom, *see* Informativeness, axioms

B

Bar Hillel, Y., 69–74
Barry, C., 49, 52
Bates, B. J., 27
Bates, M., 167
Bayesian statistics, 74–78
Beheshti, J., 127
Belkin, N., 10, 14, 23, 143, 166
Benefits, 19
Benenfeld, A. R., 172
Berenson, M., 155, 169
Bollmann, P., 126
Bookstein, A., 61
Borda count, 44–45
Bradford, S. C., 50
Brookes, B. C., 10, 14, 51, 61
Browsing, 23–24, 164, 168–171
Buckland, M., 3
Burrell, Q. L., 126–127

C

Carnap, R., 69–74
Cataloging, 162
Category, 6, 22, 35
Chain, 45–46; *see also* Ideal chain; Optimal retrieval chain
Chaitin, G. J., 81–82
Channel, 69
Cherniavsky, V. S., 126
Circulation, 79, 126–127, 157
Classification, 22, 162–166
Cleverdon, C. W., 167
Clustering, 162
Cognitive models, 5–15, 47
Cole, C., 62
Collection, 20–22, 54, 86, 142, 154–161
Commands, search, 167
Communication, human, 58
Community information center, 21
Community, user, *see* User community
Commutative relation, 41, 49, 62, 67–68, 72, 112
Comparable records, 16, 37, 40–44, 48, 87–95, 102–107
Comparison, services, 20, 54, 153–175
Completeness, 36
Compression, 61

Computability, 8
Computational measure, *see* Algorithmic measure
Concatenation, 34, 42, 49, 62, 72, 95, 112
Concept, *see* Cognitive model
Confidence interval, 131, 151–152
Conjunction, 70
Consistency, *see* Probabilistic consistency measure
Contact time, 127–132, 162
Content element, 69
Corporate information management, 156–157
Correlation coefficient, 115
Croft, B., 166

D

Data collection, 147–149
Database, 21, 54, 86, 154–161
De Luca, A., 65
Decision tree, 59
Decision-theoretic measure, 79–81
Default ideal chain, *see* Ideal chain, default
Definition, information, *see* Information, definition
Delay discount, 54, 79–80, 111, 113–117, 132–137, 154, 191–192
Delay extent, 115–116, 133, 150
Delivery
  document, *see* Document delivery
  service, *see* Service delivery
Derr, R. L., 4, 72
Dervin, B., 143
Description, 22–23, 54, 161–166
Descriptors, 23, 39
Differences, *see* Comparison, services
Diminishing returns, 50, 97
Discount, *see* Delay discount
Document delivery, 157
Dolby, J. L., 64
Domain of function, 33, 47
Dretske, F. I., 63–64

E

E measure, 126, 167–168
Economic good, 27
Edge index, 95, 114
Effectiveness, *see* Evaluation, effectiveness
Efficiency, 172–173
Eisenberg, M. B., 49, 52, 172
Entropy, 57–68, 75
  conditional, 60, 67
  extensions, 63–68
Equivalence relation, 37
Escher, M. C., 38–39
Estimation, 75–78; *see also* Informativeness, estimation
Evaluation; *see also* Information services, evaluation
  effectiveness, 141, 157, 163, 168, 193
  types, 141
Example, 38, 90–91, 94, 117–125, 131, 136–137, 158–160, 164–166, 168–171, 172–174
Exhaustivity, 162
Expected search length, 167–168
Experimental design, 153–155, 179–190; *see also* Repeated measures design; Single factor design; Two factor design
Expert judge, 18, 74, 137–138, 142, 146
Exponential function, *see* Contact time

F

Fairthorne, R. A., v, xi, 3–4
Fallout, 125, 167–168
Feature, 38–39, 89, 93
Feature bundles, 6, 10
Fill rates, 157, 163
Fisher, R. A., 76
Forte, B., 68
Foulk, C. F., 80
Fox, C. J., 4, 9–11
Froehlich, T., 9
Frohmann, B., 26
Function, definition, 33
Future contact time, 130–132
Fuzzy sets, 65

G

Goldstein, M., 155, 169
Good, I. J., 77
Graded categories, 6, 10
Granularity, 50, 97
Green, R., 15
Guazzo, M., 64
Guiasu, S., 63–64, 75–76

H

Harman, D., 167
Hayes, R. M., 63
Heaps, A. S., 64
Hoffman, E., 74
Hull, D., 155
Human judge, *see* Expert judge
Hypergraph, 45–46
Hypertext, 168–170
Hypothesis testing, 77–79, 155

I

Ideal chain, 51–53, 88–95, 117, 125, 149, 192
  algorithm to determine, 102–107
  default, 89, 95
  existence proof, 107–110
Ideal sequence, 96
Ideal service chain, 133
Indexing, 22, 162, 164
Indicativity, 172–173
Inference, *see* Logic
Information
  aggregation, 192
  center, 22, 169–170
  definition, 3–5, 8–13, 55
  descriptive, 70
  local, 67–68
  measurement, 15–19; *see also* Algorithmic measure; Decision-theoretic measure; Entropy; Informativeness; Linguistic measure; Semantic measure; Statistical measure
  need, 12, 16, 27, 52, 85, 89, 132–133
    dimension, 144–145
    number of, 135–137
    unit, 143–145
  order dependence, 49–50, 51–53, 111
  retrieval, *see* Retrieval
  relative, 67
  sample, 75–78
  selective, 70
  services, 1–3
    evaluation, 19–28, 53–54, 141–175; *see also* Community information center; Corporate information management; Medical library; National library; Online service; Opac; Public library; Research library; Special library
  subjective, 67
  unit, 59, 96, 192
  value, 19, 27, 121
Informative chain, *see* Ideal chain
Informativeness
  added, 172, 174–175
  aggregation, 28, 111–139
    over records, *see* Retrieval trail
    over services, *see* Service delivery
    over uses, *see* Use trail
  averaging, 58, 82, 128, 142–153, 192
  axioms, 73, 85–101, 111–138
  definition, 17
  domain, 47
  estimation, 54, 127, 143–153
  function, 97–100
  initial, 113, 150
  logarithmic property, 50–51, 62, 72, 81, 97
  overall, 132–139, 143–153
  properties, 46–54
  range, 47
  record sets and sequences, 47–53
  standardizing, 95–101
  time dependence, 16, 24, 47, 53–54, 79–80, 111, 133, 191
  use, 54, 142, 158–160, 164, 168–171
  validation, 18, 121–125
Interaction, 9, 12, 18, 47, 62, 67, 72, 85, 111, 125
Interface, 168–170
Isolation of effects, 162

J

Janes, J. W., 172
Johnson, N., 128
Johnson-Laird, P. N. 7–8, 72
Journal-keeping, 147
Jumarie, G., 16, 47, 66–67

K

Kampé, de Fériet, J., 68
Kent, A., 166
Keyword, 164, 168–170
Klein, S., 61
Kleyle, R. M., 80–81

Knightley, J. J., 141
Knowledge, 10
Kolmogorov, A. N., 81
Kotz, S., 128
Krugel, P., 172
Kullback, S., 78

L

Lakoff, G., 5–15, 71, 194
Lancaster, F. W., 157
Language, 66
Levine, D., 155, 169
Library, *see* Information service
  loans, *see* Circulation
Linguistic measure, 57, 74
Loans, *see* Circulation
Location time, 163
Logarithmic property, *see* Informativeness, Logarithmic property
Logic, 6, 8, 10, 69–74
Logical measure, *see* Semantic measure
Losee, R. M., 57
Lynch, M. J., 157

M

Machlup, F., 10–11
MacKay, D. M., 70
Magnitude estimation, 48–49
Marcus, R. S., 172
Marschak, J., 79–80, 112
May, K. O., 50
McClellan, C., 45
McClure, C. R., 157
Meaning, 4, 9, 62, 66
Measurement; *see also* Additive measurement; Ordinal measurement
  definition, 31–32
  justification, 193
  justification for, 16–17
  scales, 35
  theory, 32
Meddis, R., 155, 169
Medical library, 164–166
Memory, 12, 47
Mental model, *see* Cognitive model
Message transmission, *see* Signal transmission
Monotonicity, 41
MZ metric, 126

N

National library, 156
Nauta, D., 10, 13–14
Need, *see* Information, need
Negative transitivity, 36, 38–40, 91–93, 108
Nilan, M. S., 16
Noninformative records, 28, 52, 87, 95, 113

O

Obsolescence, 80, 129, 155
Online service, 158–160, 170
Opac, 120, 125, 136
Operation, definition, 33
Optimal retrieval chain, 113–118, 126, 149
Order dependence, *see* Information, order dependence
Ordering types, 34
Ordinal measurement, 7, 32, 37–41, 85–86, 92, 95, 102–107, 155, 191
  aggregation, 44–45
Ordinal scale, 35

P

Packaging, 25, 54, 171–175
Panel, *see* Expert judge
Perry, J. W., 166
Perusal order, *see* Retrieval trail
Phillips, D. C., 18
Picard, C., 59
Pierce, J. R., 60
Popper, K. R., 14, 18, 20
Posterior distribution, 75
Powell, R. R., 141
Pratt, A. D., 14
Precision, 24, 125, 163, 167–168
Preference, 37, 43–45, 48, 86–95
Prior distribution, 75
Probabilistic consistency measure, 43–45
Probabilistic measure, *see* Entropy
Proposition, 6–10, 71
Public library, 156, 158

Q

Qualitative analysis, 193
Query, 23, 52, 121, 167, 169–171; *see also* Information, need
Questionnaire, 59

R

Radial category, 6, 10
Ranganathan, S. R., 191
Range of function, 33
Rank test, 155, 164–166, 170–171, 183–190
Ranking, *see* Ordering, types
Rating, 35, 155
Ratio scale, 35, 39
Recall, 24, 125, 163, 167–168
Record
  definition, 2–3, 46
  partitioning, 50
  management, 158–160
Redundancy, 60
Reflexivity, 36
Relation, definition, 33
Relational system, 34
Relevance, 16, 64–65, 125
Repeated measures design, 154, 158, 161, 170–171, 173, 179–180, 185–187
Research library, 156
Resnikoff, H. L., 51
Retention schedule, 158–160
Retrieval, 23–25, 51–53, 64–65, 76–77, 162, 166–171
  evaluation, 64–65, 125–126, 168–171
  trail, 52, 111–126
Review paper, 174–175
Roberts, F. S., 32, 35
Robertson, S., 10, 14, 23
Rodger, E. J., 157
Rose, L. L., 80

S

Salminen, A., 45
Salton, G., 50, 166–167
Sampling, 137, 145–149, 158
Scenario, 6, 10
Schamber, L., 16
Schreider, Y., 10, 13, 38–41, 89
Schultz, R., 86
Search strategy, *see* Retrieval
Semantic measure, 69–74
Semantic nets, 74
Service delivery, 111, 132–138
Service interval, 146
Service priority, 135, 175
Shannon, C., 4, 58–63, 66, 99–100; *see also* Entropy
Shaw, W. M., 126, 162
Shelf time, 157
Shepherd, M., 45
Signal transmission, 4, 10, 58, 61, 80
Single factor design, 153, 158–160, 164–166, 178–179, 183–185
Special library, 21, 156
Specificity, 72, 144, 162
State description, 70
Statistical analysis, 172, 174–175
Statistical measure, 74–78
Strict weak order, 37, 42, 89–91, 108
Student, *see* User, student
Subjectivity, 8, 32, 47, 66–67, 72, 194
Substitutability, 144
Surprise value, 11, 58–59
Surrogate, 22, 54, 172–173
Symmetry, 36
System developer, 167, 193

T

Tague, J., *see* Tague-Sutcliffe, J.
Tague-Sutcliffe, J., 45, 76, 86, 125, 144, 166
Termini, S., 65
Three worlds, 14
Title, 172–174
Tolerance relation, 38–41
Tompa, F., 45
Total informativeness, *see* Informativeness, overall
Tourist information center, 168–170
Transitivity, 36, 46, 89
Trueswell, R., 127
Truth, 5, 7, 9–10
Turnover rate, 157
Two factor design, 153–154, 169, 181–183, 187–190

U

Uncertainty, 4, 11, 58, 61, 66–67
Understanding, 8–9
Unserviced needs, 146, 151–153
Use trail, 111, 126–132
User, 8–9, 66, 72, 111, 191
  community, 2, 13, 17, 26, 53, 111, 126, 132, 137, 141, 191
  satisfaction, 163, 168
  student, 121–125, 136–137

Utility function, 38, 63, 79–80, 110, 137–138
Utility theory, 63

V

Validation, 18, 124–125, 138
Value of information, *see* Information, value
Van House, N., 157
Van Rijsbergen, C. J., 126
Vocabulary, similarity, 163

W

Watters, C., 45
Weaver, W., 4
Weber-Fechner law, 51
Wells, R., 72–74
Wilbur, J., 65
Winer, B. J., 154
Wittgenstein, L., 16, 194

Y

Yovitz, M. C., 80–81

Library and Information Science

(Continued from page ii)

Lois Swan Jones and Sarah Scott Gibson
Art Libraries and Information Services

Nancy Jones Pruett
Scientific and Technical Libraries: Functions and Management Volume 1 and Volume 2

Peter Judge and Brenda Gerrie
Small Bibliographic Databases

Dorothy B. Lilley and Ronald W. Trice
A History of Information Sciences 1945–1985

Elaine Svenonius
The Conceptual Foundations of Descriptive Cataloging

Robert M. Losee, Jr.
The Science of Information: Measurement and Applications

Irene P. Godden
Library Technical Services: Operations and Management, Second Edition

Donald H. Kraft and Bert R. Boyce
Operations Research for Libraries and Information Agencies: Techniques for the Evaluation of Management Decision Alternatives

James Cabeceiras
The Multimedia Library: Materials Selection and Use, Second Edition

Charles T. Meadow
Text Information Retrieval Systems

Robert M. Losee, Jr. and Karen A. Worley
Research and Evaluation for Information Professionals

Carmel Maguire, Edward J. Kazlauskas, and Anthony D. Weir
Information Services for Innovative Organizations

Karen Markey Drabenstott and Diane Vizine-Goetz
Using Subject Headings for Online Retrieval

Bert R. Boyce, Charles T. Meadow, and Donald H. Kraft
Measurement in Information Science

John V. Richardson Jr.
Knowledge-Based Systems for General Reference Work

Jean Tague-Sutcliffe
Measuring Information